LANGUAGE AND LITERACY SERIES

"You Gotta BE the Book": Teaching Engaged and
Reflective Reading with Adolescents, Third Edition
JEFFREY D. WILHELM

Personal Narrative, Revised:
Writing Love and Agency in the High School Classroom
BRONWYN CLARE LAMAY

Inclusive Literacy Teaching: Differentiating Approaches in
Multilingual Elementary Classrooms
LORI HELMAN, CARRIE ROGERS, AMY FREDERICK, & MAGGIE STRUCK

The Vocabulary Book:
Learning and Instruction, Second Edition
MICHAEL F. GRAVES

Reading, Writing, and Talk: Inclusive Teaching Strategies
for Diverse Learners, K–2
MARIANA SOUTO-MANNING & JESSICA MARTELL

Go Be a Writer!: Expanding the Curricular Boundaries of
Literacy Learning with Children
CANDACE R. KUBY & TARA GUTSHALL RUCKER

Partnering with Immigrant Communities:
Action Through Literacy
GERALD CAMPANO, MARÍA PAULA GHISO, & BETHANY J. WELCH

Teaching Outside the Box but Inside the Standards:
Making Room for Dialogue
BOB FECHO, MICHELLE FALTER, & XIAOLI HONG, EDS.

Literacy Leadership in Changing Schools:
10 Keys to Successful Professional Development
SHELLEY B. WEPNER, DIANE W. GÓMEZ, KATIE EGAN CUNNINGHAM,
KRISTIN N. RAINVILLE, & COURTNEY KELLY

Literacy Theory as Practice:
Connecting Theory and Instruction in K–12 Classrooms
LARA J. HANDSFIELD

Literacy and History in Action: Immersive Approaches to
Disciplinary Thinking, Grades 5–12
THOMAS M. MCCANN, REBECCA D'ANGELO, NANCY GALAS,
& MARY GRESKA

Pose, Wobble, Flow:
A Culturally Proactive Approach to Literacy Instruction
ANTERO GARCIA & CINDY O'DONNELL-ALLEN

Newsworthy—Cultivating Critical Thinkers, Readers, and
Writers in Language Arts Classrooms
ED MADISON

Engaging Writers with Multigenre Research Projects:
A Teacher's Guide
NANCY MACK

Teaching Transnational Youth—
Literacy and Education in a Changing World
ALLISON SKERRETT

Uncommonly Good Ideas—
Teaching Writing in the Common Core Era
SANDRA MURPHY & MARY ANN SMITH

The One-on-One Reading and Writing Conference:
Working with Students on Complex Texts
JENNIFER BERNE & SOPHIE C. DEGENER

Critical Encounters in Secondary English:
Teaching Literary Theory to Adolescents, Third Edition
DEBORAH APPLEMAN

Transforming Talk into Text—Argument Writing, Inquiry,
and Discussion, Grades 6–12
THOMAS M. MCCANN

Reading and Representing Across the Content Areas:
A Classroom Guide
AMY ALEXANDRA WILSON & KATHRYN J. CHAVEZ

Writing and Teaching to Change the World:
Connecting with Our Most Vulnerable Students
STEPHANIE JONES, ED.

Educating Literacy Teachers Online:
Tools, Techniques, and Transformations
LANE W. CLARKE & SUSAN WATTS-TAFFEE

Other People's English: Code-Meshing,
Code-Switching, and African American Literacy
VERSHAWN ASHANTI YOUNG, RUSTY BARRETT,
Y'SHANDA YOUNG-RIVERA, & KIM BRIAN LOVEJOY

WHAM! Teaching with Graphic Novels Across
the Curriculum
WILLIAM G. BROZO, GARY MOORMAN, & CARLA K. MEYER

The Administration and Supervision of Reading Programs,
5th Edition
SHELLEY B. WEPNER, DOROTHY S. STRICKLAND,
& DIANA J. QUATROCHE, EDS.

Critical Literacy in the Early Childhood Classroom:
Unpacking Histories, Unlearning Privilege
CANDACE R. KUBY

Inspiring Dialogue:
Talking to Learn in the English Classroom
MARY M. JUZWIK, CARLIN BORSHEIM-BLACK,
SAMANTHA CAUGHLAN, & ANNE HEINTZ

Reading the Visual:
An Introduction to Teaching Multimodal Literacy
FRANK SERAFINI

Race, Community, and Urban Schools:
Partnering with African American Families
STUART GREENE

ReWRITING the Basics:
Literacy Learning in Children's Cultures
ANNE HAAS DYSON

Writing Instruction That Works:
Proven Methods for Middle and High School Classrooms
ARTHUR N. APPLEBEE & JUDITH A. LANGER, WITH KRISTEN CAMPBELL
WILCOX, MARC NACHOWITZ, MICHAEL P. MASTROIANNI, &
CHRISTINE DAWSON

Literacy Playshop: New Literacies, Popular Media, and
Play in the Early Childhood Classroom
KAREN E. WOHLWEND

Critical Media Pedagogy:
Teaching for Achievement in City Schools
ERNEST MORRELL, RUDY DUEÑAS, VERONICA GARCIA,
& JORGE LOPEZA

continued

For volumes in the NCRLL Collection (edited by JoBeth Allen and Donna E. Alvermann) and the Practitioners Bookshelf Series (edited by Celia Genishi and Donna E. Alvermann), as well as other titles in this series, please visit www.tcpress.com.

Language and Literacy Series, *continued*

A Search Past Silence: The Literacy of Young Black Men
DAVID E. KIRKLAND

The ELL Writer:
Moving Beyond Basics in the Secondary Classroom
CHRISTINA ORTMEIER-HOOPER

Reading in a Participatory Culture:
Remixing *Moby-Dick* in the English Classroom
HENRY JENKINS & WYN KELLEY, WITH KATIE CLINTON, JENNA
MCWILLIAMS, RICARDO PITTS-WILEY, & ERIN REILLY, EDS.

Summer Reading:
Closing the Rich/Poor Achievement Gap
RICHARD L. ALLINGTON & ANNE MCGILL-FRANZEN, EDS.

Real World Writing for Secondary Students:
Teaching the College Admission Essay and
Other Gate-Openers for Higher Education
JESSICA SINGER EARLY & MEREDITH DECOSTA

Teaching Vocabulary to English Language Learners
MICHAEL F. GRAVES, DIANE AUGUST, &
JEANETTE MANCILLA-MARTINEZ

Literacy for a Better World:
LAURA SCHNEIDER VANDERPLOEG

Socially Responsible Literacy
PAULA M. SELVESTER & DEBORAH G. SUMMERS

Learning from Culturally and Linguistically Diverse
Classrooms: Using Inquiry to Inform Practice
JOAN C. FINGON & SHARON H. ULANOFF, EDS.

Bridging Literacy and Equity
ALTHIER M. LAZAR ET AL.

"Trust Me! I Can Read"
SALLY LAMPING & DEAN WOODRING BLASE

Reading Girls
HADAR DUBROWSKY MA'AYAN

Reading Time
CATHERINE COMPTON-LILLY

A Call to Creativity
LUKE REYNOLDS

Literacy and Justice Through Photography
WENDY EWALD, KATHARINE HYDE, & LISA LORD

The Successful High School Writing Center
DAWN FELS & JENNIFER WELLS, EDS.

Interrupting Hate
MOLLIE V. BLACKBURN

Playing Their Way into Literacies
KAREN E. WOHLWEND

Teaching Literacy for Love and Wisdom
JEFFREY D. WILHELM & BRUCE NOVAK

Overtested
JESSICA ZACHER PANDYA

Restructuring Schools for Linguistic Diversity,
Second Edition
OFELIA B. MIRAMONTES, ADEL NADEAU, & NANCY L. COMMINS

Words Were All We Had
MARÍA DE LA LUZ REYES, ED.

Urban Literacies
VALERIE KINLOCH, ED.

Bedtime Stories and Book Reports
CATHERINE COMPTON-LILLY & STUART GREENE, EDS.

Envisioning Knowledge
JUDITH A. LANGER

Envisioning Literature, Second Edition
JUDITH A. LANGER

Writing Assessment and the Revolution in Digital Texts
and Technologies
MICHAEL R. NEAL

Artifactual Literacies
KATE PAHL & JENNIFER ROWSELL

Educating Emergent Bilinguals
OFELIA GARCÍA & JO ANNE KLEIFGEN

(Re)Imagining Content-Area Literacy Instruction
RONI JO DRAPER, ED.

Change Is Gonna Come
PATRICIA A. EDWARDS ET AL.

When Commas Meet Kryptonite
MICHAEL BITZ

Literacy Tools in the Classroom
RICHARD BEACH ET AL.

Harlem on Our Minds
VALERIE KINLOCH

Teaching the New Writing
ANNE HERRINGTON, KEVIN HODGSON, & CHARLES MORAN, EDS.

Children, Language, and Literacy
CELIA GENISHI & ANNE HAAS DYSON

Children's Language
JUDITH WELLS LINDFORS

Children's Literature and Learning
BARBARA A. LEHMAN

Storytime
LAWRENCE R. SIPE

Effective Instruction for Struggling Readers, K–6
BARBARA M. TAYLOR & JAMES E. YSSELDYKE, EDS.

The Effective Literacy Coach
ADRIAN RODGERS & EMILY M. RODGERS

Writing in Rhythm
MAISHA T. FISHER

Reading the Media
RENEE HOBBS

teaching**media***literacy*.com
RICHARD BEACH

What Was It Like?
LINDA J. RICE

Research on Composition
PETER SMAGORINSKY, ED.

New Literacies in Action
WILLIAM KIST

"You Gotta BE the Book"

Teaching Engaged and Reflective Reading with Adolescents

THIRD EDITION

Jeffrey D. Wilhelm

Foreword by
Michael W. Smith

TEACHERS COLLEGE PRESS
TEACHERS COLLEGE | COLUMBIA UNIVERSITY
NEW YORK AND LONDON

NATIONAL WRITING PROJECT

Published simultaneously by Teachers College Press, 1234 Amsterdam Avenue, New York, NY 10027, the National Writing Project, 2105 Bancroft Way, Berkeley, CA 94720-1042, and the National Council of Teachers of English, 1111 W. Kenyon Road, Urbana, IL 61801-1096

Grateful acknowledgment is made for permission to reprint quotes or data from the following:

Wilhelm, J. D. (2008). Teaching with a sense of urgency: A call to action. *Voices from the Middle, 16*(2), 45–49. Copyright 2008 by the National Council of Teachers of English. Reprinted by permission.

Wilhelm, J. D. (1995). The drama of engaged reading: Extending the reader through classroom story drama. *Reading and Writing Quarterly, 11*(4), 335–358. Reprinted by permission of Taylor & Francis LLC (http://www.tandfonline.com).

Wilhelm, J. D. (1995). Reading is seeing: Using visual response to improve the literacy reading of reluctant readers. *Journal of Reading Behavior, 27*(4), 467–503. Reprinted by permission of Sage Publications .

Cover photo by portishead1 / iStock by Getty Images.

Library of Congress Cataloging-in-Publication Data

Names: Wilhelm, Jeffrey D., 1959–
Title: You gotta BE the book : teaching engaged and reflective reading with adolescents
    / Jeffrey D. Wilhelm ; foreword by Michael W. Smith.
Description: Third edition I New York : Teachers College Press, 2016. I
Series: Language and literacy series I Includes bibliographical references and index.
Identifiers: LCCN 2016028260 (print) I LCCN 2016028505 (ebook)
ISBN 9780807757987 (pbk. : alk. paper) I ISBN 9780807775080 (ebook)
Subjects: LCSH: Reading (Secondary)—United States. I Junior high school students—
    Books and reading—United States.
Classification: LCC LB1632 .W54 2016 (print) I LCC LB1632 (ebook)
DDC 428.4071/2—dc23
LC record available at https://lccn.loc.gov/2016028260

ISBN 978-0-8077-5798-7 (paper)
ISBN 978-0-8077-7508-0 (ebook)
NCTE Stock # 57987

Printed on acid-free paper
Manufactured in the United States of America

23 22 21 20 19 18 17 16   8 7 6 5 4 3 2 1

I dedicate this work to all of my own teachers, especially:

James Blaser
William Strohm
Jack Wilhelm

CONTENTS

ℭℬ

Foreword to the Third Edition *by Michael W. Smith*   xi

Preface to the Third Edition   xiii

Acknowledgments   xxvii

Introduction: Really Among Schoolchildren   1

   The Reading Struggle   1

   Personal Readings   4

   Children's Hour   6

   Compelling Questions   7

   Tentative Answers   8

   Setting the Task   10

   COMMENTARY: The Human and the Cultural   12

1 ♦ Moving Toward a Reader-Centered Classroom   22

   The Bottom-Up Approach   23

   Why Johnny Won't Read   24

   There Is an Alternative   28

   Getting Started   30

   Building on Rosenblatt   33

   COMMENTARY: Be *THAT* Teacher   36

2 ◆ Looking at Student Reading — 48

The Year Begins — 49

What Makes Valid Reading? — 50

Studying Student Response — 51

Three Highly Engaged Readers: Cora, Joanne, and Ron — 53

Why Read Literature? — 62

COMMENTARY: Looking Toward Tomorrow Instead of to Yesterday—The Power of Teacher Research — 64

3 ◆ The Dimensions of the Reader's Response — 81

Classroom Research Methods — 81

The Dimensions — 87

Surprises — 90

Evocative Dimensions — 92

Connective Dimensions — 108

Reflective Dimensions — 117

Epilogue: What We Learned Together About Reading — 129

COMMENTARY: Literary Theorists, Hear My Cry! — 131

4 ◆ Using Drama to Extend the Reader — 143

Why Drama? — 145

The Students: Kevin, Marvin, and Libby — 150

Before Drama — 152

Dramatic Happenings — 156

The Moves They Made — 159

Reading as Pleasure: "You Have to Live the Story" — 167

Epilogue: The Potential of Drama — 169

COMMENTARY: Motivation, Materials, and Methods — 171

5 ◆ Reading Is Seeing — 183

Still Struggling: Tommy, Walter, and Kae — 184

Seeing the Visual Possibility — 187

The Visualization Project: Art in the Classroom 191

The Art of Reading 195

Moving Toward a Reflective Response:
"The Book Said All That" 206

Epilogue: Opening Doors with Art 209

COMMENTARY: Seeing the Substantive Possibilities 214

6 ◆ **Expanding Concepts of Reading,
Response, and Literature** 224

Reading as Engagement 225

Alternate Texts as Literature 226

Using Student Experiences: Art and Drama Activities 227

The Role of the Teacher 228

The Teacher as Researcher 232

Toward a Critical Literacy 233

COMMENTARY: A More Humane and Democratic Classroom—
For a More Humane and Democratic World! 238

**Appendix A: Questions and Activities for the
Ten Dimensions of Reader Response** 249

**Appendix B: Revolving Role Drama Lesson Plans
for *The Incredible Journey*** 262

References 268

Stories and Poems Cited in the Text 278

Index 280

About the Author 292

FOREWORD TO THE THIRD EDITION

❧

It's been 20 years since the publication of the first edition of *"You Gotta BE the Book."* As I know well from my own dwindling royalty checks, not many professional books have lives that long. So why has this book lasted? I think the answer has two parts, one a testimony to Jeff Wilhelm's accomplishment and the other a critique of current times.

Let's start with the testimony. Over the years I've been to many conferences with Jeff and have had the pleasure of being on the same panel with him at most of them. Inevitably, after we've finished speaking and are packing up, someone from the audience will come up to Jeff and say something like the following: *"'You Gotta BE the Book'* changed my life." Pretty powerful stuff. My eavesdropping on the ensuing conversations has made it clear to me the two primary reasons why so many teachers feel that way.

First, the book engages teachers in reconsidering the very purpose for the work they do. As Peter Smagorinsky (2011) explains, all cultural groups, classrooms included, are guided by a sense of *telos*, that is, "a sense of the optimal outcome that a culture provides for its participants" (p. 297). The optimal outcome in a classroom might be to pass a high-stakes test or to place out of a developmental reading class. These are undoubtedly important goals, ones that Jeff would embrace. But Jeff asks teachers to add something to the equation: to have the goal of students' being joyful and engaged readers who understand that reading has the capacity to make a real difference both in their own lives and in the communities in which they live. But having new goals is not enough. Smagorinsky continues to note that telos "suggests not only a direction, but a means for getting there" (p. 297). The second reason that this book is transformative is the extent to which it provides such a compelling portrait of how those goals can be achieved. It points the way for us to understand how we can help our students enter a story world through drama, symbolic story representations, and the use of visual art and other non-traditional texts. It points the way for us to cast our students as experts and collaborators in the educational enterprise. It helps us develop the pedagogical content knowledge to which Jeff refers in his Preface. It empowers readers by teaching them the strategies they need to enact the powerful new vision it urges teachers to adopt.

Now for the critique of current times. I think the book has lasted because too few professional publications recognize the importance of joy. Too few professional publications see the importance of the work we do in school to the work students can do outside school. Think about how many books have focused on achieving the Common Core State Standards. Think about how those standards are silent on how reading and writing can provide pleasure and foster civic engagement.

I hope in another 10 years this book is not as indispensable as it is now. But indispensable it remains.

—Michael W. Smith

Note: The Forewords for the first and second editions can be found online on this book's page and the free downloads page at TCPress.com

PREFACE TO THE THIRD EDITION

WHAT REALLY MATTERS

'm somewhat astonished to now be working on the Third Edition of *"You Gotta BE the Book."* I'm finding it as fun and stimulating to work on now as it was back then.

It's been 10 years since I prepared the Second Edition, and 20 years since the original publication. What has caused the book to continue to resonate with teachers over time? Why does it continue to inspire their teaching?

During these last 20 years, I've written over 35 different books about literacy and literacy learning. Even so, *YGBB* seems to be my foundational work.

When teachers talk to me at a conference, they most often want to talk about what *"You Gotta BE the Book"* has meant to them as teachers—or as parents, or as readers. I likewise get more emails about *YGBB* than about any of my other works. These messages are most frequently about the joy of reading, the interactive response dimensions of reading, and, recently, how these dimensions apply to the reading of nonfiction (short answer: my current research shows that they apply perfectly!; see Wilhelm & Smith, 2016). Sometimes I also get questions about methodological issues of pursuing teacher research, or fine-grained pedagogical questions (e.g., about how to use symbolic story representation with students). All of these are issues that I will take up in more detail in this edition.

Yet I think the resonance of *YGBB* is mostly due to its emphasis on joy and engagement, and how the processes of powerful transactional reading promote joy and engagement, and then deep understanding, and even transformation—transformation as readers, but even more significantly, as people. These goals are what called me to teaching and keep me engaged with it. That's true as well for the teachers I work most closely with in my own teaching, coteaching and thinking partnership, consulting, and work as a National Writing Project director.

There have been significant shifts in education over the past 20 years, and we now live and teach in the time of next-generation standards, such as the Common Core, with an emphasis on higher-order strategies, text complexity, and the reading of nonfiction. But the processes of engaged reading remain the same (and are prerequisite to strategic reading), and the call of the profound joy of lived-through experience and the transformational possibilities that we get from such reading remains the motivating allure.

THE JOY OF READING

"What in the world is this emotion?" Rebecca West asks after reading *King Lear.* "What is the bearing of supremely great works of art on my life that makes me feel so glad?" (Manguel, 1996, p. 106).

West's famous quote highlights that engaged reading—beyond involving cognitive processes (as the Core and next-generation standards emphasize)—is also a deeply emotional, participatory, dramatic, embodied, visual, artistic, psychological, and potentially transformational pursuit. This must not forget as teachers or as readers, or we will not tap into the immense power of reading, and thus we limit our capacity to be effective teachers or readers.

YGBB explores how expert readers make this kind of powerful and transactional experience happen for themselves as readers, and how teachers can model and help all readers make this experience happen for themselves, including those students who struggle with reading.

Literacy is essential to learning and to citizenship. In order to meet new standards and—much more importantly—be prepared for a complex future, our students will need to be highly motivated and highly literate. Literacy is necessary to modern life. Those who are not highly literate suffer from limited agency, and this leads to fewer life chances, decreased social mobility, more incarceration, and many other challenges. Literacy is a personally powerful and transformative activity, and also a political problem-solving pursuit on individual and cultural levels. Literacy is therefore a civil rights and social justice issue (for a review, see Wilhelm & Smith, 2014). Reading nonfiction is important to success in school, and to navigating life as a democratic worker and citizen. I'll explore in this edition how the findings and methods from *YGBB* pertain to non-fiction reading as well as fiction (see also Wilhelm & Smith, 2016).

To prepare students for the demands of disciplinary understanding and for literacy in the world, we need a robust vision of literacy, and an understanding of what really happens when expert readers read. Still more importantly, we need pedagogical content knowledge (Shulman, 1986, 1987) about reading. *Pedagogical content knowledge*—knowing *how* to teach students *how* to read, compose, problem-solve, and do disciplinary work in ways approaching how experts do it—is the hall-mark of expert teaching.

It is my observation that most research and books about teaching reading, particularly from the upper elementary through secondary levels, significantly under-articulate the complex task- and text-specific demands placed on readers engaged with different kinds of texts. Dominating the day are a few general strategies for teaching general cognitive processes of reading like making text-to-text connections. This book, in contrast, provides a finely detailed account of what expert and highly engaged adolescent readers actually do when they read, and an account of how to help less-engaged readers take on those same stances and strategies.

TEACHING IN THE TIME OF THE CORE AND OTHER NEXT-GENERATION STANDARDS

The intervening time between the First and Third Editions has seen the creation and implementation of next-generation education standards worldwide. In the United States, this movement has been expressed through the Common Core State Standards adopted by most states, and commensurate sets of standards created by the remaining states.

I want to highlight a significant point in regard to the standards: What is most powerful to learn and most generative and transferable to new situations are *procedures and strategies*. And these next-generation stan-dards worldwide are almost entirely procedural/strategic. Take a look at the Core anchor standards: They are all descriptions of strategic pro-cesses, of what students need to learn to *do*, with just brief and passing mentions in appendixes of what materials or facts students should know (familiarity with founding documents, a play of Shakespeare). The few references to lower-order strategies (e.g., RS 1: "Read closely to determine what the text says explicitly") are in immediate service of higher-order strategies (RS 1 cont'd: "and to make logical inferences from it; cite specific textual evidence when writing or speaking to support conclusions drawn from the text").

The focus is squarely on knowing *how* to engage in higher-order cognitive processes to make and apply meaning. This is consistent with what we know from cognitive science and literacy research about both "understanding" and "transfer."

TRANSFER AND "THRESHOLD KNOWLEDGE"

Here's another way to think about this tremendously important issue of transfer. Cognitive scientists describe what is most useful to teach and learn as "threshold knowledge." *Threshold knowledge* is a term used by Land and Meyer (2003) to describe "core concepts and processes that once understood, transform perception of a given subject" (n.p.), or problem-solving processes. Threshold knowledge is *unconstrained* and can be developed and refined throughout a lifetime. *Unconstrained knowledge is always strategic or involves using strategies to put concepts into play in real-world application.* Unconstrained knowledge can be transferred to new situations and often across domains. In cognitive science, "understanding" is defined as the capacity to do just this (e.g., Wiggins & McTighe, 2006).

Next-generation standards are examples of threshold knowledge. Again, threshold knowledge always involves the procedural/strategic, because even when we learn concepts those concepts must be applied and put into action through various strategies. If not, the concept is just an inert fact that cannot do any work or lead to further learning; until the concept is enacted, it is not transferred, does not demonstrate understanding, and is not knowledge.

Learning the alphabet is "constrained" knowledge—once you've learned it, it's done. The alphabet is a cultural fact. There is nothing further to develop. The same is true of learning how to decode text and answer literal-level questions. You learn it. Done. BAM. There are no new strategies or learning that are necessarily generated from this capacity.

But if one learns to analyze and see patterns, make connections, and infer complex implied relationships in texts and data sets, then this constitutes unconstrained and generative learning. (Analysis and inference are *throughlines* [an idea that runs through the text, is repeated, and connects and develops other ideas] of the Core standards and documents.) This is also true of learning to visualize, participate in story worlds, and elaborate and fill gaps, in order to monitor and self-regulate one's reading and thinking. These strategies can be further elaborated and developed throughout a lifetime. They lead immediately to the creation of further capacity and learning.

Therefore, next-generation standards represent profound cognitive achievements that, as far as they go, rightly promote the threshold knowledge necessary to the expert practice of readers and composers, speakers and listeners, all users of language, and problem-solvers doing the work of disciplines and of democratic citizenship.

I like the next-generation standards worldwide, and I like the Core, too. I have critiques, but these critiques are limited to: 1) How the Core is presented and construed, rather than the standards themselves,[1] and 2) What is missing from the Core. And what is missing is something that we, as teachers, can and must add for the good of our students (see Smith, Appleman, & Wilhelm, 2014).

ENGAGEMENT AS THE BIG MISSING PIECE OF THE STANDARDS

What is it that the standards miss? Rereading *YGBB* in the time of the Core and next-generation standards, it strikes me that the book is about engagement and motivation (missing from the Core), and the development of expertise through the learning of threshold processes (some of these also MIA from standards documents), which must be developed for students to become lifelong readers, learners and citizens.

So when I say that *YGBB* is about engagement—about joy, love, imagination, and creativity—I mean that the book explores, in addition to strategic process and stances of expert readers, *what must be added* to these and to the cognitive processes detailed in the Core standards in order for students to be motivated to meet the standards; to actually meet them; and to experience the magic of reading, its power, its profound transformational capacity. I mean that this book explores what *must be added* to promote *real* reading with students, that is, the necessary pre-

---

1. In fact, this critique is robust enough that I coauthored a book-length treatment to detail it entitled *Uncommon Core*.

requisites to providing the *context* and the *assistance* students need to read as experts do, to connect personally to the alchemy of meaning-making that is so transformative and that engaged readers love so much. I mean that the book highlights and explores what needs to be embraced as teachers to keep us tapped into the magic; to help students enact and experience and reflect on the magic; and to remind us of why we read, and why we teach, and what must be learned by students to transform reading from a technical pursuit (as it is largely described in the Core) to the magical journey of making meaning, doing inner work, and outgrowing and transforming the self to know and become and be something new.

This is what I mean: that with the advent of new standards and cultural challenges, *YGBB* is *even more relevant and needed.*

To channel Alberto Manguel in his masterful *A History of Reading* (1996), I mean that *YGBB* is a reminder that reading is a movement through various landscapes, whether fictional or real, that we often navigate in wonder, like Don Quixote on Rocinante, questing to embrace both the immense struggles as well as the magnificent pleasure and the power, seeking new lived-through adventures, deepened understanding, and transformed being—grasping for that something more, for that best possible self, for that becoming of something new. I mean that we read for the story, for the experience, but also for the application, and always for the sake of the reading itself. We read to reach conclusions and the story's end. We also read *not* to reach conclusions, to live on a threshold in liminal spaces of possibility, to hold disparate ideas in our minds all at once and to let them linger and bother us. We read like hunters and trackers, seeking a prey and prize, oblivious to our surroundings. We also read more openly, exploring nooks and crannies, taking detours. The reader is both like a hiker heading purposefully down the trail, and like her dog, rollicking around wildly, snuffling in the plants and trees. We read passionately, longingly, angrily . . .

In the standards documents, reading is described in technical, cognitive terms. If we are to preserve the wonder of reading necessary to true engagement, then this current historical moment provides a deep challenge to teachers, a challenge that *YGBB* can help to meet.

TEACHING AND LEARNING AS STRUGGLE

In addition to the challenges that have emerged on the professional level, we have all faced personal challenges as well. In my own case, 9 years ago my wife, Peggy, collapsed of what was thought to be brain cancer, but turned out to be a massive cerebral hemorrhage. Her health journey has been a harrowing one, involving years at the Mayo Clinic and the National Institutes of Health Undiagnosed Diseases Program, countless operations, 23 more brain bleeds causing traumatic brain injuries, compromised balance and vision, and many other challenges. She spent 2 months in a coma, and we were told that she was terminal on four different occasions. At the present moment, we have a working diagnosis and Peggy is improving, no longer in danger of losing her life.

What is the takeaway of challenges in the professional landscape and of the inevitable personal challenges? To me, the takeaway is that teaching and learning are struggle; that reading and composing are struggle; and that life, in fact, is struggle. These struggles can be highly productive and illuminating and even fantastically fulfilling IF one possesses a dynamic mindset, gets assistance at the point of need, and knows strategies for how to proceed and move forward. This is true for teaching; true for reading; true for everyday living and democratic life.

How did "we" succeed in meeting Peggy's medical challenge? Of course, Peggy is a woman of immense grit and grace. But there is also this: We were thinking partners and teachers for each other throughout this health journey. We never gave up in the face of her dire diagnoses. We tirelessly researched medical options, and kept open minds toward all perspectives and possibilities. We had friends and family to support us. We found doctors and health practitioners who became our thinking partners, who were willing to think outside the box as researchers, always asking "What if?" and "What if it were otherwise?," exploring conventional and then alternative treatments like traditional Chinese medicine (TCM). In the end, it was TCM that offered a solid diagnosis and a path toward health, verified by her symptoms and by all metrics of both Eastern and Western medicine.

We and these thinking partners maintained a growth mindset (Dweck, 2006), a belief that we had the capacity to more deeply understand and improve our situation through effort and expert strategic applications, and we used our strategic knowledge as readers and researchers to continue moving forward. We all demonstrated resilience as learners.

This is something I tell the student teachers and practicing teachers with whom I work: Don't give up. Keep after it. *"Schild immer vorner!"* (German for: "Keep your shield in front of you—always moving forward!")

In our studies of the literate lives of boys (Smith & Wilhelm, 2002; 2006), Michael Smith and I found that boys would undertake profound challenges—with literacy and otherwise—if and only if they felt totally assured that a teacher would provide the assistance they needed and would not give up on them. Without such assurance, the boys typically punted on significant challenges. Teachers, like a life partner or any thinking partner, must stay with the relationships with students and stay with the problems and not give up. They must engage in *bricolage*, trying out new and creative ways of solving problems. I personally think that what students most learn from us, and what I hope my own children learned from our family's medical journey, is that life is an inevitable struggle, but there is beauty, grace, and inspiration in this struggle, and there are always untapped resources for addressing problems. This book is meant to help you deeply understand engagement with reading, to understand what highly engaged readers do as they read, and to model and mentor and monitor as *you* teach and *your students* learn to experience and take on the stances and strategies of highly engaged readers. It is meant to help you stay with the struggle and have a wide repertoire of strategies to use when students, as so many do, are challenged by reading.

BEING THE BOOK OVER THE YEARS

On my own personal professional level, I've continued to teach—both in middle and high schools (I'm currently teaching 8th- and 11th-grade English in Saarbrücken, Germany, as a Fulbright fellow), and at the university level as a National Writing Project director working with practicing teachers in classrooms on a variety of initiatives.

As a much younger teacher, 12 years into my career, and as a novice researcher writing *YGBB*, I worried and wondered about how to 1) stay enthused and passionate as a teacher, 2) stay fresh and keep developing my pedagogy over time, and 3) set up and pursue a research agenda that would support my ongoing development as a teacher.

It turned out that the answer to all three questions was the same: become a reflective teacher and an action researcher. Or, to put it in other terms: keep trying new methods and techniques and then reflect, with students and colleagues, on how it went, what could be different, how to revise that practice to make it even better for the next time. In other words, to embrace a dynamic growth mindset.

I've found over the last 20-plus years (wow—can this be possible?) that I needn't have worried. The classroom action research that I pursued in writing *YGBB* provided the springboard to my future instructional experiments, joy and engagement, research and reflection ever since. I know, too, that for many of the readers of this book, they too have found the innovative pedagogies they have developed as a result, and their deep reflections and revisions based on these implementations, to be both informative and inspiring to the continuing trajectory of their practice.

One thing leads to another; road leads on to road.

In preparing this Third Edition, it strikes me that in fact, my research agenda since the writing of *YGBB* has been organized around the same central question and project I pursued here: How can I help reluctant and struggling readers and learners to engage with their reading and learning, and to take on the stances and strategies, the purposes and procedures, of experts, so that they can understand and independently pursue the power of learning on their own, in ways that they value personally and that are valued out in the world and in the disciplines?

It surprises but gratifies me that the work I did over 20 years ago has continued to inform all of my work since that time. In fact, even today— just like 20 years ago—I can't think of anything that is more compelling or challenging than helping disenfranchised and disengaged readers to enter into the expertise and excitement of those who are members of the innermost sanctum of the literacy club. It is a journey that can transform students as readers, as learners, and even as people. It is an arduous journey, but one worth taking. And there is no way to help students on this journey unless we as teachers model the growth mindset and resilience to take it with them.

TEACHING WITH URGENCY

If anything, I undertake this journey now with even more energy and urgency than before. Which one of our students is expendable? Whose needs can we afford to leave unmet? Who will not need to be a reader and problem-solver? A believer in her own potential? Since the answer is obviously none at all, then what we, as individual teachers, can do today for our students, let us do today. What we can then do tomorrow, let us do tomorrow. What control we have, let us exercise it fully. Certainly, there is much to do.

The challenges facing our world are compelling, and it will be up to the next generation we now teach to address these challenges. What is already known will not suffice; our students must learn to frame problems and solve them with imagination, in new and creative ways.

In many studies (see, e.g., Smith & Wilhelm, 2002; 2006), students have been found to crave personally engaging, challenging, and socially significant work. They crave competence. The problem does not lie with students. Yet the quality of students' lived experience in school has been shown to be dire (Goodlad, 1984; Smith & Wilhelm, 2002; Steinberg, 1996). School, particularly the academic experience, can be mind-numbing. As all of us can attest from personal experience, such a situation does not promote motivation or learning. Emphasis on standardized testing has only exacerbated the problem. But most heartbreaking to me is how easily, even in the face of existing constraints, student experience could be different, and learning in school could be significant, engaging, and fun. Reading could be more powerfully supported and encouraged. This will happen only if teachers take the necessary steps through the crossroads in their own classrooms. We must also take steps forward in our own schools, communities, and professional networks. The steps forward are ours to take.

To do so, we must use contexts of inquiry as cognitive apprenticeship and interactive strategies that meet kids' current needs for personal relevance, and for social as well as disciplinary significance—ones that develop and use imagination and new ways of creating meaning with text.

Many studies show the importance of using engaging, interactive, hands-on techniques for developing new processes of meaning-making and deep conceptual understanding (see, e.g., Smith & Wilhelm, 2002, 2010; Wilhelm, 2007). I would also make the case for the importance of developing and using imagination.

THE POWER OF PLEASURE READING

Imagination is essential to all learning. We must be able to imagine what it was like to live in a different time or place, to imagine what might happen if we extrapolate data patterns, to imagine a story world or a mental model of how feudalism would affect us or how inertia works. Most importantly, perhaps, we must be able to imagine ourselves as the kind of person who would want and be able to use what is being learned when we are out in the real world, and we must imagine ourselves doing so. We must be able to imagine making a difference through who we are and what we are learning to become.

Pertinent to this new edition is my recent research on the satisfactions and benefits of pleasure reading (Wilhelm & Smith, 2014), and how pleasure reading serves democracy and operates as a vehicle toward civil rights, social equality, and mobility. The stakes are indeed very high when it comes to becoming an engaged reader.

That research leads me to argue that we must include free-choice pleasure reading as part of our teaching—both integrated into inquiry units, and as an informal adjunct:

◆ Because it is the single most powerful way to promote cognitive progress;
◆ Because it is a civil rights issue for social mobility, coming out of poverty, educational attainment, avoiding incarceration . . . ; and
◆ Because pleasure reading in youth has more to do with overcoming social inequalities than any other verified factor.

There's much research supporting these contentions (see, e.g., Krashen, Lee, & McQuillan, 2012), but to my mind the most compelling is the British cohort study, following the lives of more than 17,000 people born in England, Scotland, and Wales in a single week of 1970.

The latest analysis (Sullivan & Brown, 2013) of this evolving data set establishes that reading for pleasure in youth outside school has a highly significant impact on people's educational attainment and social mobility, in part because pleasure reading actually "increased cognitive progress over time." This effect is much more significant than parents' education or socioeconomic status, a stunning and revolutionary finding that shows how powerful pleasure reading can be in helping students overcome life challenges.

Our study *Reading Unbound* (Wilhelm & Smith, 2014) explains the pleasures readers get from their free-choice reading, and how these in turn develop cognitive progress, as well as personal progress, over time. The pleasures include:

◆ Immersive play pleasure, which develops the capacity to enter textual experiences, to visualize and participate in such worlds;
◆ Intellectual pleasure, which develops the capacity to see patterns, fill gaps, and figure things out like how and why things happen, and how and why texts work to create meaning and effect;
◆ Work pleasure, which develops the capacity to develop functional applications and transfer what is learned to new situations;
◆ Inner work pleasure, which develops the capacity to use reading to evaluate who you are and rehearse who you want to become, and to navigate psychological and emotional challenges; and

◆ Social pleasure, which develops the cognitive processes of identifying oneself, affiliating with groups, and differentiating oneself.

WHAT THE TEACHER LEARNED

When I pursued the research leading to *YGBB*, I learned to listen to my students. I learned that you have to get to know your students to be able to teach them. I learned that when you ask them and listen, you'll be surprised by what they already know, think, and feel, and what they are capable of learning next. I learned not to underestimate my students: that they are capable of more than I thought—especially if I provide a meaningful context of use for their reading and writing, and if I assist them in practicing new strategies.

Anders Ericsson's research (popularized by Malcolm Gladwell; see Ericsson, 2016, for a critique of Gladwell's presentation and a discussion of the research and its implications) demonstrates that learners need (as a very rough average) 3,000 hours of "deliberate practice" to become competent with a complex repertoire like reading or composing. Just spending time reading is *not* deliberate practice—reading while consciously trying out new strategies is *deliberate* practice. And you could practice for 3,000 hours and still suck. You need assisted and focused practice that works toward what is known as the "correspondence concept" (Bereiter, 2004), i.e., that corresponds to expert practice. This book is about what we need to deliberately practice (strategies meeting the correspondence concept) and ways to practice these strategies in real reading and real contexts of use like inquiry as cognitive apprenticeship leading to application and social action.

I learned that to listen and learn from students you have to find ways for them to make their thinking and reading and writing and productive struggles visible and available to you, to themselves, to peers. This research project is when I first began to explore the possibilities of visualization strategies, symbolic story representation and reading manipulatives, drama and action strategies, questioning and discussion techniques, and a variety of group structures. I've continued to experiment with all these techniques and to write about them ever since, and I'm sharing some of the most effective with you by adding them to the new edition of this book at the end of each chapter.

I learned and became passionate about what I've come to call "the authority of practice": that the authority of teachers comes from their experience, deliberate practice, and reflection on teaching, from continual learning from students how best to teach them. I learned how to study learning in the context of school and lived-through experience outside of school.

Like a giant web growing outward from the rich soil of this research, I have subsequently considered the conditions that motivate and support literacy, the effects of inquiry environments on learning and literacy, and the effects of teaching and learning for service; studied boys' literate lives inside and outside of school; and continued to study the power of pleasure reading. All of these threads are about engagement, and how to guide students to deeper engagement and understanding by using various interventions and expert strategies in new and more powerful ways as they are actually reading.

This web extends to the learning and teaching of this book's readers, their reflections, and their own innovations. It gratifies and inspires me to continue sharing this learning through this latest edition, and to continue extending this giant web. It gratifies me to hear from readers who are using inquiry, experimenting with visual and drama strategies, and creating their own situated expertise in concert with their students.

MAKING THE MOST OF OUR EXPERIENCE

Writing a new edition certainly invites reflection upon the intervening time. In *A Pilgrim at Tinker Creek*, Annie Dillard (1998) writes that the way we spend our days is ultimately the way we spend our lives. It's both a thrilling and a chilling thought. As a teacher, am I using each day to teach my students in the most challenging, interesting, exciting, and worthwhile ways? If not, then why not, and how might I overcome the obstacles to doing so?

Because if I do not face this challenge with wide-awakeness, attentiveness, and courage, then I teach years of days and multitudes of students in ways that are not all they could be. I fail to actualize the potential of my teaching and of my students.

Time passes. Sometimes the experiences of time cause our guiding principles and thinking to undergo radical revisions—as happened to me during the time of the reading, research, and writing that went into this book. Sometimes these principles and ideas become deepened and more complex over time, as has generally been the case for me in regard to the central insights expressed in this book in the time since its first publication.

This Third Edition keeps the original version, both because of the success of the original text and because of its data-driven nature, which cannot be revised after the fact. Instead, in addition to the original text, each chapter concludes with a new reflection on how changes in policy, insights from research, and my subsequent experience as a teacher, a teacher educator, and a researcher working with schools and with students has informed my evolving thinking about the research and the insights I report on in this book. I've also added some key practical resources that I've developed along the journey that may help you along your own.

In your class, at this moment, many of your students may have their last best chance to engage, learn, and succeed, to become readers with a literate identity and a growth mindset, to begin actualizing their potential. Grasp the moment. Pursue it. With *urgency*.

In this book, I hope to help you on this quest, and even more importantly, to help you help your students on their quests to become all that they can be.

Here goes.

ACKNOWLEDGMENTS

෨

I wish to thank many people who were important to the thinking, conversing, and drafting that went into the completion of this book. The completion of such a project would have been impossible without the help and support of many people, to whom I am very grateful.

Above all, thank you to my wife, Peggy Jo, for her understanding support through the past several years. Her loving kindnesses and her constant belief that I would grow significantly through the long process of sustained study and writing—not to mention her constant belief that I would actually finish what I had set out to do—were of great and necessary importance to me.

My appreciation and thanks go to David Schaafsma and Stuart Greene for their generosity of time, energy, and thoughtful response to much of my work. Their encouragement and expertise have been much appreciated.

Thanks also to Wayne Otto and Deb Brandt for their reading of this manuscript and their very helpful suggestions.

A special thanks must go to Patricia Enciso for guidance, help, and sharing of her own expertise and many insights. Michael Smith also offered constant encouragement and support. Brian Edmiston was a great help to me as I planned, implemented, and analyzed the drama activities.

I would like to thank my team teaching colleague Paul Friedemann for his support; my friend Brian Ambrosius for serving as a model reader and a model tennis partner; Leon Holley Jr. for his collegial support and friendship through the years; and Erv Barnes for many discussions on our companionable trips down to Madison, Wisconsin. Thanks to my colleagues Brenda Power, Jim Artesani, and Kelly Chandler at the University of Maine for their help during the final drafting. Thanks to Steven Olsen-Smith for his collegiality and assistance chasing down literary citations.

Thanks to my father and my mother (both deceased) for instilling in me a love of learning and of reading, and some growth mindset stubbornness besides, and to my many dedicated teachers through the years, most notably James Blaser and William Strohm.

For this Third Edition, I deeply wish to acknowledge and thank my colleague and co-director of the Boise State Writing Project, Jim Fredricksen, and the many Boise State Writing Project fellows who have been my thinking partners over the years, further and bravely experimenting and developing many of the teaching techniques explored here. There are many more of them worthy of acknowledgment then can be recorded here, but I would be remiss not to give a hearty hug and a cheer of profound gratitude and a place on the roll of honor to the National Writing Project, to friend and colleague Tanya Baker of the National Writing Project, all of my BSWP co-directors and teacher leaders, especially Paula Uriarte, Ramey Uriarte, Frank Dehoney, Rachel Bear, Chris Butts, Jackie Miller, Karen Miller, Jonelle Warnock, Debra Smith, Brandon Bolyard, Emily Morgan, Micah Lauer, Nancy Tacke, Jerry Hendershot, Jess Westhoff, Patti Wiseman-Adams, Cecilia Soto-Pattee, Greg Wilson, my so capable assistant Dawn Brown—the list goes on. The rest of you know who you are: please accept my anonymous but still heartfelt thanks! Thanks to friends Todd Fischer, Bob White, Dale Reynolds, Ralph Comstock, Patrick Harren, One Arm Willie Stewart, Mike Weber, Steve Olsen-Smith, Whitney Douglass, Kathleen Rose, Shelle Marks, Connie Bates, and many others who were always there for me and my family during my wife's long health struggle. Thanks too to my friends and fellow book-clubbers who always indulge me in using our club meetings to think about why and how we read: Paula and Ramey Uriarte, Gregor and Wita Wojtkowski, Mark and Gemma Utting, Debra Smith, Steve Bushi, Ceredig and Hannah Roberts, as well as my wife Peggy Jo. Also many thanks to my daughters Fiona and Jasmine, readers and composers both (not to mention being fine and courageous young women) who submitted willingly (mostly) over the years to many of my reading and learning experiments and who were willing to share their thoughts on literacy and much else with me. Of course, many thanks to the persistent Emily Spangler and the whole editorial team at TCP. They make their authors look smarter with their wonderful editing and design. Also many grateful thanks to all the students with whom I have engaged and learned over the course of 33 years of teaching and 57 years of living. Finally, thanks as always to Michael W. Smith, who has been my unfailing thinking partner and friend over these many years.

INTRODUCTION

Really Among Schoolchildren

A s I read my early teaching journals and reflect, I look back through cloud banks of memory and am more than a little bit dubious of the confidence my younger self often expressed. I was certainly enthusiastic, totally in love with what I was experiencing with my students. There are days now when I would like to plug into that sort of positive energy. I wrote about *knowing* how to teach literature and *knowing* how to teach writing. For a young guy I was pretty smug. "I'm getting it down cold," I wrote one day over 10 years ago. "I'm cruising down the curricular highway, nailing lesson after lesson, skill after skill. I feel like a batter on a hitting streak" (March 1984).

My association with the National Writing Project supported and excited my thinking about the teaching of writing. The cornucopia of college and graduate literature courses I had enjoyed made me think I knew literature, and therefore how to teach it. I knew lots of stuff, for sure.

THE READING STRUGGLE

Today I find this sort of highly competent feeling about my own teaching almost unimaginable. All my original beliefs about learning and instruction have undergone intense changes over the past few years. I now regard all of my current positions as categorically tentative. I converse daily with colleagues and with students, looking for a slightly better way to do things. Margaret Meek's (Meek et al., 1983) question about learning,

"What if it is otherwise?" has become almost a mantra. I search daily for ways to help my individual students learn more fruitfully. There are practices, such as directly intervening in student literary interpretations, that I have rejected, embraced, and rejected again before coming to some sort of compromise position that I am sure will be compromised again.

My reflections these days have more to do with how often I may have missed opportunities while navigating my students from September to June through the course of a school year. Was I oblivious to tremendously important issues occurring in the minds and hearts of my student crew, sealed off from the view of my chart room? Did the evidence I garnered to support the idea of my earlier successes come only from my most enthusiastic students? Were there students whose needs I missed or dismissed? What might I be missing now? Did I know how to look into the secret hearts of my students' reading lives? What windows are now available to me into student attitudes and reading processes? What opportunities and students might be slipping away at this very moment?

These days, the complexity and responsibility of teaching 130 individual students often weigh upon me as a series of almost awesome possibilities.

What changed for me? For 7 years I had taught high school English and speech with panache and assurance. Then I transferred to the middle school to teach language arts and three courses of "remedial reading."

It was the experience of teaching eighth-grade "remedial reading" that really shook me up for the first time. In retrospect, those classes were the knocks in my mental engine that became thrown piston rods. After "remedial reading" I no longer possessed the confidence that my teaching theories and practices could help many of my students on their journeys to becoming independent readers and learners, nor sustain me on my own journey as a teacher.

You see, those kids knew what it meant to be labeled a "remedial reader." With every move and comment they made, they damned the very label, the class they were in, and their whole history of reading education in school. My confusion and frustration began on the first day I met my "remedial readers," and it never let up.

Over the first few days of school they strode into class and greeted me with hurled gauntlets such as, "I'm Jeff and I hate reading!"

"You can't make me read!"

"I'm a terrible reader. That's just the way it is. Sorry."

This message was repeated through a myriad of other explicitly and subtly insistent ways during that confusing first semester. Early in February, I made this journal entry:

> What a day! What a week of days! What a year of days! The eighth graders simply hate reading, or say that they do, and they refuse to even try to do it. Whether this is a defense-mechanism, a learned behavior or what, I don't know, but they won't be shaken from it. And another thing I don't know is how to help them change so they'll have a chance to become better readers. I have tried plan A, B, C, and D and I don't have a plan E! And if I don't find a parachute quickly I believe that I am going to crash and burn and take all of my little kiddies with me. And then I will be the biggest smoking black hole in family history. (February 1989)

This is how the year unfolded: After a first few dismally unsuccessful weeks, I put the basal readers and reading skills workbooks onto the shelf. Then I tried using newspapers, short stories, and journal writing, then free-choice reading and literary letter writing. Nothing worked. The students wouldn't bring any reading materials to class. They wouldn't choose books from our classroom library. Neither comic books nor magazines appealed to them. Trips to the library left them unmoved. They refused to write literary letters to each other, or would write the most cursory letters imaginable: "Hi Trudy. My books stupid. See you after school."

Finally I went exclusively with what I prayed would work: the reading of stories and trade books together as a class.

On this particular February day we were reading *Deathwatch* by Robb White, a story of a young man who guides a rich hunter into the desert. When the hunter "mistakenly" kills an old hermit and his guide insists that it must be reported, the hunter strips the boy and drives off without him, vowing to wait and watch until the boy dies of exposure. It's a disturbing yet powerful story, full of visceral injustice, action, and adventure. The students selected it themselves from several options.

We began the unit with a desert survival simulation that actually worked! The students imagined that we had been stranded by an airplane crash in the middle of the desert. Each class eagerly bought into this imaginary situation, which surprised and relieved me. As a group, the students had to rank the items available on the plane in order of importance to their survival. Finally, the class had to reach consensus about a plan for achieving their survival. All three of the classes were animated and fun. I wrote that "it was the first time all year I didn't feel it was a struggle to get through class" (February 1989).

The girls enjoyed the first few chapters as well as the boys, reacting mostly to the "unfairness" and injustice of the protagonist's situation, much as the boys engaged with his struggle for survival against an evil enemy and the forces of nature.

But after just 3 days of reading, things slowly fell apart. The students would listen when I read aloud, but many would not follow along. When I asked them to read in pairs or small groups, they resisted. So I asked them to read on their own. On one bleak Thursday afternoon, half the class closed their books and put their heads down. Three girls began chatting about their weekend plans. Two girls were actually reading, but none of the boys. I went to each student in turn, asking why? why? and WHY?

Perhaps because I was polite, the students were generally polite in return, but insistent. "I don't like to read," Jamie told me. "It's OK when you read out loud," Troy said, "but there's no way I'm going to read it by myself or with any idiot from this class."

In short, the class simply shut down. They would listen to me read, but there was "no way" they were going to try it on their own.

By now I was pretty thoroughly entangled in the strings of parachute D and I had nowhere to turn, except perhaps down—where I could see the hard cement of classroom reality rushing up to meet me.

PERSONAL READINGS

During the same time frame, I was hugely enjoying several books on my own, books that I read in every free moment, books that I stayed up late into the night to read, books that haunted me, books that made me not want to speak for hours or made me call a friend to talk, books that stayed with me for days and were replayed in my dreams, books that insistently tapped on my memory and wove themselves into the tapestry of my life.

I read Flanagan's *The Year of the French* and imagined myself, each morning at breakfast, as an Irish peasant eating bacon for the first time in my life and enjoying it intensely. I savored the food all the more because I deeply suspected that the French would betray us and I would be hanged as a traitor. And I would never eat bacon—or anything else—ever again.

I read Ishiguro's *The Remains of the Day* in one sitting and was compelled to take a long silent walk in the woods. I sat down on a bench and silently cried for the main character and for my own foolish losses and decisions. As I thought about my experience with the book, I wrote my wife a series of intense letters that I left for her each morning at the breakfast table. I read Paton's *Too Late the Phalarope* and finished it when I should have been coaching. My assistant coach, a brother in the reading fraternity, had told me to "finish it, and then go home." He had read the book, too, and knew that I would be worthless for coaching after the experience of its conclusion. He would take the practice. It was a generous offer, and good advice, because I was so deeply inside the book that I could have been at the bottom of the sea. There was no way to quickly resurface without getting the bends.

I have had these experiences with books as far back as I can remember. My best friendships involve books; some friendships are because of books. There are authors and characters that I feel I know so well I regard them as friends, great-hearted people whom I get to know better each time I read. Seeing that they have written a new book or story is like receiving a dinner invitation: a chance to get to visit and know each other more.

When I finish a book, I have in some way finished a chapter in a relationship that I will continue to nurture. There are always two or three more books awaiting that I have already started, and another pile near my bed that have aroused my interest from their former place on a friend's bookshelf, the library, or a bookstore. I carry a book with me everywhere, just in case a train comes by or I'm stuck in a waiting room. I cannot imagine a day of my life without reading. This is why I studied literature in college. This is why I became a teacher: to share in grand conversations about books, to spread the joy, to initiate and welcome students into the fraternity, into what Frank Smith (1988) calls "the club of clubs," to travel with them into wondrously familiar or incredibly strange imaginative worlds.

As I considered the intense meaning of reading in my own life, I felt that there were significant numbers of students who were sleeping in their seats as I developed my own classroom literary flight plans. The plans and the journeys were my own, and seemed inaccessible to many of these eighth graders. What experiences did they lack that might help them to develop a love of reading like my own, or at least to glimpse the potential of stories? How might I change my teaching, adapt my chosen modes of curricular transportation, to make the students active planners and participants in their own sojourns?

CHILDREN'S HOUR

At night, after struggling with my eighth graders, I often found myself happily reading to small children: my niece, the neighbor boy, and my own small daughter, Fiona. The experience was always the same. At the sight of me, the child would run to find a book, yell something like, "Let's read!" and jump into my lap, sometimes before I even had a chance to sit down. And one book was never enough. Oh no! These children consumed books as if they were Lay's potato chips. It didn't matter what book; no one could read just one. Fiona to this day opens her own negotiations with the question, "Two books or three?"

After reading, I would pronounce "The End" like a solemn "Amen," bringing closure to our shared reading experience. There would be a moment of thoughtful silence, perhaps a question, then the cathedral-like silence would shatter like a baseball thrown through stained glass, with "Read A-nudder One! Please, please, please, please, PLEASE!" (And how can one refuse a request like that?)

Reading with these children was a series of joyous surprises. Sometimes they would sit silently, soaking up the world of the book. But more often than not, they would interrupt me, pointing at pictures, telling stories about their own lives, laughing, asking questions, judging, elaborating, and even getting up to make faces and act out scenes from the book. I made several journal entries about our reading, commenting always on how reading, for them, was much more than "words." In fact, I was sometimes irritated with all the interruptions to what I regarded as "the story." For them, reading was an adventure that was unique each time. The books were suggestions, maps to be consulted, edited, deviated from. For these children, a book was a promise, and reading was an experiential fulfillment of the promise.

While reading a simple little story by Hans Wilhelm entitled *Waldo Goes to the Zoo,* my daughter interrupted on the very first page, telling a story about how "we went to the zoo and we saw the walrus and he spit at us, didn't he, Daddy?" She later pounced to the floor and roared like a lion, strutted like a giraffe, and then glided back to my side to continue reading, without commentary or explanation.

After *Waldo* it was *Madeline's Rescue* by Ludwig Bemelmans, which we must have read for the next 10 nights running. When I asked if we could read *Madeline* or *Madeline and the Bad Hat,* Fiona was most insistent; only *Madeline's Rescue* would do. "I want to read this one!"

she insisted. (In my journal that night I ruminated about how I discouraged students from re-reading a book or even an author that they had already read.)

On the first page, Fiona chimed in to read the final rhyme of each couplet, cheering out the words and laughing. She pointed at the vines on the house and said, "Look, here's the vines!"

On page two, before a word could be uttered, Fiona yelled, "Oh no! Madeline shouldn't do that!" upon seeing that Madeline was walking on the railing of a bridge.

Without letting me read out the words, she turned the page and told me, "Don't worry, the dog will save her," as we studied the picture of Madeline sinking into the Seine. She pointed out various details: the blue house, the painter—"he's mad, isn't he, Daddy? Why were you mad at Jasmine [her baby sister] today?"—the policeman, and even Miss Clavell holding her head. "Don't worry, Miss Clavell!" she advised Madeline's teacher and caretaker. She even attempted to comfort Miss Clavell's picture, by patting the nun's back with her finger.

And on it went. Lord Cucuface was "mean. He's a bad man!" Miss Clavell was "nice," Madeline "naughty . . . sometimes, like me." A monologue followed explaining how she was mostly good but could still be "contrary" sometimes. Two stories were told about our neighbors' dogs, Cody and Monty, who had run away that past week.

At the end, when the puppies are born, Fiona laughed wildly, as she had each day for the past 10 days. "Look at all the doggies!" she gulped between giggles, proceeding to count the pups.

And before I could say "The End," Fiona turned to me and informed me, quite diplomatically, "I don't want to go to bed yet!" She shook her head sideways. "I'm not tired. Let's read another one!"

It was on this same night in February that the neighbor boy's mom came over in a distraught mood. At that night's parent-teacher conferences she had been told that her first-grade son was doing poorly in reading, and that in fact he seemed to resist reading. The teacher had suggested testing and possibly enrollment in extra-help programs.

COMPELLING QUESTIONS

Something was going on here, something as fishy and distasteful as cod liver oil. How could a boy who loved books, who loved sitting on a couch to read, who in fact continued to insist upon it in the comfort of his own home or my own, how could such a boy *not* like and succeed at reading in school?

There was clearly some sort of chasm for him between home reading and school reading, between what I came to consider engaged and unengaged experiences of reading.

And what about my daughter? As much as she loved reading now, could she become a nonreader who had lost the sense of reading's mystery, drama, magic, and camaraderie? Whatever had happened (or not happened) to my eighth-grade students that they would not now give the act of reading another chance? As I thought about this, I began to formulate the questions that guided the subsequent years of classroom research and revised practice that I will report on in this book, primarily through the telling of three teacher research stories.

Why do some kids love reading? What is rewarding and engaging about reading for these students? What do these engaged readers "do" as they read that makes the experience fun, satisfying, and engaging for them?

Why do other kids hate reading? What in their experience has contributed to their negative view?

I realized that year after year, I had encountered students who obviously resisted reading. But they seemed to be a minority, and eventually—I'm ashamed to say—I'd really just given up on them as far as their becoming readers was concerned. It was when I encountered a whole class of them that I could not blame them instead of myself, the materials, or the method. Eighth-grade remedial reading produced a crisis that required a new way of thinking about and teaching the act of reading. If I wished to pursue my job of developing readers, then resistance and lack of engagement were compelling issues that had to be deeply considered.

These considerations led to the central concern of this book and the theme of my most recent teaching: How might less engaged readers be helped to read in the way that engaged readers do, and maybe (just maybe!) become readers themselves?

TENTATIVE ANSWERS

I considered these questions for several years, thinking about them, reading and writing about them, and testing out revised practices in my classroom. I kept track of what happened in class and interviewed students about their own attitudes, views, and experiences. I talked to my engaged readers and those who were unengaged and reluctant. I encouraged them to talk to each other.

As part of a graduate course, I used audiotaped protocols of students observing their own reading processes. The next year I used cued protocols, asking students to stop at various points in their reading and report their thoughts, feelings, imaginings. I kept questioning. I looked for any window that would make reading visible and offer me a glimpse of information about my driving questions. What has resulted is an evolving story about how my own student readers read and how they may be helped to read in more engaged and satisfying ways. The story I tell here is primarily the story of my students, how they revealed the moves they make as readers, what they made happen, and what happened for them when new classroom practices such as art and drama were put into play. But it is also my own story, and that of my own developing perspective on the teaching of reading and of the practice of literacy in classrooms.

For a problem such as this, I wanted advice, but I knew I had to find my own answer. No one else could know my students, or see what happened when we tried new things together. I took myself, as jazz musicians like to say, "out to the woodshed" for some heavy thinking. I tried to become aware of my implicit theories, think clearly about what I could do in the classroom and what ends I thought might be achieved through new practices. I became, for the first time, what I regard as a teacher-researcher: a teacher who is consciously questioning, observing, theorizing, testing, adapting, and learning something every day in the classroom. Teacher research revitalized my passion for teaching, for reading literature with students, and it helped me to both read and teach in more aware and powerful ways. The story of what happened to the students involves what happened, and continues to happen, to me as the teacher. I see my experience as a teacher-researcher as one of reclaiming my classroom for myself and for my students, of taking control, together, of what and how we will do things together. This active control, and the awareness and willingness to use it, is what "empowerment" means to me.

The professional landscape of education has long been occupied by people who aren't teachers, and though I know these experts add valuable voices to the educational conversation, they can't be expected to have a teacher's perspective.

My experience as a teacher-researcher leads me to encourage teachers to become researchers who collaborate with students and share a community of multivoiced stories, providing a variety of classroom-based viewpoints from which to survey different parts of a highly complex topography of readers, literary experience, and learning. By combining our various voices, perhaps we can devise a map and a sense of the landscape that will help us all to become better and more independent readers of words and, as Freire encourages us, readers of the world.

SETTING THE TASK

For the past four school years, my students started the year by anonymously completing attitude inventories. These inventories indicated that most of my own middle school students did not regard themselves as readers. Between 30 and 50 percent of the responses indicated that though the students generally regarded themselves as "competent" readers, the activity of reading was something they saw solely as a necessary life skill and school activity. In their private lives, nearly half of my student population noted that they were "nonreaders," that they read "rarely," that they regarded reading as something required by "school," instead of something to do on your own, at "home," for "personal satisfaction," or with "friends" or "family." They wrote that they would not choose to read as a leisure-time activity, ranking it far below television, video games, sports, and, for some, even below "chores"! A variety of other responses also hinted that they generally held negative attitudes toward reading.

Each year, I am continually astonished by these results. I had always been aware of a few highly resistant and unengaged readers, some who were out of the closet and some who did their best to hide. But I had never dreamed that so many would anonymously express a total lack of interest in reading as a personally fulfilling pursuit. There were so many!

I began asking students to voice their opinions about everything that they read. I provided time during each class to log and write letters about what had been read the previous day: books, magazines, newspapers, cereal boxes, STOP signs, anything. And the results were consistent with the inventories. About half of the students just didn't read on their own. Half.

God, that there would be so many!

The inventories, logs, and subsequent interviews showed that students regarded reading as the finding of meaning in the text or as the passive reception of another's meaning. One student told me that reading is being able to answer the questions at the end of a story. This is an attitude, I think, that schools and textbooks actively endorse and reinforce, and that disenfranchises readers (see, for example, Durkin, 1979; Hillocks, 1987). Many other students maintained that reading was "answering questions" or "finding answers" and that this sort of "snipe hunting," as my case study student Joanne put it, was what "makes me hate reading for school." I began to suspect that it was this view, and their school experience of reading, that contributed to many students' lack of interest if not outright disdain.

If we take the theoretical stance that reading is, in fact, producing and creating meaning, then the way reading education is traditionally practiced in schools must be rethought. If reading is creating texts in response to texts, something new must start happening in our classrooms. This something must take response beyond boilerplate questions and "correct" answers.

The students who *do* know that reading is producing meaning have gone underground to harbor and nurture their secret. School has forced them to be secretive. Most forceful to me was the coy testimony of Joanne. "You're not really interested in how I read," she told me early in the school year. "No teacher would ever be interested in that." What teachers are interested in, she told me, was "my getting it right—or what you all think is right." Because of this, Joanne continued, "I do what I have to in school and then I take my own book home and do real reading."

If reading truly is the producing of meaning, then all the materials of the curriculum become pre-texts, by which I mean an excuse or a reason to pursue personal inquiry and create personal meanings. If we are interested in student learning and transformation, then textbooks and stories become the texts that catalyze the real text that is the reader's response and new understanding. The questions and the answers will become those of the student and may be most fruitfully embedded and expressed through creative, artistic, and student-centered response "texts."

The studies and the stories that follow will pursue two intertwining paths of inquiry suggested by these initial findings and impressions:

- ◆ What can we discover about how highly engaged adolescent readers produce meaning?
- ◆ What can be done in the classroom to help reluctant readers reconceive of reading as a creative and personally meaningful pursuit? Can this be done in a way that guides and scaffolds their use of meaning-making strategies so that they actually develop as readers? How, in short, can they be helped to become developing readers?

COMMENTARY

THE HUMAN AND THE CULTURAL

Here's the central idea about teaching and learning that resounds in my head after rereading this chapter: Teaching and learning are both relational and cultural pursuits. Two finer points: Implicated in all relational teaching and learning are both human and cultural factors, operating both at the microcultural levels of the classroom, school, and community and on the macrocultural levels of policy and policy implementation.

The Human Factor

Effective teaching is necessarily relational and reciprocal. This insight, which I first articulated for myself while composing *"You Gotta BE the Book,"* regards the essentially and intensely human dimension of teaching. As George Hillocks so eloquently expressed it to me: "Teaching is a transitive verb, and that means that it takes both a direct and an indirect object."

In other words, we don't teach English, or reading (or science or math). We teach English or reading TO our students, or we teach our young charges English or reading. This accounts for all the challenge and also all the joy of teaching. We teach *something* to *somebody*. If we forget the somebody, we can hardly be said to be teaching, and there will certainly be no learning.

Unfortunately, my reading of a long history of research reviews on classroom teaching demonstrate that as students move through school, teaching is ever more dominated by information-transmission and curriculum-centered approaches that bracket out the students and relationships. Likewise, significant and robust findings from research on human development and learning, for example, about the power of inquiry (as cognitive apprenticeship) to motivate learning in all disciplines, do not seem to find their way into most classrooms (see, e.g., Hillocks, 1986a, 1986b; 1995; Joyce & Weil, 2014; C. Moore, in preparation; Rogoff, Matusov, & White, 1996). This is despite the fact that research also indicates that teachers are coming to accept constructivist and co-constructivist theories of learning (Ravitch, 2000; Ravitch et al., 2000).

This human factor has been reinforced to me in several ways: by reflecting on my own individual and intensely personal journey as a teacher, which now involves teaching many refugee students who require differentiated methods, moves, and materials; by my subsequent research—particularly into the literate lives of boys both inside and outside of school, in which the social was always necessary to motivation (Smith & Wilhelm, 2002, 2006), and into pleasure reading, in which social pleasures were revealed to be vitally important (Wilhelm & Smith, 2014); and most of all by my experience as a parent, as my two daughters have made their way through school and into their lives beyond their schooling.

Because I am a teacher researcher, I often find myself telling the stories of my students and my own teaching. Though I have collected data in a variety of ways using various methods, all that I have learned fits into a larger narrative of inquiry—a personal story, if you will—a living-out of my own mythic journey around the themes of who I want to be as a teacher, how I want to relate to my students, how I want to assess myself, how hard or soft I want that evaluation to be, and what it is I am really working for. What are the ultimate objects of my quest, for both my students and also for me? What is the quest after all, the grail; who are my helpers; and what dragons really need to be slain, and which ones can I sneak around?

As a researcher, the insight that all teaching is relational was made crystal clear to me during the *Reading Don't Fix No Chevys* study I undertook with my friend and mentor Michael Smith (Smith & Wilhelm, 2002). Our informants were motivated to read and to learn when these activities involved exploring or developing relationships with family, friends, classmates, authors, characters, or teachers. As one boy eloquently put it: "It's always better with friends . . . *always*." Across the board, the boys expressed their expectations of teachers in what we came to see as an implicit social contract.

The Social Contract

- ◆ My teacher will try to get to know me as an individual.
- ◆ My teacher will care about me.
- ◆ My teacher will address my interests in some way (inside and/ or outside the classroom).
- ◆ My teacher will assist me in learning and will work hard to make sure I have learned.
- ◆ My teacher will be passionate about the subject and about teaching.

These findings, which I now also see lurking in the data from *"You Gotta Be the Book,"* have changed me as a teacher more than anything else. When I recently took over a class from an 8th-grade teacher, he pointed out a girl dressed in black Goth clothing whom I will call Sasha. He said that she was trouble, never did her work, and was often absent. In the past I might have tried to work around her, but I knew that I could not teach or help her unless I engaged with her, not as the student I hoped she would be, but with who she was as a human being. I knew from the social contract that if she was not assured that I genuinely cared for her as she was, and that I would not give up on her, she would be unable to learn from me.

On the first day of class I asked her what she was reading. She held up a tattered copy of Marilyn Manson's biography. When I said that I did not know his music, she barked, "Too bad for you!" But this exchange began our relationship and a complex negotiation of assignments (comparing Huck Finn to Marilyn Manson instead of Tom Sawyer; doing her poetry project on gothic rock poets instead of one from an approved list, etc.), lunches spent listening with Sasha to MP3 files of Manson's music (which, by the way, I found to be hideous!), and checking out websites she had bookmarked for me. It wasn't all peaches and cream, believe me, but Sasha was coming to class and doing her work, and was integrated into the classroom on terms she seemed to enjoy. She was also being allowed to stake her identity in the class in ways that were obviously important to her, and to do so in ways that contributed to the common project and the work of the class.

At the end of the year, we were inquiring into the question, "What are the costs and benefits of conformity?" Sasha accused her classmates of being conformists, "part of the machine!" At that time I projected a few images of Marilyn Manson's wedding (you see, I had been monitoring the website, so I knew all about this!) and said, "Check this out. Marilyn Manson just got married. Pretty conformist and conventional, huh?"

I thought the classroom was going to erupt, but there was Sasha in the middle of it all, mediating the discussion. She led a class discussion for 42 uninterrupted minutes in which every student participated at least once and most several times.

I say this with humility: I helped to save her. She completed all her assignments, earned an A, and improved her performance on the state test by 30%. I say this with humility because I wonder: How many students have slipped through the cracks in my classrooms because I did not make the same efforts, because I did not consciously choose to relate to them and approve of them in these same ways?

Likewise, in my *Reading Unbound* studies on the power of pleasure reading, social pleasures and relationships were always a part of engaged reading (Wilhelm & Smith, 2014). These social pleasures involved relating to characters, often as friends; relating to authors and other individual readers; affiliating with groups of readers; and relating with the self, particularly in terms of identity exploration and formation.

The famous psychologist Erik Erikson has made the point that staking one's identity is the primary task of early to late adolescence, during which time adolescents must resolve role confusion through their evolving interests and competence. To the degree that school and reading serve this purpose, they assist with the human journey. To the degree that school and reading do not serve this purpose, they undermine the human journey.

Finally, and most powerfully, the human factor of teaching has come home to me as a parent. Before I had children of my own, I remember returning from parent-teacher conferences or IEP meetings thinking, "What *are* they *on* about?" I thought being a parent must make you crazy. Of course, when I had children of my own, I immediately perceived the answer. I was connected to the world and to craziness in a way that I never thought possible.

Two of the most wrenching experiences of my life were dropping my daughters off at school on their first day of kindergarten (repeated, I must admit, each subsequent year to lesser degrees). I remember thinking: My daughters can be experienced in many ways. How will their teachers choose to experience them? Will their teachers choose to perceive and teach them for their best possible selves? Will they love them as learners? When I teach the many refugee students now in the Boise schools, I think particularly of their personal histories and challenges, and of what their parents would want from me as I am entrusted with their children.

I am grateful, probably eternally, to those teachers who have done this for my own daughters. And, of course, I am regretful for the opportunities missed for teaching, learning, and enjoyment where the positive possibilities were not actualized—both in my own teaching and learning, but also during my daughters' education.

Interestingly, readers of *YGBB* quite often ask me whether I am still in touch with the case study students featured here, or whether I ever did follow-up work with any of them. This highlights that readers of this book are engaged not just by the data itself and the various instructional implications that follow, but by the human stories played out here, of readers being readers and pursuing their reading lives in ways encouraged and discouraged by school, and even more of readers disenfranchised by school, who want so badly to be competent but don't see the way, nor how school might help them.

The Culture of Teaching and Learning

The answer to the question of whether I am still in touch with these students is complicated by some restrictive elements in the culture of American schooling: I left my middle school teaching job a year after writing this book. Because I left that teaching position, however unwillingly, I no longer live in the town where I taught. I have had several email contacts from Cora over the years, and I have visited with her twice, once quite recently; I have seen Ron twice by chance on return visits to my hometown. Both are doing well, having become successful young professionals who continue to enjoy a wide variety of reading. I've not heard from, nor much about, any of the other students.

But my departure from teaching is a story in itself. Michael Smith, in the Foreword to the First Edition, writes that by leaving teaching, I was critiquing the educational system. This is true in more ways than one.

I had never intended to be anything other than a middle or secondary school teacher. I pursued my doctorate solely for the purpose of improving my capacity to assist my students. But as events transpired, the achievement of my doctoral degree and several publications directly led to an untenable teaching situation for me. Though most of my administrators and teaching colleagues were and remain supportive of my teacher research and writing, there were a select few who made it clear that I had overstepped some invisible boundary. For example, it was decided that I would not be able to attend professional conferences any longer "because you have had your chance." There was anonymous hate mail. There were complaints (from colleagues, not parents or students) about the inquiry projects I pursued with students, about my teacher research, and about my writing—which must be distracting me from my "real job of teaching."

I don't take any of this personally. I've heard from many other teachers who have earned advanced degrees, or begun to present professionally or write and publish, who have experienced the same phenomenon of being rejected or mistreated by some of their administrators and colleagues. I feel that one of my most important jobs as a National Writing Project director is to create a safe place for teachers to explore and express the professional authority of their practice in ways that may not be possible in the current status quo culture of schools.

However prevalent mistreatment of ambitious teachers may be, and however limited the minority of perpetrators, it is a troubling professional phenomenon. Why is it that we lack a professional culture that actively and articulately supports professional growth, thinking partnerships, and leadership, that professes an attitude that *anything any* teacher does for students or professional culture makes us all richer? This is certainly worth consideration and study.

Then, of course, there are macrocultural factors like the Common Core and next-generation standards, which exert an effect on teachers worldwide. As I've argued elsewhere (e.g., Smith, Appleman, & Wilhelm, 2014), I like the Core. It reflects much of what we know and research supports about cognitive expertise (and this expertise for reading is mirrored almost perfectly by the interdependent dimensions of reader response promoted in this book). The plus: The standards focus (for the first time in my teaching career) on *strategies* that constitute *threshold knowledge* of expert readers and writers.

The downside: There are many important facets of engaged expertise that are missing, and I don't like how many people talk about implementation or actually do implement the standards. But that is something in our power as teachers to add and to do in our own ways, depending on the specific human beings we teach.

Another plus: The standards documents themselves articulate that decisionmaking power about curriculum and instruction should reside with teachers and local schools. The downside: When you have any kind of standardization, it tends to become reified. While many teachers and schools have taken the invitation to rethink their curricula and methodologies creatively, many more have moved toward entrenchment in the form of overly scripted curricula and limits to teachers' professional freedom and decision-making. However, this is not a problem of the standards, but of implementation and of an impoverished sense, in many schools, of teacher professionalism.

I tell the teachers with whom I work that even if I didn't like the Core, here is what I would say: When we deal with a policy mandate, we must decide how to best leverage it for our professional practice and for the good of our students. I have taught with the methods described in this book for many years, even in unfriendly policy environments. In my opinion, with the Core these methods and other innovative pedagogies are actively invited and rewarded. For example, I don't see a way to meet the Core's anchor standards unless students are cognitively apprenticed to master these profound achievements over time in various inquiry environments. The standards demand robust teaching that assists students to intensely participate in textual meaning-making, visualize and create mental models of meaning, and connect and reflect, exactly what the interdependent dimensions of reading response described here help students to do.

Since the last edition, there has been a troubling trend of marginalizing teachers both professionally and politically. I'm thinking of Wisconsin Governor Scott Walker's coordinated attacks on teachers to limit teacher voice, their professional decisionmaking power, the work of unions, their benefits, and much else. In Idaho, we recently experienced a state superintendent of education who had never been an educator, and who wanted to require high school students to do at least a year of school online with undifferentiated information-driven courses and multiple-choice tests, shunting funding for schools to online academies/for-profit businesses.

How can we fight this trend? First, by being professional and reflective teachers and teacher researchers, and by becoming public intellectuals sharing our professional work and knowledge. Second, by involving ourselves in professional groups and projects, like the National Writing Project, that dedicate themselves to professionalism and know how to work toward professional respect.

Cultures of Schools and of Teaching

It's also important to consider macrocultural expectations and constraints on microcultures of schools and of teaching.

The latest expression of next-generation standards, although an improvement in ways I've described earlier, is also a continuation of high-stakes teaching and assessments. In such a context, there's an implicit demand for us all to be Superteachers and to contribute in immediately visible ways to student learning achievements.

I'm worried about this cultural mythology and find it corrosive. For the mythic Superteacher, every class period runs like a Cuisinart and comes to a banquetlike conclusion with toasts all around. I have never met such a Superteacher, nor have I experienced the perfect class. I love Tom Newkirk's (2009) injunction that we don't further the profession by telling only of our successes. We need to tell the underside of these stories, including the struggles, the risks, and the falling short, and what we learned from these. Teaching and learning are highly complex struggles involving failures and approximations. They need to be portrayed as such. Standards and assessment movements oversimplify what we teach, why we teach, how we teach, and what is learned through a very messy process.

Another worry: that standards mandates tend to come from outside the profession, are created by noneducators without intimate knowledge of teaching and its contexts, and are imposed upon us. This imposition devalues teaching as a profession because professions create, implement, reflect on, and revise their own standards, which professionals work together to meet. Until teachers are afforded the same autonomy as other professionals, we have to work with the policies we have. But in the meantime, I would encourage ongoing discussions between teachers and policymakers about what is best for our students, based on our personal experience, authority of practice, and teacher research.

As professionals, teachers should be involved in designing and revising assessments. I was part of Smarter Balanced Assessment Consortium thinking partnerships (acting as a reviewer for the creation of the SBAC assessments used in many states to measure student progress on meeting the Core standards). The original "requests for proposal" (RFPs outline the criteria and requirements for particular projects) and drafts of this assessment involved portfolios created by students over the course of 11th grade. The portfolio creation portion of the assessment incorporated clear guidelines for students and teachers, yet allowed much flexibility in how students would demonstrate competence through engaging and useful projects and products. Students were also required to write reflections naming what they had done, how they had met challenges, how they came to understand, and what they had learned that they could use now and in the future.

This part of the assessment has since disappeared, but it could be revived and teachers could work to revive it. If students can demonstrate their learning and meeting of standards through our classroom projects, real-world work, and actual archival knowledge documents; and can code their work to the standards, naming what they know and how they have demonstrated it; then why we would need an artificial standardized test? The more we teach toward actual demonstrations of learning in real-world projects and usable knowledge documents, the more we make the case against any need for standardized tests.

Here's another worry about a cultural myth: that teachers are born and not made. I am totally compelled by the growth mindset research of Carol Dweck (2006) and others (e.g., Johnston, 2012), and this research means that any student can learn the next available skill if given the right assistance and the opportunity for deliberate practice in a context of use. In fact, this research tradition goes back to Vygotsky and his powerful vision of effective teaching as always being on the cusp of what students can next become. If the growth mindset research is right—and the data are compelling—then it has to be true of teachers as well as students. If teachers have access to the right forms of professional development over time in the context of their own classrooms, and take the opportunity to reflect and revise their practice together, then the research demonstrates that they can and will grow.

Yet so many mandates, such as the current ones, come without money or support for professional development.

Here's another worry: There is a long and robust research tradition demonstrating that if you have a high-stakes test (or actually a test of any kind), teachers naturally teach to these tests (Earl, 2013). Standards that lead to high-stakes tests are going to guide and constrain teaching. Are current standards good? They could be better. We can fix this in our own classrooms. Do we want the tests to drive all or even some of our instruction? If not, then we must be vigilant and teach for higher purposes that we define in addition to the standards. Do standardized assessments capture our students' growing competence? Then we need to provide assessments *for* and *as* learning in our classroom.

Standards and assessments obviously inform what teachers will teach, and to some degree how they will teach, how they will relate to students, how they will encourage students to relate to texts, and how they will assess students' learning. I also worry that an emphasis on "text complexity" ignores the interpretive complexity that students engage in and the strategies they can learn from picture books, young adult literature, and multimedia texts; and marginalizes materials that may be the most engaging and appropriate for students.

The Challenge: Modeling What We Want Students to *Be* and *Do*

How are we to call ourselves teachers if we do not promote and reward risk-taking, let alone encouragement for innovation, particularly in regard to our own teaching and assessment, as well as in regard to helping students who are hard to reach, creating as we do so professional knowledge through our experimentation? Teaching, as I argue here and have argued before, is creating appropriate challenges and assisting learners in meeting those challenges. We certainly need to help one another do this as thinking partners and professional colleagues. Teachers need what all learners need: assistance and deliberate reflective practice over time in a context of use. We cannot let standards, assessments, and required curriculum of any kind deter us from these necessary goals of growth, both personal and for wider cultures of teaching.

It doesn't do to marginalize or silence ourselves, our struggles, or our colleagues or students. We are in a human profession, and we need to learn how to listen to one another, learn from one another, and to name and celebrate one another's successes, learning together how to use struggle as a tool toward more conscious competence with the complex tasks of reading and learning, as well as demonstrating that learning through actual accomplishments.

1

❧

Moving Toward a
Reader-Centered Classroom

This past year, on reading workshop days, my seventh-grade students had to show me an "entrance ticket" to enter the class. That ticket was a free-reading book. Each student would show me the book and, in an enjoyable ritual (that could probably only happen with young adolescents), would give me a high five and call out "I am a reader!" as she or he entered the classroom. Every student would do this except Marvin, who would flash me his book, give me a high five, and yell out, "Reading is stupid!"

Marvin and many previous students much like him have literally changed my teaching, if not my life. It's because of him and classes such as eighth-grade remedial reading that I came to rethink the reading act. Because of students like him, I've come to express this argument about the teaching of reading: In order to develop readers, we must encourage and foster the creative attitudes and activities of engaged readers. We must do this instead of teaching sets of skills or teaching texts—which was what was probably done for (or to!) us—and which was what I was certainly taught to do in my teacher education courses. It's also what traditional anthologies and workbooks and all other prepackaged programs require us to do. By instead focusing our instruction and support on the construction of meaning, the classroom can become a place where students not only produce and share meanings, but a place where they share ways of reading and being with text, becoming aware in the process of their own strategies and those of others. And then, with a little luck, reading won't seem so stupid to our students.

Creating this new kind of reading environment was a new and difficult direction to move in as a teacher. It was uncomfortable to leave the security of an anthology that blanketed the year with reading selections, suggested activities, and questions. And it required really recognizing my beliefs about reading so that they could be reworked in ways that would serve my students.

THE BOTTOM-UP APPROACH

On the first day of this past academic year, I was walking to school. It's a small town, and I know the kids whom I'll be teaching. I was following two of them, Randy and his friend Chris. We had to walk through the neighborhood elementary school grounds to get to the middle school, and I continued along about 10 paces behind them. Near the front entry stood a child, probably a kindergartner who'd just been dropped off by his mom, and he was *wailing.* He was a sandy-haired little boy in new clothes clutching a green Ninja Turtle backpack. Big, gulping sobs were heaving out of his chest like giant burps, and he was struggling to catch his breath before the next sob racked his body. I was hurrying over to him as Randy and Chris passed by. Randy leaned toward the child and said, "Chill out, kid. It only gets worse."

At this point the playground aide hustled the weeping child away, and I was left thinking about Randy. I said to myself: *This is my challenge, isn't it? How can I help Randy so school doesn't get even worse for him this year?*

A couple of weeks later I was conferencing with Randy and asked him about the incident. He told me that "school is a bunch of crap that doesn't mean anything . . . you just do a bunch of crap for someone else so you can get through the year." This description of being a student is strikingly close to Plato's definition of a slave: a person who does someone else's work. Randy especially hated reading, and told me that reading was "like . . . pain."

Randy, Marvin, and most of their classmates learned to read using a phonics-based approach. This model of learning to read is also labeled the "bottom-up" or "parts to whole" approach. According to this approach, the foundation of learning to read is understanding letter-to-sound correspondences, better known as "phonics."

I understand that students have to know some phonics to read. But I also think that this approach to reading has encouraged students like Randy and Marvin to think of the meaning of reading as something outside themselves. My students who did not recall being read to at home often reported negative memories of elementary school reading instruction, because, I think, their experience with reading consisted of worksheets instead of stories and conversations about stories. My LD (learning disabled) students (and Marvin was one of these), who often had been given extra reading help through approaches such as DISTAR—an intense phonics and word recognition approach to reading—had very negative and resistant attitudes toward reading, summed up by Marvin's favorite little chant.

Libby told me that "All I remember [about learning to read] is sitting around all the time." Another student, wondering about my language arts class, asked me, "How can you do reading without worksheets and vocabulary lists?" (It's interesting that you don't read, you *do* reading.) When I asked if she thought doing worksheets helped her to be a better reader or to enjoy reading, she just said, "No. I hate reading, but that's what we've always done." Again, I think that these students have never been helped to pursue reading in any personally meaningful way. By the time they arrived in my classroom, an intense demythologization of the reading act was in order.

Leading experts call this "bottom-up" approach the longest and greatest influence on reading instruction, and the one that is usually reflected in basal readers and reading programs. This view regards reading as a data-driven process, and is rather mechanical in that it emphasizes mastery of specific subskills and skills, moving from small units such as letters to bigger units such as words, phrases, and sentences (e.g., DISTAR). The idea is that once students have understood and mastered the subskills of reading, they can apply these in context to decode letters and words; they are then well on their way to becoming readers. The emphasis is on breaking the code because meaning is seen as being in the text. Print is therefore in control of the reading process, which starts with letters and words. The page is greater than the reader.

The majority of my own students seemed thoroughly indoctrinated by this approach, and several students a year tell me that reading well is being able to recognize words or being able to answer the questions at the end of a story.

WHY JOHNNY WON'T READ

Once students have learned how to read, and move through middle and secondary school, reading is still regarded as a passive act of receiving someone else's meanings. This is due in part to a literary theory known as New Criticism that implicitly informs much if not most of our nation's literature teaching. The New Critical orientation toward literary reading, in a way, is a natural kind of extension of the bottom-up approach to learning to read.

Basically, New Criticism is a highly systematic and formalistic approach to rigorous, analytic readings of literary texts. The New Critics paid tremendous attention to literary form, and the structures of the "whole text." They called for an end to a concern with matters outside the work itself—the author, his life, the historical situation, and the implications of the work for society or for the individual reader. In fact, they denied "the psychological effects of the poem" in an effort to make an objective science of interpretation. Textual details work together to express one thematic meaning.

Teachers influenced by this approach may emphasize knowing and recognizing literary devices, getting at the "internal logic" of a text's construction by studying various patterns and codes, and relating a work's central "organic" meaning to how this meaning was expressed. There may be an emphasis on "rightness" of literary interpretation. Interpretive questions about the text will be answered after reading; thesis essays assigned; and discussions mediated by the teacher, who acts as the authority on the text. The text is what is studied, and it is an artifact regarded with something rivaling reverence.

Throughout my own first years as a teacher, I suffered from what I might now call a sort of theoretical schizophrenia. I adopted the implicit New Critical conceptions that surrounded my own school education. Reading was finding meaning in text, and there were strict methodologies to be followed to get at that "correct" meaning. I certainly wasn't alone; studies by Durkin (1979) in elementary schools and Hillocks (1987) in high school settings demonstrate that most reading and literature instruction involves seatwork and recitation that focus on cracking codes instead of creating meanings.

Through my high school and college literature courses, a blend of classical and New Critical theory was the order of the day and informed classroom instruction, literary interpretation, and grading. My notes from college classes recorded the "intentional fallacy" and the "affective fallacy"—which warned me not to be moved or affected by my reading—as pitfalls to be avoided, and New Critical tenets pepper my notes as a way of directing "correct" interpretation. Thesis essays were written to show how well I had read and interpreted the text, with evidence provided in the form of formal analyses and textual quotations.

Creative, personal response was taboo. One college professor was severely stricken by my parody of Shakespeare's *Troilus and Cressida* starring Steve Martin as a comedic Ajax. "The play is a tragedy! What right do you have to violate the text of Shakespeare?!" he practically gagged. Holy smokes, I thought, I had engaged in illicit, practically blasphemous activities! I was sure to be put on some literary blacklist and called up by the Congressional Committee on Un-literary Activities!

The result of my own education was a tragicomedy of sorts: my situation as a teacher-theorist. You see, I didn't even know that New Criticism was a theory; I thought it was just the stance and strategies you used to read well. I had digested it, unaware that it was just one theory of reading among a constellation of theories.

I was certainly not alone in my ignorance (which is a place where you usually find a lot of company). The elder Roger Applebee's survey of literature instruction (Squires & Applebee, 1966) found that New Critical beliefs about literary interpretation dominated American secondary and undergraduate education in the 1960s. The younger Applebee's more recent national survey (1989) found that little has changed in the practice of literature instruction since that time.

Despite the best of my own intentions and a lot of very hard work, I've come to believe that my implicit theory and methods (shared as they are by much of the school establishment) were a large part of the reason for many of my students' discontent.

You see, New Criticism assumes the text to be an integrated and coherent whole, and it monolithically determines meaning, which can be gleaned through "close readings" of the text. As such, the reader's role is akin to dentistry (or Plato's slavery): to extract someone else's meaning. The role of the reader as an active meaning-maker, one who connects personally to what is read, who spends pleasurable and stirring time with stories, and who might judge or resist the text and its author, is essentially precluded from the reading act.

A study by Newell, MacAdams, and Spears-Burton (1987) of three secondary literature teachers found their situations to be entirely similar to my own. These teachers' literary theories and beliefs did implicitly inform their instruction, though not in particularly consistent or conscious ways, and did not lead to significant study, discussion, or changes in their practice.

Richard Rorty, cited by Jerome Bruner (1986) in *Actual Minds, Possible Worlds,* characterizes Anglo-American philosophy as the pursuit of the epistemological question "how to know truth," which is an empirical question, versus "how we come to endow experience with meaning," which is the epistemological question that preoccupies the poet and the storyteller (p. 12). And as I wrote in the margin, this latter question is the procedural one that should preoccupy the teacher. How do we endow experience, especially the experience of reading, with meaning? How can readers who do not endow the reading experience with meaning be helped to do so?

Many teachers influenced by New Criticism work against the purpose of this procedural question. They often communicate that literature is not about the students and their most vital concerns, but about whatever some superior intelligence tells them it is about. As Aidan Chambers (1985) asserts: "Nothing could be more dishonest and more productive of a cynical and disaffected community" (p. 126). Such an orientation can also serve to disaffect teachers. There came a point in my own career when I wrote:

> If literature does not speak to student lives, then what good is it? If students don't come to love reading now, when will they ever read later? If teachers cannot help students to read better, with more purpose, better attitudes and greater power, then what good are we? I am sick and tired of teaching the "classics" and blaming the kids who can't answer my questions as "lazy" or "below grade level." If I am really going to be worthy of the title "teacher" then I had better start understanding what this act of reading is all about, and I'd better find out how to let kids in on the secret. (April 1987)

I had always asked what content I should teach, what literary works and terms and ideas were most important for students to know. I tried to convince myself that by teaching *To Kill a Mockingbird* I was helping students to internalize types of questions and ways of reading that would lead to "correct" interpretations. The harder I looked at this assumption, the more reductive and incomplete it seemed to be.

This is what I was asking students to do when they read literature: someone else's work instead of their own. This is why Randy thinks of school as a "bunch of crap to get through" and why Marvin can maintain that "reading is stupid!" As I tried to make reading literature a kind of personal work that my students would do for themselves, my implicit New Critical views began to give way to a reader-response orientation that reading is the enjoyable and affecting act of producing meaning.

THERE IS AN ALTERNATIVE

Instead of looking at reading as receiving the meaning in texts, reader-oriented theories regard reading as the creation, in concert with texts, of personally significant experiences and meanings.

Proponents of the "top-down" psycholinguistic model of learning to read regard too much phonics instruction as misguided because of the ultimate irrelevance of phonics to the competent reader, the complex nature of the rules, and the time that such instruction takes from real reading and writing activity. They also see phonics programs as symptomatic of the way schools drain away the juicy joys of reading and set out obstacles between children and becoming literate.

Proponents of this approach, such as Ken Goodman (1982) and Frank Smith (1978), see reading less as an ability and more as a highly social, purposeful, and meaning-driven activity. The Whole Language movement, though this is an umbrella term for a wide variety of classroom practice, has been largely informed by the thought of Goodman and Smith. The point for these theorists is not the array of skills the reader can deploy, but how the reader actually makes use of skills as she explores and experiences meaning. Reading is seen as an intensely human pursuit with intensely human purposes that must be foregrounded. Reading, instead of a complex set of skills, becomes a social practice and a search for meaning.

Goodman argues that reading

> is the search for meaning which preoccupies the reader. . . . That is why aspects of the process and how it works cannot be isolated from the construction of meaning that is the ultimate goal. Learning to read involves getting the process together. That is harder if instruction takes it apart. (1985, p. 839)

Still, with such an approach, the teacher must ask when to intervene, especially with students such as my own who are often reluctant or resistant readers. How can their attitudes be changed, their repertoire of strategies developed? Are there no bottom-up skills that would be useful to them?

One answer to these concerns comes in the form of a compromise "interactive" model that has been proposed by David Rumelhart (1985) and that conceives of reading as both top-down and bottom-up. Yes, readers search for global meanings, but they sometimes use decoding skills on a local level to achieve this end. Both the text and the reader play a part in the meaning-making process, and the relationship is constantly changing. When reading lyric poetry, for example, the reader plays the more powerful and vital role by supplying memories and emotions. When reading a legal document, however, the text exerts more rigid controls over the meaning-making process. As the reader interacts and constructs meaning with text, she uses multiple sources of information. She is a pattern synthesizer who uses syntactic, semantic, and orthographic clues to arrive at a most probable interpretation that both considers the text and is satisfying to her own purposes and needs.

This model stresses the prior knowledge structures or "schema" of the individual reader. Reading becomes a meeting of the reader's prior knowledge *and* textual meanings that work together to create a greater sense of things.

Frank Smith (1978), in particular, stresses the importance of what the reader brings to the page, a body of knowledge he calls "nonvisual information."

> There is only one way to summarize everything that a child must learn in order to become a fluent reader, and that is to say that the child must learn to use nonvisual information efficiently when attending to print. Learning to read does not require the memorization of letter names or phonic rules, or large lists of words, all of which are in fact taken care of in the course of learning to read, and little of which will make sense to a child without experience of reading. Nor is learning to read a matter of application to all manner of exercises and drills which can only distract and perhaps even discourage a child from the business of learning to read. (p. 179)

As I prepare the final draft of this manuscript, my now 4-year-old daughter Fiona knows her letters and is beginning to recognize words. Yet we have never used flashcards or drills. We have magnetic letters on the refrigerator, which she will sometimes ask her mother and me to help her use to write out a message. She writes notes that are a mixture of real words and scribbles. After reading with us, she will make serial illustrations of scenes on computer paper. She makes character books in which she draws characters from books and real people engaged in typical pursuits. At other times she will write her own story by drawing pictures and asking us to write the text, but she is eager to write for herself the words she already knows. She knows many of her books so well that she can "read" to her sister Jasmine, age 2, by flipping through the pages and reciting the story—nearly verbatim.

Last night she and little Jasmine asked me to be the Big Bad Wolf as they acted out a rendition of "The Three Little Pigs." They gathered pencils to signify sticks and blocks to signify bricks. After I slid down the back of the couch they had designated as the chimney and into the box that was their soup pot, they pulled me out and invited me to stay for dinner, an ending they liked better than the one in the book!

And then, before bed, flipping through a *Newsweek* article on airplane safety, Fiona asked me to point out the word "airplane" and then spelled it out for herself, then asked me to read "the story for this picture." She asked questions such as "What's a bomb?" and "Why don't they take more care of the airplanes so they won't have accidents?" Even as a child just learning to recognize her first words, reading is a search for meaning and understanding. She applies what she knows and asks adults to help her understand and learn what she does not know. Reading is something fun to do together with others to both explore the world and to express how we would change it. And responding to her reading through a variety of artistic and dramatic texts is quite natural for her.

The interactive model of reading allows readers like Fiona to pursue their own reading and construct their own meanings, yet asks adults to teach background knowledge, skills, and strategies helpful to the reader's purpose in the context of real, personally purposeful reading and writing.

This kind of interactive approach allows for everyone to have a place in learning and experiencing the reading act: the author, the text, the teacher, and especially the reader. This approach to learning to read is a natural complement to Louise Rosenblatt's transactional approach to experiential reading that can inform how we teach preadolescent and adolescent readers.

It was the transactional approach that provided the antidote to my own New Critical orientation, training, and teaching practice. This resulting reader-oriented approach led me to a changed classroom filled with both goal-oriented instruction and independent reading clubs of students who express their understandings through art, drama, hypermedia (a multimedia computer platform), and videotape. This new approach helped my students to become more positive and productive readers willing to explore and create for themselves the pleasures of text.

GETTING STARTED

As I considered how to change my classroom practices, I turned to the work of Rosenblatt, who is widely recognized as the founder of reader-response theory.

In Rosenblatt's theory, reading is a "transaction" in which the reader and the text converse together in a particular situation to make meaning. The reader makes meaning *with* the text, instead of solely on his own, as top-down literary theorists such as David Bleich (1975) would have it. The reader's experience with the text is called the "poem," and it is unique to each reader and reading. The reader's situation, the text, and the interpretive conventions it puts into play guide the process of making the "poem," but not nearly to the degree asserted by Fish (1980), who argues that meaning is constrained entirely by the "interpretive communities" to which the reader belongs. For Rosenblatt, the reader's own individual purposes, mood, and background experiences with life and reading become primary influences on the meaning that is evoked. As she expressed in her first major work, *Literature as Exploration*:

> The special meanings, and, more particularly, the submerged associations that these words and images have for the individual reader will largely determine what the work communicates to him. The reader brings to the work personality traits, memories of past events, present needs and preoccupations, a particular mood of the moment, and a particular physical condition. These and many other elements in a never-to-be-duplicated combination determine his response to the peculiar contribution of the text. (1983, pp. 30–31)

Her later book *The Reader, the Text, the Poem* (1978) is more specifically useful to classroom teaching. In this work, Rosenblatt criticizes literary instruction (such as my own) that focused on correct answers. She cites an anthology question that asks: "What facts have we learned from this poem?" as a way of highlighting the shortsightedness of such an approach.

As part of her argument she makes an interesting move away from the view that "reading is reading" by drawing a distinction between "efferent" and "aesthetic" reading. Efferent reading is pursued when readers adopt a stance in which they are concerned with what information they can "take away" from the reading. The text is treated as consisting of information. The aesthetic stance, however, is maintained for the purpose of "living through" an experience that is enjoyed while reading. Texts themselves are not intrinsically literary or nonliterary; the stance taken toward a text is what makes the reading aesthetic or efferent.

Rosenblatt emphasizes that readers will operate, during the reading of a single text, on different points of a continuum between efferent and aesthetic reading. As she points out, most classroom reading, questions, and texts are designed to elicit efferent responses, and assume that there are correct answers to these questions. In fact, the way literature is generally taught, she argues, predisposes students to take the efferent stance, and in many subversive ways invalidates the taking of the aesthetic stance that makes literature an experience to be enjoyed.

Empirical research conducted by Alan Purves (1973) on the typical response modes in the classroom supports Rosenblatt's dreary view. By setting a correct interpretation to be reached by students in advance of the experience of reading, the students are led to particular interpretations and an efferent mode of reading. Purves asserts that "the penchant for experiential reading . . . is driven out of the heads of readers by instruction" (p. 72).

When Brad explains that the purpose of reading is "to find out stuff" and Kevin tells me that it is "to answer the questions at the end of the story," they are taking an efferent stance.

If students do not know how to take an aesthetic stance as they read, then they will be denied the opportunity to "live through" the experience of a literary transaction. In my journal, I almost exulted:

> This is what is happening. Suddenly it is clear! These students have not ever experienced the world of a story. They read for information. Every anthology selection, every quiz, every class they have ever taken has reinforced the efferent stance of reading at the expense of the aesthetic stance. Even their literary letters were just summaries, with an occasional judgment. My God, no wonder reading is uninteresting to them. No wonder they don't understand the wonder of it. (November 1989)

This also threw light on another phenomenon I had been observing in my classroom. Those students who were avid readers had all gone underground. They did not want it pointed out that they liked to read, and they only agreed to speak about their reading in private situations.

> Today the strangest thing happened. We were talking about our reading and Sarah was discussing *That Was Then, This Is Now* and I was approving of her and her effort in various ways when Clancy yelled out, "But she's reading at home!" to which everybody else started yelling, "Yes, yes! She's reading at home" like this was a crime or the ultimate stupidity or something. There was this attitude that it was OK to read in school, in class or even in a study hall, but—as Jeff put it, "if you have nothing better to do at home than read you'd better think about getting a real

life!" Reading as only something you do at school, to finish assignments? Where in the hell did they get that idea? (February 1990)

I was often surprised during the school year when in journal writings or through observation I discovered that some students were quietly trading books and writing notes about their reading. When I asked why they would not share their reading more publicly, I was told, as in the case of Stacey, "Mr. Wilhelm, try not to embarrass us. We like to read but we don't want it to destroy our reputations or anything and seem like geeks or nerds or something. Try to understand! We'll do the reading and stuff but don't embarrass us about it." I hypothesized that

> these students have discovered the aesthetic experience of reading, and that is something that many of their peers cannot conceive of or understand, and in fact they deride the very notion of it. Perhaps if all could be introduced to the aesthetic stance and experience of literature, a great nationwide movement could be undertaken to make reading "COOL" and "POPULAR." Yes, perhaps teens across the nation would buy and trade books like they were baseball cards. Maybe book clubs could replace gangs. . . . Maybe. . . . If this mission could be undertaken a great sweeping change would occur across the nation! (March 1990)

Rosenblatt had unleashed my prophetic powers and a vision of an America of readers. She was making a move that had explanatory and suggestive power for the classroom teacher and researcher. As Robert Probst (1988) points out, her model suggests that "students must be free to deal with their own reactions to the text," which also means that teachers should "ask students what they see, feel, think and remember as they read, encouraging them to attend to their own experience of the text" (p. 31). This focusing on the process of reading, instead of solely on what was read, became a major thrust of my own classroom practice and research, which I will describe in the next chapters.

BUILDING ON ROSENBLATT

When I was in graduate school I always found myself teaming up and working with other practicing teachers. The following joke struck a chord with us, and we told it over and over.

There's a famous education professor at a large midwestern university and he hasn't taught a night class in 20 years. He's prevailed upon to do so, though he knows what kind of clientele he'll get, and he'd really rather avoid them. Yes, he's going to get practicing teachers. Sure enough, that's exactly who flocks to his course, and some of them are a real headache. Two in particular keep bothering him to come visit their school. School! He hasn't been inside a school for over two decades. But teachers can be persistent, and he finally gives up and agrees.

When he comes to the school, the two teachers really roll out the red carpet, and they proudly show him around. There are students working in literature circles and other cooperative groups. Kids are creating their own hypermedia and video documentaries to teach other kids. Teachers are working in integrated teams. There are reading and writing work-shops; students are publishing their own weekly newspaper and a monthly literary magazine.

At the end of the day, the teachers escort their professor out to his car and wait expectantly. He pauses and says, "Well, yes. It all looks very good in practice. But my question is: will it work *in theory?*"

As I pursued my research with students, I struggled to put reader-response theory into practice. I became convinced that for most of my student readers, engagement with literature through the aesthetic stance did not occur naturally or spontaneously. Rosenblatt, like many literary theorists, seems to assume an Ideal situation versus the Real situation of the classroom. Despite free reading and reading workshops, journals, literary letter exchanges, and a variety of response activities, many of my students did not seem to improve as readers, and many more continued to resist reading.

In fact, many of my better readers did not experience literature in a way that I considered to be complete. They did not recognize and make use of conventional invitations to make certain sorts of meaning (Culler, 1975; Rabinowitz, 1987). They missed irony, didn't understand unreliable narrators, didn't fill in textual gaps, didn't seem to converse with or critique characters, authors, or other readers. Their interpretations of a text's meaning often seemed very far off the mark.

My students, I came to believe, would not be able to "converse with texts fully unless they learn how to take particular stances, deploy strategies to engage with text, and to make use of literary conventions to truly make meaning with text" (June 1991). I worried that their ability to learn and be transformed by literary transactions would be severely impaired unless Rosenblatt's theory could be made more specific and user-friendly in regard to what readers must do to elicit meaning from the text in order to converse with it. Of primary concern to me was that

> Rosenblatt rings so true to me, but she doesn't give an answer about what can be done to help my middle schoolers see themselves as readers. Sure, take the aesthetic stance, but what do readers do to achieve an aesthetic reading? What are the moves that constitute the aesthetic stance? (August 1991)

Certainly there are general processes of reading useful in any situation: determining importance, summarizing information, drawing inferences, generating questions, and monitoring comprehension (Dole, Duffy, Roehler, & Pearson, 1991). But literary reading was, I agreed, a highly particular sort of meaning-making that involved particular strategies and moves. What were they, though? Rosenblatt never identified them.

It became clear to me that the general strategies used by many students to read a textbook in the efferent stance were not sufficient to achieving an aesthetic reading with literature. What special knowledge and specific strategies did they lack for achieving literary experience and understanding? And what perspectives on their lives, what experiences did they possess that they could be helped to bring to their reading?

Rosenblatt made it clear that it was the reader's responsibility to attend to the author's careful crafting of literary signs, to the conventions of text that were exercised. But how do readers learn to do this? And what must readers do with particular genres, or when faced with sophisticated literary conventions? How do expert readers recognize and respond to these conventional markers and invitations? How could students be helped to develop problem-solving strategies for doing so?

Margaret Meek and colleagues (1983) remind us that we must make public "those secret things" that expert readers know and do. Rosenblatt is not specific in this regard. These issues were of primary importance to me as I used Rosenblatt's theory in my classroom, and eventually led to interesting questions about the actual moves readers make with narrative fiction, and my attempts to help resistant readers make use of and enjoy these stances and strategies.

Though there are reports and research that explore the use of reader response in the classroom, there is no body of work available that is highly detailed, specific, and broad in its look at the actual meaning-making processes of avid and highly engaged adolescent readers. We have lists of what adolescents read, and brief summaries from survey research of what they say they do. But I wanted something more: What could be found out from looking very closely, in great detail, at the particular moves of highly proficient readers? This is what I set out to do over the course of a whole school year.

In my journal I listed these questions, which eventually came to guide the research that I report on in the following chapters:

- What can be done in the classroom to develop reluctant readers and extend the abilities of all readers?
- What do "mature" readers do to engage in "rich and powerful" readings?
- How can less engaged readers be encouraged to do these things, and with what effects?
- How can my students be helped to experience literature, and to tell the story of their reading, helping them to discover for themselves the power and variety of the literary experience? (May 1990)

COMMENTARY

BE *THAT* TEACHER

In the locker room of my Master Blaster (aka old geezer) Idaho Nordic ski team, there is a photograph of skiers sprawled on the ground just past a finish line. There is one skier who is still standing. An arrow points to him with the caption: "BE THIS GUY!"

In this chapter I wrote about seeking alternatives to what was not working for my own students. It was essentially a teacher research question, which resulted in a quest of reflective teaching about how to best meet the needs of all the very specific human beings who are students in my classroom. The way to fulfill this quest: Move to teaching reading and writing as inquiry, in contexts of inquiry. Help students to inquire into expert reading and writing, into how they personally practice literacy and can practice literacy more widely and expertly. Do this in a wider context of inquiry into personally compelling and socially significant questions.

This means that students are actively apprenticed and assisted to read, write, and think in new and more expert ways in a context of meaningful use. They need inquiry, but *inquiry as cognitive apprenticeship* into the understanding and use of threshold knowledge. When we teach in such a way, we naturally meet all of the anchor standards of the Core or any set of next-generation standards.

My big question, as I think about my own teaching and my daughters' school experience, is: Where is the teacher, like the skier in the photograph, who stands out from the fray? How can I BE *THAT* TEACHER?

Why does information-transmission teaching still dominate American teaching? Why aren't student interests and their capacity for joy leveraged more often? Why aren't progressive and engaging kinds of inquiry environments more available to learners? Many teachers profess a constructivist point of view, but a preponderance of these teachers still teach through information transmission: lectures, worksheets, and formulas like the five-paragraph essay. Middle and secondary teachers, and those working with struggling students, tend to be more information transmission and less constructivist (Ravitz, Becker, & Wong, 2000). Therefore, the students who most need to become active in deliberate practice and learning how to read, write, and make meaning get the least support in doing so. This has a negative effect on motivation and learning (Hillocks, 1986a; 1986b; 1995; 1999).

Information transmission is fundamentally at odds with research into human learning over the past 80-some years, as well as with what research shows are the most powerful ways to teach in the English language arts (Hillocks, 1986a; 1986b; 1995; 1999).

In sociocultural/apprenticeship learning theory, described and contrasted with competing theories like information transmission in the chart at the end of this commentary (see Exhibit 1.1), teaching and learning are pursued to transform the participation of students from passive receivers of information to expert analysts and producers of meaning, from learning alone to learning together in continuous collaboration with more expert others, and as thinking partners with peers.

Is it our emphasis on standardized test scores? A lack of vision? A construal of our teaching task as "delivering curriculum" or as "purveying information" instead of developing lifelong readers, problem-solvers, and democratic citizens? Is it legislation and policy? Is it that we do what was done to us, despite all the advances in research and methodology?

If it is policy, it is not the policy itself, but our interpretation and implementation of it at the classroom level. The Common Core and other next-generation standards offer us a powerful lever to shift toward inquiry and cognitive apprenticeship modes of teaching that deeply engage students and lead to the most substantive learning of any teaching model.

There are many studies that demonstrate the case for inquiry as cognitive apprenticeship (not to be confused with unstructured discovery learning, a mistake many metareviews and reviews of research tend to make). My favorite is the Restructuring Schools Study, conducted by Fred Newman and his colleagues at the University of Wisconsin (Newman & Wehlage, 1995; Newman & Associates, 1996), involving 23 schools and over 2,300 students. Learners were found to have significantly higher engagement and achievement on challenging tasks when they learned in an inquiry environment. Inquiry practices were shown to have more positive impact on student performance than any other factor, including prior achievement and background.

The anchor standards of the Core are all strategies and procedures of expert reading, composing, and problem-solving. The Core consists of what is known in cognitive science as "threshold knowledge" (Meyer & Land, 2006), that is, of generative processes (or concepts put into use through procedures) that can be developed and used throughout a lifetime, and that provide a gateway into thinking and perceiving the world and disciplines in the ways that experts do. When students learn to read and compose as inquirers in a context of inquiry, they pass a threshold into more expert awareness (Hillocks, Kahn, & Johannessen, 1983).

For teachers, inquiry practices are threshold knowledge. If we learn how to teach reading and composing as forms of inquiry, and in a context of inquiry, we will experience a threshold to a new world and so will our students. And when one has passed the threshold, then one does not go back to more impoverished notions and practices.

A study published in *Science* (Pianta et al., 2007) critiques schools for spending too much time on purveying information and on basic reading and math skills, and not enough on problem-solving, reasoning, and inquiring. The study also maintains that the United States focuses too much on teacher qualifications and not enough on what teachers actually do in classrooms to engage, support, and assist students to become more expert, that is, to apprentice students into inquiry and problem-solving. The study found that students spent over 90% of their class time passively listening to a teacher, and little time working together on significant problems of interest, practicing the skills and strategies of experts. Classrooms, the researchers found, are basically dull, lifeless, and uninspiring places and do not introduce students to threshold knowledge or give them practice with it.

I am sorry to say that this mirrors my own daughters' experiences, with some wonderfully notable exceptions. These notable exceptions were teachers who related to them and appreciated them as people, showed great interest in their learning, and thought outside the proverbial box by using materials and projects and rigorous but creative instruction that looks different from the traditional, and that apprenticed them to outgrow themselves as readers, writers, and people. This is my message: BE *THAT* TEACHER!

I have seen this in my daughters' experiences and in my own studies of teaching and literacy: If a teacher meets a single criterion of the social contract, or uses new and creative instructional techniques, the students will almost uniformly love that teacher, and this will translate into a willingness to learn from that teacher.

I am reminded of hearing the educational philosopher Eric Johnson's injunction that "All educational experiments are doomed to succeed—except perhaps on Friday afternoons or during the month of February!"

I take it that what Johnson means is that in most situations trying something new as a teacher will lead to learning for everyone. And if it doesn't go as smoothly as you might like, at least you will have had some fun and learned how to adjust for next time—IF one uses the opportunity to reflect with students and learn from the experience. In other words, we learn from mistakes as well as successes. You can't learn by doing the same thing over and over again, and neither can your students.

One of my favorite jokes is about the teacher who didn't really teach for 30 years, he taught for 1 year 30 times. Here's another message: DON'T BE THIS TEACHER!

Why is this joke funny? Why are we not continually exploring alternatives? Why are we not engaged in educational experimentation?

Ken Zeichner's answer is "the salience of the traditional" (see, e.g., Zeichner & Tabachik, 1981). Zeichner's research shows that preservice and inservice teachers who go back to school will articulate new theories and develop rich repertoires for implementing these new theories, but then quickly revert to teaching the way they were taught or in the ways they have taught before.

The salience of the traditional shows up in school schedules, 45-minute periods; expectations of students, parents, colleagues, and administrators; traditional materials and traditional texts; traditional assessments; and the like.

When I wrote this book nearly 25 years ago, I focused on helping students to read more like experts. One aspect of this project I want to highlight here is the importance of a meaningful context that promotes and coproduces meaning-making. In the Introduction, I wrote about how the culture of learning must be relational, reciprocal, and social, how classrooms must leverage the social context of peer teaching and the Vygotskian insight that we are smarter together than we are alone. The culture of school must reconsider how we work together and do so more collaboratively, with teachers as master practitioners inducting students into expertise through joint productive activity and mutual projects in which they learn together. Schools must also change how they conceive of time and how to support innovation through social networks such as Professional Learning Communities (PLCs), which at their best can be robust thinking partnerships working on instruction.

Social learning is essential to our students, but also to us. As a learning profession, teachers must work together socially as thinking partners—as they do in National Writing Project sites—to transform their own participation both in the classroom and in the community of practice of teaching. In NWP sites we do teaching demonstrations of our effective practices; justify and explain these with our own experiences, with theory and research; and help others to connect what we have done to their own teaching.

Here I want to consider how creating a classroom inquiry environment can work wonders to engage and support learning, by teaching with clarity of purpose, and including more of the social in the classroom.

My daughter Fiona was recently reading about the rise of the textile industry in 16th-century Europe. She didn't know what to pay attention to because she didn't know the purpose of what she was reading—and she couldn't conceive of how it could possibly matter to her personally or out in the world. (Have you ever seen a student who highlighted everything in a text? That was Fiona, and it was because she didn't know the purpose of the assignment or the class.)

Now imagine if the purpose had been made clear to her. Say the teacher had announced, on the first day of school, that they were going to consider the essential question "Why do civilizations rise and fall?" Imagine that the teacher had told the students that every time they studied a civilization or an aspect of it, they would compare that study to modern America.

He could then ask: What industries of early-21st-century America will historians write about? Answers would certainly include hydrocarbon energy (e.g., oil) and electronic technologies. Then he could ask what students predicted historians would say about our devotion to hydrocarbon energy and electronics. Which might be thought to contribute to the demise or rise of American culture and influence? In this way, Fiona's reading would become purposeful and personal. To do this work, she would be learning threshold concepts and procedures used by historians and social scientists. She would know what to pay attention to and highlight (how did the textile industry contribute to the rise of Central Europe and how did this affect history?). She would naturally make connections between history and the present day, and connections from her own life to history and to world events. She would learn to read, write, and think like a historian and social scientist. And if I know my daughter, she would be moved to read about historical events on the Internet and in YA books, to check out movies about the events and trends she was studying in school, and to compare and critique these. She would learn to look for and explain patterns, to infer and analyze. She would learn, in other words, how to engage in historical inquiry.

Over the past 20 years I've been working on an adolescent literacy project in the content areas (currently we are concentrating on literacy in science learning), and one thing we have found is that when you read (or learn), you are reading *about something*. If that something is made purposeful through an essential question (see Jacobs, 1989; Smith & Wilhelm, 2010; Wilhelm, 2007), then the dull dynamic of the classroom is exploded and revitalized. The relationship of students to the content is changed, the relationship of the content to the world is clarified, and the relationship of teacher to student, and student to student, is transformed into one of collaboration—working together as thinking partners on issues that really matter in the world and in the disciplines.

As one teacher in our study of teaching literacy in inquiry environments, Dallas Smith, proclaimed, "Using an essential question changes everything!"

This highlights my second point, that learning is social. In the *Science* study cited earlier, anything that could be construed of as group work was engaged in for only 7% of class time. And I'm guessing from my reading of the data that much of that group work wasn't structured to maximize the benefits of working together. Why is so much work in school done alone? Vygotsky's work (1978) is explanatory of how working together can move us through our zones of individual proximal development: "What children can do in cooperation today they can do alone tomorrow." We also know much about the social nature of literacy and of all learning, about the importance of collaboration around significant work. And it seems to me that the unique capacity of the classroom is that we can do significant work *together*.

BE *THAT* TEACHER who includes more social collaboration in your classroom. This collaboration is essential to practicing the sociocultural learning theory and, I would argue, to deep understanding and the meeting of next-generation standards.

When students work together, or even alone using a reader-centered pedagogy (work I argue for and promote in many ways), I do worry that they might not be challenged to read in new and more powerful ways, to see new perspectives, or to learn to understand the contended nature of knowledge. Failure to undertake these challenges means that our teaching is too student-centered and not teaching/learning-centered, working to apprentice them to greater expertise. Teaching that is too student-centered keeps students from true understanding.

For example, I worry that when students read multicultural literature, they will need to be given "equipment" and "tools" to see and respect and understand from the perspective of authors and characters who are distant from them in time and place. I worry that if they are not assisted in doing so, they will merely look in the mirror over and over again, and that they will fail to actualize the opportunity to outgrow themselves, pass over thresholds, develop new strategies and understandings, and as a result become something new.

The social is important on many levels: There is a need for a knowledgeable and sensitive teacher who can assist students in using new strategies in new ways in a variety of contexts so that they will learn to be and become more than they already are, as readers, as problem-solvers, and as people. There is a need to learn relationally from characters, authors, and experts through our transactions with various texts. And learning is always more engaging and powerful when we learn through dialogue and joint productive activity with others.

Exhibit 1.1 summarizes a comparison of the three different theories of teaching and learning identified by cognitive science (e.g., Rogoff et al., 1996) and implies how to reorient teaching and move from curriculum-centered information-transmission approaches to those that are teaching/learning centered through inquiry and cognitive apprenticeship. The online unit planning templates are guides for planning inquiry units.

There is an alternative to traditional information-transmission teaching: BE *THAT* TEACHER who actualizes the unique power and possibilities of inquiry and the sociocultural theory of teaching and learning!

Exhibit 1.2. can be found online on this book's page and the free downloads page at TCPress.com

Exhibit 1.2. Model Inquiry Unit Templates

Exhibit 1.1. Theories of Teaching and Learning Chart

	ONE-SIDED MODELS		MULTI-SIDED MODEL
	Curriculum-Centered: Information Transmission	Student-Centered: Discovery	Sociocultural Teaching/Learning—Centered: Inquiry as Cognitive Apprenticeship
Historical Roots	Skinner, Pavlov, Thorndike	Piaget, Chomsky, Geselle, Rousseau	Vygotsky, Rogoff, Bruner, Hillocks; Dewey: *Child and Curriculum*, *Experience and Education*
Theoretical Orientation	Behaviorism Focus on the *what* to be purveyed and reflected back	Progressivism Cognitivism Radical Constructivism Focus on the *who* of the learner, including their current interests and capacities	Coconstructivism Socioculturalism Focus on the *why* and *how* using the *what*, but on the conceptual level—addressing the *who* of the individual and their potential (*what and how they might learn next*) and, even more importantly, the *who* of the disciplinary community to be entered and emulated, and the context of situated cognition (the *when and where* of knowledge production and use)
How Learning Occurs	Transmission of Information: Teaching is telling; learning is receiving and repeating	Acquisition of Knowledge: Teaching is creating contexts for discovery; learning is personal discovery	Transformation of Participation: Teaching is creating environments and instructional supports that assist and apprentice learners into ever more expert practice
Context of Learning	School	Personal Space	Real World or spaces analogous to real world (e.g., inquiry contexts, drama worlds)

Exhibit 1.1. Theories of Teaching and Learning Chart (continued)

	ONE-SIDED MODELS		MULTI-SIDED MODEL
	Curriculum-Centered: Information Transmission	Student-Centered: Discovery	Sociocultural Teaching/Learning–Centered: Inquiry as Cognitive Apprenticeship
Mindset Orientation	Past Orientation: Fixed mindset—what you can learn depends on your past learning and background and capacity	Present Orientation: Mild growth mindset—you will learn what you want to learn and what you pursue with energy	Present/Future Orientation; Dynamic/Growth Mindset: The next available learning is always accessible through deliberate effort and practice with strategies in a context of use.
Theoretical implications for instruction	Both teacher and the student are passive; curriculum determines the sequence and timing of instruction	Students have biological limits that affect when and how they can learn; teachers must not "push" students beyond their limits. Knowledge is a "natural" product of development.	All knowledge is socially and culturally constructed. What and how the student learns depends on what opportunities the teacher/parent provides. Learning is not "natural" but "cultural" and depends on interactions with more expert others, and apprenticeship into using expert threshold knowledge in contexts of meaningful use. Any learner can learn the next available thing if given appropriate assistance and deliberate practice in a context of use.
Student's Role	"Empty Vessel": Passive receivers of information	Active constructor of personal meaning	Collaborative participant learning how to create meaning in ways established and justified by expert practitioners, so that one is inducted into that "community of practice"/discipline and can participate in and contribute to it, and eventually even extend or revise that community's knowledge.

44

	Transmit the Curriculum		
Teacher's Role	Create the environment in which individual learners can develop pretty much on their own in set stages— implies single and natural course		Observe learners closely, as individuals and groups. Scaffold learning within the zone/s of proximal development; match individual and collective curricula, methods, and materials to learners' needs through differentiation. Create inquiry environment where all can participate with you and peers in a common project, even if doing different kinds of work with different methods, levels of assistance, groupings, and materials.
Reading	Learners are assigned required textbooks and canonical texts. Focus is on what texts mean, not how they mean or what readers must do to make meaning. Little reading instruction, and if it exists it is done separately from the actual reading of assigned texts, e.g., with worksheets.	Learners read whatever they like; learn reading strategies by reading on their own.	Learners read widely from different text structures and perspectives. Some of this is shared reading, much is free choice. Students are assisted in reading more expertly in the context of their reading through teacher and peer modeling with think-alouds, drama/action strategies, visual strategies, and the like.
Writing/ Composing	Very little writing, and if there is writing, it is formulaic, like the five-paragraph essay, and does not reflect new meaning-making but mirroring back what has been purveyed by teachers and textbooks.	Free-choice writing of any form.	Lots of structured and assisted informal writing practice to apprentice students to understand the concepts and processes of composing different text structures in different modalities, leading to usable and archivable "knowledge artifacts" that can be shared and read by others.

Exhibit 1.1. Theories of Teaching and Learning Chart *(continued)*

	ONE-SIDED MODELS		MULTI-SIDED MODEL
	Curriculum-Centered: Information Transmission	Student-Centered: Discovery	Sociocultural Teaching/Learning–Centered: Inquiry as Cognitive Apprenticeship
Dominant Instructional Activities	Teacher-controlled activities: Teacher lectures, students memorize material for tests	Student-selected reading, student-selected projects, discovery learning	Teacher-guided participation in both small- and large-group work; constant use of formative assessments *as and for learning* to make student progress and challenges visible, recording and analyzing individual student progress; provide explicit assistance in the context of meaningful activity to reach higher levels of competence. Modeling, mentoring, and monitoring. Gradual release of responsibility to students.
Metaphor— Cooking Spaghetti Sauce	Students, you do not know enough to make spaghetti sauce, so I will give you the one best recipe for spaghetti sauce. You will memorize it and follow the recipe without deviation.	Students, you must invent your own spaghetti sauce! No one else can do it for you! I have provided all the ingredients you might need. Have fun figuring it out!	Students, we will work together to learn general principles of cuisine and food chemistry that inform great cooking. We are going to work together on using several spaghetti sauce recipes to figure out these principles of cooking chemistry. Then, using these principles, you will develop your own personal sauce recipe.

46

Who Is Responsible if Student Does Not Progress?	The student: He/she can't keep up with the curriculum sequence and pace of lessons or meet the demands of a prescriptive school program. Since this is inscribed in stone, there is really nothing to be done.	The student: He/she has a "developmental delay," a disability, or is not "ready" for the school's program. Since learning is natural, there must be a problem with the natural process. Often, family or social conditions are at fault.	The more capable others: They have not observed the learner closely, problem-solved the learner's difficulty, matched instruction to the learner, made informed decisions, helped the learner get ready, and assisted the learner over time in developing competence and in seeing and naming her growing competence so that she has a "tool box" for learning and problem-solving activity. Since everyone can learn with the proper assistance and deliberate practice, the teacher must search for alternatives.
The Results	If successful, the learner will remember the purveyed information and can repeat that information to pass a fill-in-the-blank test, multiple-choice test, or formulaic writing mirroring back the information.	If successful, the learner has constructed personal understandings about a topic and can express these in some form to herself.	If successful, the learner is inducted through gateways to participating in the role of "novice expert" in actual disciplinary problem-solving and meaning-making. The learner who has mastered threshold knowledge in a discipline can begin to create new knowledge and participate in ongoing disciplinary conversations and problem-solving. The student can create a culminating project or service that demonstrates and makes use of conceptual and procedural threshold knowledge.

Significantly adapted from Wilhelm, Baker, & Dube-Hackett (2001)

2

Looking at Student Reading

As I pursued the answers to my questions, I became very close to many of my students, sharing stories about reading and life with them on an almost daily basis. Later in the year, when I told Joanne that I was interested in her "story as a reader," she told me, "No, you're interested in the story of my life." But after thinking for a moment, she said, "But for you that means almost the same thing." And maybe she's right, because though she will be one of a few thousand students I will eventually teach, I will always be her seventh-grade English teacher, and I hope that will somehow make a qualitative difference in her life.

The stories I'm going to tell here come from a school year during which I taught 123 students. All of the students were involved in the activities that I will describe. I analyzed and report the data from only nine hand-picked students who represented a wide range of student interests, abilities, and difficulties, and it is their stories that I will tell in the following chapters.

I was part of an integrated middle school teaching team that served all of what I jokingly called the district's "severely labeled population." This meant that our team taught all of the students labeled LD (learning disabled) at the seventh-grade level. During this year 13 LD students participated in two mainstreamed language arts classes with regular education students. Our team also served other labeled students such as ED (emotionally disturbed), ADHD (attention deficit/hyperactivity disorder), and ESL (English as a second language) in mainstreamed situations.

The students live in a unified school district in a medium-sized midwestern town and a large surrounding farming area. Most parents from town work in light industries such as metallurgy, shoe-, cheese-, and food-processing factories, or in the professions.

THE YEAR BEGINS

At the very beginning of the school year, as I began to systematically collect information about how all of my students were reading, I was immediately struck by several central themes that corresponded to my main frustrations and questions as a teacher.

First, through the initial interviews and conferences, it seemed that the real reading lives of my students were led outside of school. They did not expect school reading to be fun, engaging, or personally satisfying. If they regarded themselves as readers, then the reading they valued was pursued in study halls, at home, with friends and family—usually any-place but the classroom.

Ron expressed to me that his experience as a reader was not captured by school activities. "I've read things in school that were pretty good, but it's kind of just good luck. Usually if I'm learning something or really into something it's nothing to do with school." Later he explained that "you can read something good and the teacher ruins it by asking you questions that you already know, that don't matter, that you disagree with. . . ."

Some of my students who loved reading most, students like Ron, Mandy, and Lisa, had achieved marginal grades in school and became "antistudents," as Mandy put it, as they "tr[ied] to ignore what's going on in class." These three students were often in "trouble" for reading in class, or even in study hall—when they "should be doing their home-work," as the math teacher told me (just one example of how literary reading is marginalized in school).

Even engaged readers who were highly successful students, like Cora and Joanne, expressed that teachers and school activities did not share or abet what they valued most about their own reading. "I do what's asked [in assignments], but it often has . . . very little to do with what I'm thinking and feeling and caring about [as I read]," Cora said.

There was another type of student who read and seemed to enjoy stories, but had great difficulty answering typical anthology or worksheet questions. Their lack of success at these activities undermined these stu-dents' confidence. Libby, labeled LD, told me, "I like to read, but I'm not very good at it, I guess, or at least I can't remember what I read because I'm not good at answering the questions." Kae, an ESL student, told me that "I read and I sometimes like and I think I know it but then I do bad on quiz. . . . I like reading by home better."

There were students like Marvin who simply refused to read, and made an issue out of it. "Can't make me," he told me when I encouraged him to read early in the year. Then there were students who played along and appeared to be reading, like Brad, Kevin, Tommy, and Walter, but who just didn't seem to comprehend or experience what they had read. They all sometimes resisted reading, and expressed that they were not good readers. "Let's face it," Brad told me, speaking for his LD-labeled cohorts, "We suck [at reading]. And who cares?"

For these resistant students, the factual or interpretive questions typically asked by teachers and commercially prepared materials appeared to be no help in revealing, developing, or extending their reading abilities. Even when I was able to navigate them through a reading, their responses seemed totally off the mark, unconnected in any way to what I had understood the story to be about.

WHAT MAKES VALID READING?

What makes a reading "valid"? Is any response a good one? This has been a thorny issue for me. Given the readers with whom I work and their often negative and submissive attitudes toward reading, my primary concern has been to help them gain confidence as producers of meaning. I wish to help them gain control over their reading processes and to merge into textual worlds in which they will exert this control.

Rosenblatt (1978) addresses this issue when she asserts that a "valid" reading requires that "1) the interpretation is not contradicted by any element of the text, and 2) that nothing is projected for which there is no verbal basis" (p. 115).

Though I accept and even encourage divergent readings from many of my reluctant readers, because I believe growth is being demonstrated as they begin to create meanings, I do keep "valid" reading as an ultimate goal to work toward. I think it is critical to consider the author's intent and meaning, embodied in the "actual accomplishment" (Rosenblatt, 1978, p. 109) of the text. This authorial consciousness gives the reader access to insights, experiences, and perceptions otherwise beyond her reach, thus allowing a reformulation of the reader's consciousness. In other words, reading can lead to self-discovery and learning—but only if we understand what an author has to say! Still, personal meaning will differ from reader to reader and remain valid. Rosenblatt takes pains to argue for honoring the individual nature of the reading act when she states that teachers need "to help *specific human beings*—not some generalized fiction called the student—to discover the pleasures and satisfactions of literature" (1978, p. 34, my emphasis).

From the very start of my project to understand the activities of my student readers, this is what I wanted to find out: How could the students and I create a learning climate that would be meaningful for all of us, one that emphasized our current readerly activities and human concerns? How could we run a class that helped to encourage vital and enriching reading experiences by building on what individuals already knew and could do, and that extended and developed them as readers from whatever starting point they now inhabited?

I was especially troubled by the students who appeared to be reading but who did not find it meaningful, and who did not discuss or answer questions about what they read. In my journal, I asked myself "How can they be brought into the fold? [How can they be] convinced that there is something worthwhile about this pursuit [of reading]? . . . What are they doing that the questions miss? that I miss?" (May 1992)

STUDYING STUDENT RESPONSE

So I became a researcher. As a teacher, I teach individual students, individuals whom I invite to become part of a community of readers. Every individual is my project; I know that I really cannot afford to neglect one. Each year now, I try to get to know each student as a person and as a reader. The methods and projects I will describe in the following studies have helped me to do this. It is an arduous and complex job, this process of knowing and teaching students. And I have never felt when a year ended that I have dealt with each student in nearly the best possible way. This is part of teaching, and why teaching really is an act of faith. You do what you can and believe that it will suffice. As I wrote in my journal:

> I only ask to win three of every five. I can't win them all, and if I can win at least three of every five lessons, three of every five school days, three of every five encounters or conferences, then my students and I can go to the World Series. (September 1991)

As a teacher, I study every student who comes into my classroom. To do less would be to not take each student with the seriousness she or he deserves. I share with each student what I have noticed about what she does as a reader, and ask her to share with me what I may have missed. We identify and celebrate what they do, and set about pushing back the boundaries of what might be done. I ask my students to tell me what they are trying to do next, and to set goals that I will help them meet.

As a teacher, I am concerned with big pictures, with overall development, with the long term, with vistas of the future. Some of my past students (whom I still regard as my own, and in whom I am still intensely interested) are married and have children. Some are highly educated professionals or highly skilled laborers who might write up my will or fix my car. Many write me notes and letters, call on the phone, or stop by—often to discuss their reading, but always to discuss their lives.

I am concerned with the sort of lives they are leading and how what we experienced together in a language arts classroom contributes to that. I am concerned with helping the students now in my classroom to live enriched lives. These are the big pictures I concern myself with, learning from one student what can benefit the teaching of all future students.

I would like to make it clear that as a teacher I am interested in both the uniquely individual and in what is regular and patterned. I need to know about both to be able to teach (cf. Bissex, 1987; Chambers, 1985). What I describe in the next chapter is what three individual readers do as they read, but what is described seems generally true to me of what all my most engaged readers do and have done as readers over the past several years that I have carefully observed and written about them.

To gain a window into my students' reading activities, my students and I used a blend of interviews, conferences, literary letters, a variety of protocols (or think-alouds), and a technique that I call the symbolic story representation, in which students use cutouts or "found objects" to dramatize both what they are reading and how they are reading it. (I discuss these methods in more detail in Chapter Three.)

These first three individual readers are the figures against a ground made up of more than 1,000 students. The special knowledge of a teacher is made up of an accretion of thousands of daily events, discussions, observations, reflections. The special knowledge of the teacher-researcher is not the knowledge of the university researcher who may choose to study a very few students on chosen occasions. There are costs and benefits to each approach. When I speak of what I know, it is from the perspective of 13 years of carefully observing and thinking about what children do when they read. But this observation is in the context of 180 days of busy classroom interaction, clouded by problems, interruptions, conflicts, a continual lack of time, sometimes by tragedy, often with laughter.

Therefore, though I concentrate first on the stories of three engaged readers and later on the stories of six reluctant ones, I do so to achieve some clarity and focus. Their stories will have to do the work of the thousands of stories I would wish to tell.

THREE HIGHLY ENGAGED READERS: CORA, JOANNE, AND RON

During the first 12 weeks of the school year, I chose three highly engaged readers to be case study students. I chose Cora, Joanne, and Ron because they (1) said they loved to read, (2) proved it by reading constantly, (3) exhibited high levels of engagement while reading, (4) exhibited wide varieties and highly divergent types of response to literature, (5) were highly articulate about what they did as they read, (6) expressed a willingness and interest in becoming co-researchers, and (7) exhibited proficient readings that seemed to embody the ways I had observed other engaged readers reading over the past several years. In other words, their readings were rich, valid, and displayed a conscious sense of the reader as a meaning-maker.

I chose to work with these excellent readers so that I could come to understand more clearly what they did to make their reading meaningful. I then planned to use what I found to help my less engaged readers begin to use these same strategies.

Cora, Joanne, and Ron were all delightful kids to teach. Cora seemed to be a private person in some ways, but she loved to contribute in class and was very articulate. She struck me as mature and philosophical, a loner by choice who could nonetheless blend in with various groups. She had dark brown hair and experimented with a few wildly varied hairstyles throughout the year. She had her own uniquely stylish way of dressing that she called "funky but chic," kind of what you'd expect from a female lawyer who was going a little bit out on a limb.

Joanne seemed very shy. She didn't talk much in large group discussions, but she had a soothing voice and worked well with other students as a peer tutor and in smaller groups. She was willowy and tall for her age, with blonde curly hair that flowed over her shoulders, and that she would whisk out of her face with a quick flicking gesture. She always dressed very neatly, often in a corduroy jumper over a turtleneck or blouse—which was rare among her peers. She had a simply tremendous smile that flashed when she was enjoying a story or classroom exchange.

Ron was a nut. He seemed to always be in some kind of minor trouble with other teachers, but I loved him. He described himself as "a wild and crazy seventh-grade guy." He was big for his age, extremely gregarious, and was going out with an eighth-grade girl who caused him occasional but very temporary heartache. He liked jeans and T-shirts with environmental slogans or flannel shirts. He had some good friends in class, especially Chris, and they would exchange high-fives and simultaneously chant "Glory BE!" hum the ESPN *SportsCenter* theme, or engage in some other humorous inanity whenever the spirit moved them—which was quite often.

Cora and Joanne were both students who excelled in the language arts, though both were described as "average" students by their math and science teachers. They earned mostly A's, with a few B's in math and science. Ron achieved average grades of B's, C's, and an occasional lower grade in math, though his teachers agreed that he was "bright" and "creative."

These students were all conscious of and articulate about what they did and felt as they read. As was true of many of their classmates, they immediately knew what I meant when I asked what they "did" as readers or where they found themselves in relationship to a story. They were generally eager to share these details with me. Cora especially spoke spontaneously and at great length about her role as a reader, about authorial technique, and about the relationship she naturally took up with the characters and authors of books that she was reading. Joanne was initially guarded about sharing how she read, revealing that, "It's not the sort of thing teachers are usually interested in knowing or hearing about." Joanne, as did other students, indicated that she had gone "underground" with her intense interest and experiences as a reader. "I talk to a few friends about it, but no one else. I imagine being considered weird or something if people knew about it." In fact, in light of data regarding my students' attitudes toward reading, this fear was not unfounded.

Attitudes Toward Reading

Of the three case study students, Ron indicated that reading should be graded on "the amount of time people read and how deep they get into it"; Joanne by "what they learned, how it effected [*sic*] or changed them."

Cora explained that "I don't believe reading can or should be graded. Reading is really important and personal. It's more of a hobby than a job you have to do, which is what tests sort of tell you it is. It just seems foolish to me to try and grade reading unless you have a way to get inside people's minds . . . there are so many things that are important about what and how I read that I could never tell anyone . . . [and in response to a follow-up question] because it might be too private, or because I just couldn't put it in words. And a teacher would grade me down because I couldn't!"

All three case study students indicated that they read for both enjoyment and to learn, or as Joanne said, "to grow knowledge, [to] kind of water your head," and that they willingly attempted to enter any story they encountered. Cora told me that she would rather read than do anything else. "I love it. It offers you worlds and people to know and . . . well . . . there's nothing like it, it can offer you everything." She told me that she only watched TV "when I'm too sick to read and I don't want to think."

Early in the study, before we began to explicitly discuss and share our ideas of reading, I specifically asked these readers to discuss metaphors for their reading experience. Interestingly, their metaphors are all consistent with Rosenblatt's notion of a literary transaction. Both girls directly state a relationship with an author, and Ron implies one. All three express an active sense of agency as readers within the flexible parameters set by the text. All three clearly imply that reading is an experience.

CORA: *Reading is like a relay . . . it's more than a conversation. It's as if the author decides on the race and the terrain and the strategy and gets it all going, and you have to figure out the rules of the race and how it's run and then you get the baton and have to continue on your own. And you can make, then, the sort of race you want to run on the course the author has set out. Basically, once you're out on the course you can make what you want. You can stop if you want, or go exploring if you want.*

JOANNE: *[Reading is] like a safari and the book is your vehicle and the author is like the driver inside who takes you places and points out things, but what you notice—either with or without his help—and think is yours, that's the real story.*

RON: *It's sort of like map-reading, except the map—like in the Narnia books—will turn real if you start to believe in it and then KA-ZAM—there you are in the real world of the map doing stuff with the people there.*

Intensity of Engagement

The intensity of these students' responses to literature and the powerful reality of the secondary worlds these readers created were striking to me. Ron, reading a story about a boy whose dog was killed, told me that he felt so strongly that he was the boy in the story "that I couldn't stand how sad I felt about it." He reminded himself "that I was just reading, but it took a long time to convince myself. . . . I was like totally upset." When he did convince himself, he reentered the story, not as the boy, but as "the kid's grandfather. . . . I thought the whole thing would be easier to take and I would be in a better position to help out if I could sort of be the grandfather. . . . it still hurt, but not as bad."

Joanne told me, "Sometimes I'm thinking something and I can't remember if it really happened or if I dreamed it or read it. Then I'll go back and . . . I found it. I'd read it. I couldn't believe it hadn't really happened to me because I thought that it had, you know, *really* happened to me."

This fuzziness of the border between actual and virtual worlds was echoed by Cora. She constantly referred to literary characters as "people I know": "I knew a girl who . . . ," "I know about a person who. . . ." She revealed that "when the author is good at writing then I get to know the people in the book and I carry them and their ideas around with me just like we were best of friends. And in a sense, we are, we really know each other, better than you almost always know people in real life."

The experiences reported by these students echo D. W. Harding's (1962) reports that participation in story worlds is far more complex than terms such as "vicarious experience" and "identification" can possibly suggest. These readers used a wide variety of moves (described in Chapter Three) to engage with stories, to become active participants in the story world, to then connect with that virtual world as real readers, and to reflect upon their experience as readers.

So, What *Is* Literature?

These three students were constant readers. They read a lot, and they read a real variety of materials. Cora read *Spin* magazine; Joanne sometimes read *YM*. Cora read books ranging from the Nancy Drew and R. L. Stine series to Chris Crutcher (who usually appeals more to boys), the Scary Stories series, the young adult novels of Katherine Paterson, biographies of Marilyn Monroe and Eleanor Roosevelt, and decidedly adult books such as Gage's *Eleni* or heady documentaries such as Gitlin's *The Sixties.*

Joanne read books such as *Alice's Adventures in Wonderland, The Wind in the Willows, Watership Down,* and Anne Frank's *Diary of a Young Girl.* While preparing to create a video documentary, she read the works on female psychology of Carol Gilligan (1982) and Jean Baker Miller (1976), and a slew of nonfiction texts about women in the workplace.

The two of them shared both traditional and quite contemporary young adult novels ranging from *Little Women, The Secret Garden, A Gathering of Days,* and *Anne of Green Gables* to Voigt's *Come a Stranger* and Cole's *Celine.*

Ron read through many Tom Clancy and John Grisham novels, hefty as they are, but interspersed them with young adult books such as *The High King, Deathwatch,* the Holocaust comic books *Maus* and *Maus II,* and contemporary comics such as *X-Men.*

What does this suggest about the kind of materials we might want our students to read? Given the reading habits and choices of these highly engaged readers and a transactional view of reading, how should we define the idea of literature?

The transactional view, focusing as it does on the experience of reading, does away with any traditional idea of a "literary canon." What constitutes a literary text is any text that provides a particular reader with a deeply engaging aesthetic experience. This depends largely upon the reader: her interests, abilities, preoccupations, experiences as they are brought to bear on the literary transaction in a particular moment of time.

This implies a new role for the teacher as one who will help familiarize students with all kinds of stories in various forms and with various content, and who will validate the reading of these materials. An important goal will be for students to learn to find and select the sorts of materials throughout their lives that will speak to their current needs, desires, and concerns.

We must remember that the ways in which we mediate literature with students will have a profound effect on the kinds of readers they will become. Cora told me that she resented people, including teachers, who "expect me to read only one kind of thing. That would be like eating only one kind of food all the time. I hate it when people say, 'I can't believe you're reading *that*,' like it's a book for children or something." Ron said he liked to know about a wide variety of books and always loved it "when someone introduces me to something new. That's so cool!" Joanne asserted that the best thing a teacher could do was "to recommend a good story to me, and give a chance to talk about it. . . . Most teachers must not read," she said, "or they'd know how to teach reading and not ruin it for us."

Part of encouraging adolescents to read is knowing a variety of materials and encouraging kids to read different genres and authors to learn the scope of what is available and the field of their own taste. Part of knowing how to teach good reading entails learning what techniques and what texts will work best with particular groups and particular individuals, and what books will be new, surprising, and challenging—helping the student to grow. This requires getting to know students, their current interests and abilities, and their own stories of what and how they read. The research techniques that I used with my students (described in Chapter Three) provided windows into my students' reading activity and helped to make what they did as readers visible to me. This story of the reader must be known before the story can be written about what sort of reading they might do and what sort of readers they might become. These stories are helped to unfold by providing the opportunity for students to choose their own reading materials and share what they are reading with each other.

There are vital genres of literature known as Children's and Young Adult literature that speak directly to the concerns of these age groups, attempting to connect directly with their "current state of being" (cf. Chambers, 1985). There are comic books, mysteries and horror stories, historical fiction, fantasies, stories of death and dying, and nonfiction that different students of mine love and read with great intensity. In middle school, I teach many students like Cora, Joanne, and Ron who engage with all of these age-directed genres, with children's books as well as with popular adult books. When I began to work with Tommy, Walter, and Kae, picture and comic books were highly intriguing and helpful to them. Marvin eventually read High Interest–Easy Reading books. This was not the sort of literature I had studied in college as I prepared to be a teacher, nor was it the sort of literature I had read either in or out of the classroom, on my own or with students, since that time. I now see the necessity of immersing myself in it so that I can suggest books to students and converse with them about them.

This is only to reassert that learning to read begins with the reader. After Marvin and Kevin were helped to find stories that spoke to their interests and were accessible to them, they began to take some steps toward selecting their own books. They showed me that readers will develop the interests, willingness, and abilities to dive and swim in more challenging literary currents if they have first learned the pleasures of the swim in waters that are meaningful, safe, and engaging for them. Readers need to have books that understand them as they are and help them to consider and perhaps outgrow their current points of view. Then they will have the desire to deepen and expand their experience.

Ron, Cora, and Joanne all independently indicated that reading was an important way to get to know yourself, who you are, what you believe, and what you should or might do in different situations. Beyond this, Cora felt that reading meant getting to "know other people, getting to live with them in other times and places to see what it was like or would be like for you." Joanne said that "reading is a way to get inside other people. . . . It's a way to learn stuff that's impossible to learn any other way because you learn from the inside." For Ron, reading gave him the opportunity to know people in his own life better. "The best thing about reading is it gives you something chewy to talk with other people about."

The reasons these students give for reading indicate something I have long believed about maturity. Maturity entails, first, the recognition that you have a unique perspective and a view of the world that has value, and second, the recognition that there are different perspectives in the world and that these have value and are worth knowing about, too. This is the issue of developing social imagination so central to literacy education and to democracy. Our adult relationships, with books and with others, entail a balancing of this paradox. When students are helped to outgrow their current selves, they will have the desire to deepen and expand their experience. Any text that serves these ends must be regarded as literature.

To this end, readers should be appropriately encouraged to read both literature written for them and literature written beyond them from traditional literary mainstreams and outside these mainstreams. Multicultural literature, in particular, helps students to enter other perspectives. When we pursued readings associated with a cultural journalism project late in the school year, all three of these students were excited. "I never thought about how different people live . . . about how different things are and look to different groups of people . . . until I read these [multicultural books]," Ron revealed.

Many teachers and parents are upset by their children's powerful passion for pap, those formulaic books of mystery, intrigue, or romance.

In fact, all three of these engaged readers enjoyed these books. All readers who transact with such texts are engaging in powerful literary experiences. I have been continually impressed by the depth and intensity of student response to the horror tales of R. L. Stine, though his books elicited no response but disgust during my own painful reading of them. My students often compare themselves and their situations to those fantastic ones described in the story, and have often discussed how such books provide lessons, as Brent told me, "for surviving in a teenage world." Cora told me that such stories "certainly make you feel, and they can really make you think."

Besides that, research shows that:

1. Adolescent readers of formulaic fiction go through a stage of intense engagement with such books, such as the Hardy Boys or Nancy Drew mysteries, followed by a desire for something "more," for something more challenging and sophisticated, for something offering another way of seeing and interpreting the world (Carlsen, 1980). I have seen this often in my own teaching. R. L. Stine leads to Stephen King leads to Ray Bradbury or Ursula Le Guin. Or R. L. Stine leads to Stephen King and R. L. Stine. The point is that these formulaic books speak to the students and are helping them discover the power of reading, and that they often lead to the reading of other material.

2. Adult readers of formulaic fiction often have wide-ranging tastes. They read formula fiction for particular purposes, such as entertainment, but they know and enjoy other sorts of texts for other sorts of purposes. They are readers, and they know the various purposes reading can fulfill. My wife, a constant reader, is a perfect example of this, reading mysteries to "rest" between what she describes as "intense" literary experiences such as that offered her by Pilcher's *The Shell Seekers*.

3. Perhaps most importantly, studies such as Radway's (1984) *Reading the Romance* show that readers of what might be considered trash literature (like the romance) actually use it in highly creative or resistant ways that must be considered "literary transactions." The women studied by Radway revealed that romance reading gave them power over their lives. First, it staked out a time during which they were to be left alone, to their own pleasures, and not to be bothered by duties of serving spouse and family. Second, their actual readings of the texts helped them find a powerful way of

being in the world, and a vision and potential for transforming the contexts of their own lives. Finally, reading the romances connected them to communities of women with similar concerns, thereby providing them with a powerful support group of readers and writers. Any texts that provide such experiences must be considered literature.

Aidan Chambers (1985) argues that the seminal quality of literature is that it is "transformational" or life-changing in some way—whether this is a change in our views, our relationships with the world, or the way we read and regard books. Joanne echoes him when she says: "Every good book I ever read has changed me, it's like adding another layer of more sensitive skin on my body . . . or maybe on my brain." Literature, if read transactionally and creatively, may have the effect of transforming us as readers and as people. Transformative reading begins where the reader currently is, and works from there.

Chambers cites Kafka, who wrote: "We have need of books which act upon us like a misfortune from which we would suffer terribly, like the death of someone we are fonder of than ourselves . . . a book must be the axe that smashes the frozen sea within us. That is what I think" (1985, p. 17).

One job of teachers, I have come to believe, is not to define a narrow and exclusive view of "literature" and to familiarize students with it, but to put children in touch with a wide variety of books and ideas that will help them develop into readers who can recognize the books that can be their personal axes, readers who can take them up and wield them mightily to smash the frozen seas within. Any story that can do so, for them at this particular moment, must be regarded as literature.

Because literature encourages the reader to enter the experience and perspectives of others, and to measure one's understanding in relationship to others' ideas, it is a doorway into the world of conversing with and understanding others. It offers choices and possibilities for the world and how we want to be in that world. As will be seen, Ron, Cora, and Joanne all articulated this "imaginative rehearsal for living" as part of their reading experience.

But there are hurdles to overcome. Applebee (1989) asserts that though readers best learn how to read and respond to literature by spending time reading, today's adolescents spend little of their leisure time pursuing reading. Other studies indicate that students spend very little time actually reading in school. Some experts estimate that the average child spends less than 5 minutes a day reading—including schoolwork (cited by Healy, 1990, p. 23). And students express repeatedly that they see little reason to do so. By putting books that speak to them and fit their abilities into their hands, we can give them many reasons to read.

WHY READ LITERATURE?

So, what might we say to critics and reformers (such as Willard Dagget) who maintain that we should be teaching technical and textbook reading, and that literature is pleasure reading that serves no important purpose?

I put this question to my case study students. Ron had this to say: "Because school is supposed to help you live better, right?"

Joanne asserted that "a story helps you to think. It involves you totally in thinking about things you could never think about except in a story."

Cora maintained that reading was like "a microscope and a telescope . . . helps you see things that are invisible—because they're too small or too far away. . . . It makes you think so much more than a video or TV."

In a school where the sole purpose is to manufacture competent workers for the nation's technological-industrial complex, perhaps the need for literary instruction and reading would not be keenly felt (though this position can certainly be argued; cf. Brown, 1991). But if schools serve a greater function, to help create empowered and attentive citizens who can both pursue fulfilling and fruitful individual lives and who can contribute in transformative ways to the life of a democracy, then literature must take a central place in the curriculum.

If "functional literacy" is to be replaced with a "literacy of thoughtfulness" (Brown, 1991), if students are to develop critical and creative habits of mind, then literature must be a major player in this enterprise.

As Ron, Joanne, and Cora informed me, literary experience is on the one hand intensely personal and individual, helping the reader to understand his or her self and situation. On the other hand, literature can be a social experience in which we share meanings and ways of making meaning.

Narrative, as Hardy (1977) and Schank (1990) argue, is a primary way of knowing and organizing our personal knowledge of ourselves and the world. Storying defines humanity, makes us human, empowers us in being who we are, and makes it possible for us to conceive of being more than we are. As Bruner (1986) tells us, storytelling is a unique way of knowing that cannot be replicated by any other epistemological form. Literature, Aidan Chambers (1985) explains, offers us images with which to think, imagine, and communicate. It is in our nature as a "culture building species" to make sense of our surroundings and ourselves, and to communicate our understandings (p. 6).

Just as Cora suggests, Chambers argues that it is "with words, by words and through words" that we make sense of ourselves, and that this pursuit is the special province of the sense-making function of language in the form we call narrative. Literature is more profound, even at its simplest level, than any other form of words. What we can do with ourselves is limited or enabled by what we can do with language to tell and imagine stories (pp. 4, 5, 6).

Literature is transcendent: it offers us possibilities; it takes us beyond space, time, and self; it questions the way the world is and offers possibilities for the way it could be. It offers a variety of views, visions, and voices that are so vital to a democracy. It is unique in the way it provides us with maps for exploring the human condition, with insights and perceptions into life, and with offerings for ways to be human in the world. Literature helps us to define ourselves as we are, and to envision what it is we want ourselves and the world to be.

Joanne told me that "I feel like reading a good book makes me someone new." I think she's right. The literary transaction helps to shape us; it can help us to shape the world. Perhaps this is why literature flourishes in repressive political situations: it can not only critique and protest, it can reach out to others and toward something better.

As the world becomes a more complex and smaller place, it seems that self-understanding and the willingness and ability to understand others will become ever more important. That is one big reason why I think literature is important for adolescents.

Ron, Joanne, and Cora helped me to ask and answer the questions of why literary reading was important for all students, and how I could put all my students in touch with a variety of books that might speak to them.

Perhaps most importantly, these three students helped me see how I could teach all of my students—especially the many reluctant and resistant readers—how to more actively and expertly read and enjoy books. What follows in the next chapter is a highly detailed description of their reading response throughout the course of their seventh-grade year. The descriptions take a very close and fine-grained look at examples of all the kinds of moves they made as readers. I look specifically at the whole wide range of their reading activity because, to date, we do not have a specific and comprehensive case study of what highly engaged adolescent readers do as they read. That is the story that comes next, and it has a lot to say for how we can better teach our more reluctant readers—as will be seen in Chapters Four and Five.

COMMENTARY

LOOKING TOWARD TOMORROW INSTEAD OF TO YESTERDAY—THE POWER OF TEACHER RESEARCH

Research is a high-hat word that scares a lot of people. It needn't. It's rather simple. Essentially research is nothing but a state of mind . . . a friendly, welcoming attitude towards change . . . going out to look for change instead of waiting for it to come.

Research is an effort to do things better and not to be caught asleep at the switch. It is the problem-solving mind as contrasted with the let-well-enough-alone mind. It is the tomorrow mind instead of the yesterday mind.

—Charles Kettering (quoted in Hubbard & Power, 1993, p. 1)

In this chapter, I describe my first foray into teacher research, and articulate the first burning teacher research questions I pursued.

Reading this chapter again makes me think about how important teacher research has been to me and to my students in school as well as to my preservice and inservice students at the university, and the importance it could have to teaching as a profession.

In *YGBB* I write only about the benefits of teacher research, and I admit that my belief in the benefits has been strengthened over time. I certainly don't cover all of the benefits here, but I also missed some of the costs.

For one, although I know from experience that reflective teaching and instructional inquiry can be made a natural part of each teaching day, I also know that shaping this research into a formal presentation, an article, or even a book can come right out of my teaching hide. Yet this kind of work is necessary to move my teacher research from something that is personally meaningful to something that might be part of a thinking and teaching partnership, into something professionally influential whether at the level of my department or school, or at regional and national levels. It does seem to me that as professionals we need to not only continually understand, justify, and improve our own practice, but we also need to see how our work speaks to social practices and policies. And for the good of ourselves and our students, I believe that teachers must become part of the research conversations and policy creation surrounding education. Teacher research makes what we do, why we do it, and how it works visible and justifies it to ourselves and to others. Doing teacher research means that you are entering into conversation with other teachers and researchers about what is most challenging and what matters most to us as educators, and it means that we not only have a voice and speak, but that we must listen and take in the voices of others. Without teacher voices, grounded in experience and clear-eyed interpretations of the data in our classrooms, policies will be top-down and ill-informed, and implementations will be inefficient.

At my National Writing Project site, our central project is the creation of teaching demonstrations of teacher expertise, justified through theory and research. We share this work and converse about it during our institutes and workshops but also through annual Nights of Inquiry, where teachers share their action research with one another and the public, and with Administrators and Friends dinners, where we share our work with administrators, state officials, and the public over a meal and short program. Even more influentially, we work closely with our state department of education to develop, deliver, and archive professional development in areas of need. This past year we delivered over 110,000 contact hours of professional development to teachers in Idaho. The workshop content included teaching demonstrations based on our NWP fellows' own teaching and their own teacher research. This year we are working for the first time with science teachers from around the state, creating model curricula and methods of literacy development and inquiry along with them.

I've come to see that my time and my energy are my greatest commodities, and I try to privilege attending to my students, my teaching, my planning, and my reflection as the first authority. But I've also come to realize that to best serve my students, I also need to serve my profession, and that means involving myself as a conversant at levels that extend beyond my classroom. That's exactly what we involve the fellows and teacher consultants at my NWP site to do.

Finally, though I argue here and elsewhere for the power and importance of teacher research as an essential element of teacher professionalism, how does this argument stand up for those living in the time of the Common Core and other next-generation standards?

I know that expertise about teaching resides with teachers and therefore must inform policy, and that implementation of all policy depends on teaching and the expertise of teachers. Successful implementation will require constant reflection and continuous professional conversation as we make the path by walking it.

Aside from being necessary to larger policy discussions, teacher research is important because it also counts personally: for us, our students, and our own practice. In so many ways we are prisoners of the traditional; Dan Lortie's (1977) research findings regarding the "apprenticeship of observation" and Zeichner's (Zeichner & Tabachik, 1981) on "the salience of the traditional" show how teachers tend to do what was done to them, and what they most often see being done, even when they know better and know how to do it differently. When under pressure of any kind, any professional, including teachers, may often revert to what is most transparent and commonplace. For teachers, this may be the traditional curriculum-centered practices that Zeichner argues constitute a "salience of the traditional" that is tremendously difficult to overcome, especially when we are overburdened or stressed. And the best and perhaps only way to overcome it is to work with others to reflect on and justify practice, working toward the development of *conscious competence*, of knowing when something works and why it did, and likewise when something doesn't work and why that might be and what we could do about it.

So here is the challenge in a nutshell: What can we do to replace the "yesterday mind" with the "tomorrow mind," particularly when times are tough in our classroom—which is certainly when we need the tomorrow mind the most?

The Personal Importance of Teacher Research

Teacher research has meant many things to me. First, it has meant learning from my students how they need to be taught. Teacher research has helped me to understand my students as readers, writers, learners, and people in ways that were previously unavailable to me. Every time I have looked carefully at an issue, or come to know a student and her work more fully, I have been surprised and challenged in ways that have made me outgrow myself. In essence, what I have learned from teacher research has made me breathe Eleanor Duckworth's question as a mantra: "What if it were otherwise?"

Recently, I undertook a teacher research project with several of my preservice teaching students and inservice teachers around the question of how we might affect student attitudes, risk-taking, and learning through the use of feedback, including "procedural feedback."

Procedural feedback is nonevaluative. It requires learning to look carefully and objectively at student work (which is much harder than it sounds). My NWP site has also found it tremendously useful and even more productive to look at student work with that student, or with colleagues. Exhibit 2.2, located at the end of this commentary, presents our guidelines for looking at student work with others, along with guidelines on providing procedural feedback to students, and getting students to provide procedural feedback to one another, themselves, and authors.

Procedural feedback involves simply describing what the student has done as a reader or writer (or what a professional writer or problem-solver has done), and the meaning and effect these "moves" had for you (e.g., "The way you began your poem by comparing your nervousness to a squirrel in your stomach helped me to visualize a squirrel darting to and fro and helped me to really experience your anxiety"). Procedural feedback is meant to express a growth mindset (Dweck, 2006), a belief that with effort practicing expert strategies, one can and will improve and become more expert. Please see Exhibit 2.3 for tips on formulating and using procedural feedback.

Our teacher research group focused on how the various kinds of feedback, provided at different times and stages in their writing, worked (or not) in ways that affected student attitudes toward writing and the correctness and quality of their writing, and how it informed their reading and their attitudes and achievement as readers. Though we looked across groups of students and looked at student work together, each of us focused on case study students as well. We also researched ourselves, the challenges of providing procedural feedback versus other types, and how giving procedural feedback affected and informed us as teachers.

We found out a lot of things that were very interesting and challenging to us. For example, we found that focusing on errors caused students to take fewer risks and resulted in regression in terms of overall quality in subsequent writing and reading. The more we focused on student strengths and how to build on them ("I wonder how you could continue to extend that metaphor of the squirrel through your poem and what would happen if you did?"), the more risks students took and the more self-efficacy they felt, and the more willingly they communicated what worked, what they were struggling with, and what they were planning to try next. We further found that as teachers we needed to profoundly understand expert reading and writing of particular texts to give helpful procedural feedback, and that descriptions of expert practice, like those provided in this book on the interdependent dimensions of response, helped us to notice and describe what students were doing and could do.

But probably most importantly, we all learned that the ways we give feedback affect student attitudes toward reading and writing, and their continuing impulse to read and write. We also learned that the feedback we give can promote or undermine not only student learning and engagement, but our own. When we gave procedural feedback, we were required to look closely at student work and to describe it precisely. This promoted a growth mindset for us as teachers, and a growth mindset about our students. My individual teacher researchers were all appropriately impressed by how the instructional decisions they make could so powerfully affect the students they teach, and themselves as teachers. The research reinforced to me how powerful the notion of the growth mindset is for teaching and learning, and how helpful procedural feedback can be in promoting not only better teaching but also a growth mindset as a teacher (see Wilhelm & Smith, 2016, for more on procedural feedback).

Teacher research has taken many forms in my classroom: As simple reflection on what has happened and why it happened that way; through peer coaching and thinking partnership, both formal and informal, whether during classroom observations, learning labs, or lesson studies; in school or over a cup of coffee downtown, or by looking at student work together (my new favorite thing to do with other teachers to reflect on student learning as related to our practice). All of this has helped me to see what was happening in my classroom from a new angle and with a fresh perspective. I've come to see 1) teaching students how to inquire into the subject through the use of essential questions (see Wilhelm, 2007), 2) teacher research and reflection, and 3) peer coaching/thinking partnership as parallel processes, and as multiple levels of the same kind of inquiry into how we can best teach so that students best learn.

I've also seen that teacher research provides teachers with the professional expertise and confidence to teach with the creativity and rigor required to meet next-generation standards. Emily Morgan is a Boise

State Writing Project (BSWP) fellow and teacher consultant. She has been a longtime member of our Teacher-Inquiry Community (TIC), presents annually at our conferences and workshops, and provides professional development and thinking partnerships through the BSWP's various inservice programs.

Emily teaches 9th grade English at a junior high school with a growing refugee population, and she has continually changed her unit framing essential questions as a result, moving—as just one example—from "What makes a good relationship?" for a unit including *Romeo and Juliet* to "What makes and breaks relationships in different cultures?" in order to more directly invite her refugee students to participate. She has also continually refined and developed new teaching strategies, most recently working with nonverbal drama strategies.

Emily is continually involved in teacher research with her colleagues in a practical process outlined in Exhibit 2.4 (see the end of this Commentary). When they do teacher research, they start with challenges, nigglings, and wonderings that they frame into questions. Then they justify the payoff for pursuing the question. They consider what they already know (or think they know) and where to look to see what other people have thought and written related to their question. They think about where the data reside (always to some degree with students and in their work) and how to solicit it. They decompose their plan and divide up responsibilities, set up due dates, and the like. When they have collected enough rich data from a few different sources to chew on and analyze, then they come together to do their analysis and synthesis. Ultimately, they consider how to share what they have learned in various ways, both informally and formally. For a description of Emily's latest presentation of teacher research, conducted with thinking partner Niki, see Exhibit 2.1 on p. 70.

Like all good teacher research, Emily's research involves student work and students as data sources, and involves looking at student work as formative assessment *for* learning—so that they are innovating directly for the various students and situations that they face. Emily and her colleagues serve as thinking partners and peer coaches for one another in terms of teaching decisions and learning from student work. And when it comes to the Core, they are now go-to thinking partners across the state of Idaho because not only have they reflectively considered and experimented with how to implement the Core for their diverse students, they have reflected on general principles of engagement and apprenticeship that can help other teachers to do the same.

Exhibit 2.1. Emily and Her Thinking Partner Niki's Most Recent Teacher Research Presentation (April 19, 2016 Night of Inquiry, Boise, Idaho)

Table One: What's Your Story? Seeing Through Another's Perspective

Emily Morgan

> You never really understand a person until you consider things from his point of view . . . Until you climb inside of his skin and walk around in it.
>
> —Harper Lee, *To Kill a Mockingbird*

Since we read Harper Lee's *To Kill a Mockingbird* in 9th grade here in Boise, a few 9th-grade teachers envisioned a real opportunity for our students to understand some different points of view through a collaborative writing lesson. Our teacher research was focused by the question: What will happen when we collaborate across schools and with collaborative tools to respond to each other's stories exploring seeing new perspectives?

Using Google Docs, West Junior High students were paired up with a diversity of Fairmont students, and for several weeks, they got to know each other through a variety of strategies (interviews, character GSAW [character goals and obstacles to meeting them, stakes, actions towards goals, story world/situation]). Students wrote stories and then identified and named each other's story elements and authorial moves. They used this noticing and naming as a springboard to provide procedural feedback to each other. The culminating activity was a poem written from the other student author's perspective. This project was a way for students to deliberately practice collaborating, practice noticing story elements, practice providing procedural feedback, and practice seeing the world through other perspectives. We will share with you the ups and downs of this process, what worked and what we will do to improve the process, as well as student work and what they learned and thought of the project in their own words. *SERVICE FOCUS: Service to self and peers and school community.*

What I've Learned

Just as Emily's teacher research informs her growth as a teacher, my journey as a teacher and teacher educator has been profoundly shaped by lessons I've learned through my research. Perhaps most importantly, teacher research has taught me to enjoy the journey and to get over my desire for perfection. Teaching is continually revealed to me as an intensely human and incredibly complex activity. It is messy and requires risk-taking and mistakes. It requires constant recalibration—not only because there is so much to learn, but also because students change, every student group is different, and our culture and world continually place new demands upon us as we deal with the challenges of habitat loss, food safety, alternative energies, climate change, poverty, refugees, income inequality, a deteriorating infrastructure, and so many other problems, the solutions to which have not even been thought of yet. I've learned that showing students how I roll with the punches, engage in bricolage and problem-solving, and learn from my own mistakes is some of the best teaching that I do.

I've learned that teaching can work even if my lessons don't work exactly as I expect or desire.

I've learned that falling short and even failure are part of the game, and that no learning occurs without slips and trips. If I am not learning and continually improving, I am moving backward. If I am not stepping boldly into tomorrow, then I am slinking back to yesterday.

I've learned that trying something once or twice or even three times is not really trying it. If something is worth doing, it is worth failing at, revising, and improving over time. I've learned that my students learn when I am trying to do new things, and that they don't learn nearly as much when I stick with the status quo.

I've learned that even the best ideas, when they become programmatic, become reified and lose their vitality. Teachers always need to put their own stamp on any prepared materials, by framing and adapting these to meet the needs of their specific students in their unique situation.

This is why any materials, including well-conceived and intelligently designed curricula and programs, and even the best of standards, cannot work without the expert adaptations of a reflective teacher. Teacher expertise is adaptive: it means knowing how to teach in such a way that the expertise and unique individuality of the specific human beings with whom we work can be promoted through inquiry, through safe environments of exploration and expression like workshops, and through pedagogies that foreground how real readers read and use their reading.

Here's a personal anecdote about the importance of our specific and situated local knowledge. I remember taking my eldest daughter, Fiona, to the doctor when she was 5 years old. I was worried because she had been complaining about her ears and sinuses, and she rarely complains. After an examination, the doctor proclaimed that there was nothing wrong and that her complaints were "typical" of kids her age. But I insisted on further tests, and I told the doctor that though she knew medicine, and she knew children in general, she did not know my child the way I knew my child. Upon further testing, it turned out that something was wrong, and that Fiona needed minor surgery almost immediately.

It Takes a Teacher—and a Reflective One at That

This is an object lesson to me about teaching. The authority in the classroom *is and must be the teacher.* I personally don't want to have someone outside my family making familial decisions for me. I won't let an outside expert make decisions about my children that go against my gut feelings, ethical sensibilities, or personal knowledge. Certainly, I am grateful for experts such as our pediatrician and will consult them and consider and usually follow their advice. But I will be the final authority, because I bear the final responsibility. I am the one who must implement the Core. I am the one who must notice and meet my students' needs. I am the only one, because I am the only one who is there. What I do will get done; what I do not do is left undone.

I'm currently teaching 8th and 11th grade English as well as university Pedagogical Methods courses on a Fulbright Fellowship to Europe. One of my Fulbright colleagues in science education, Chris Moore from Coastal Carolina, told me that the central lesson learned by the creators of the Next Generation Science Standards (NGSS) from the Common Core (CCSS) rollout was "not to let any publisher stamp NGSS on materials because the materials are mostly crap, and even if they are not, it's up to the teacher to implement the material in a way that would actually meet the NGSS and support scientific reasoning—no materials can do that—it takes a teacher."

Likewise, as a teacher, I don't want some outside agency or publisher creating my agenda. I am the world's only expert on the possibilities of my particular school and classroom. Therefore, the ultimate professional decision-making power must rest with me. But to wield this decision-making power effectively, I must deeply understand motivation, materials, and methods, and I must know how to apply these in differentiated ways to the multifarious situations and challenges of my own students.

Perhaps this is the most important thing I've learned from being a teacher researcher: that I am and that I must be the decision-making authority in my classroom. No one else is or can be an expert on my students in my school at this point in time. But I've learned that I have to get to know my students, get to know their work (by looking at it carefully with them, and sometimes with other teachers), and reflect and continually build my teacher repertoire to be that decision-making authority.

If I teach in an information-transmission mode, the curriculum is set and no decisions need be made. But if I accept the research and the challenge to teach socioculturally and through inquiry and apprenticeship, then I am surfing continually on the crest of the future's breaking wave, making decision after decision.

I've learned, too, that I need to be part of larger conversations. Kenneth Burke (1957) has a wonderful "parlor metaphor" for reading literature as being part of a larger ongoing conversation—moving in and out of a room to listen, learn, or contribute, moving out and then moving in again. Teacher research has affected me in just this way. I've become part of larger conversations with my students, their parents, my colleagues, and the larger profession. Being part of such a conversation makes everyone richer.

What is true of all learners is true of teachers—we need to take risks, make mistakes, have help, reflect both with others and on our own—and we need to give ourselves the time to do this, and we need to do all of this over time.

Teaching as a Profession

The definition of a "profession" includes the criteria that professionals 1) create and use their own knowledge base, that is, knowledge comes from inside professional practice and is not mandated from the outside, 2) articulate and apply their own standards, 3) set their own agendas and assessments, and 4) gatekeep the profession by mentoring, monitoring, and developing their membership. Historically, these professional prerogatives have been largely denied teachers. But what if we took on the tomorrow mind instead of the yesterday mind? What if unions began to talk less about wages and benefits and more about promoting better learning environments for teachers and for students? What if, as a profession, we questioned the status quo and helped to experiment with how it could be different? What if teacher research were part of our profession's agenda? What if we presented our research regularly at school board meetings, at parent nights, at professional meetings? What if we leveraged current policy like next-generation standards and the Core to show how teaching the core requires profound professional knowledge of learners and learning, and especially profound "pedagogical content knowledge" (Shulman, 1986)—that is, knowing *how* to teach students *how* to do what disciplinary experts do? It takes deep professional understanding to do this kind of work—a person off the street would have no chance of doing it.

Teacher research has fed my belief that teachers must be recognized as competent professionals. I believe that teaching is a profession that matters—perhaps more than any other—and I believe that teachers who engage students in active, authentic activities in a rigorous academic setting are able to reach even the most reluctant student. I believe that the work of Vygotsky and work in the sociocultural tradition show this to be true. I look to Benjamin Bloom's (1976) work on human potential, in which he shows that nearly all learners can learn the next appropriate thing if they are provided with the proper assistance. This matches the growth mindset work of Dweck (2006), who demonstrates that if anyone expends effort on practicing expert strategies in a context of use, they will make progress. It is up to teachers to notice the need, provide the assistance, and create the motivating and meaningful context of use. That is a challenge worthy of a professional. And if we meet it, the research is clear: Our students can and will learn!

Perhaps the most important effect of teacher research is that it makes teachers, as Giroux (1991) proposes, into public intellectuals who assert their place in public conversations about education, whether these conversations are academic, legislative, political, or otherwise. Involving students in the research, as I've been doing more and more (see Wilhelm et al., 2014), makes them public intellectuals as well and inducts them into disciplinary work and democratic living.

Conclusion

I love the play *A Man for All Seasons* by Robert Bolt (1996). In my favorite scene, Sir Thomas More berates Richard Rich for the political intrigues and compromises that led to his becoming the chancellor of Wales.

When Rich asks what he should do, More tells him: "Be a teacher!"

"But who would know?" asks Rich.

"You, yourself, and God," replies More. "Not a bad audience, that!"

But who would know if we all became teacher researchers? Ourselves, our colleagues, our students, their parents, our community, and perhaps even the profession itself. And who would benefit? All of these. Not a bad audience, that.

Exhibit 2.2. Guidelines for Looking at Student Work with Students and/or Colleagues

When looking for evidence of student thinking, meaning production, and growth with students:	When listening to colleagues' (or students') thinking:
• Stay focused on the evidence that is present in the work.	• Listen without judging.
• Look openly and broadly; don't let your expectations cloud your vision.	• Mirror back what you are hearing: "What I hear you saying is . . ." to make sure you are hearing them correctly
• Objectively describe what you see; bracket out judgment and evaluation.	• Tune in to differences in perspective.
• Then use procedural feedback to describe what was done and the resulting meaning and effect for you.	• Use difference and even controversy as an opportunity to explore and understand each other's perspectives. Welcome and explore it instead of shutting it down: "I wonder what would happen if . . ."
• Look for patterns in the evidence that provide clues to how and what the student was doing, thinking, negotiating challenge, etc.	• Focus on understanding where different interpretations come from: "What makes you say so? Help me to understand . . ."
• Use stimulated recall: Have students watch a video of themselves working or doing drama, or look at a piece of student writing or performance like a visual response, and have them describe retrospectively what they were noticing, thinking, feeling, and doing.	• Share your own thinking as clearly as you can, and justify it as well as you can: "I think . . . because of this evidence . . . and this reasoning . . ."
• Ask students directly about why they made certain "moves" in their writing, reading, problem-solving, etc., and what "work" that got done or didn't get done for them. This can be done verbally or in writing.	• Be patient and persistent. Ask: "Tell me more about that . . . Convince me . . . but I need more evidence, and need to hear your reasoning . . ."
	• Ask colleagues directly why they made certain evaluative moves and judgments and what they hope or think could or will happen as a result.

Exhibit 2.2. Guidelines for Looking at Student Work with Students and/or Colleagues (continued)

When reflecting on your own thinking:	When you reflect on the process of looking at student work with student/s or colleague/s, ask:
• Ask yourself, "Why do I see this student work in this way? What does this tell me about my perspectives, biases, what is important to me, my theories?" and "What if I changed my lens, perspective, bias, theory?"	• What did you see in this student's work that was interesting or surprising? Similarities and differences from your thinking partner/s'?
• Look for patterns in your own thinking.	• What did you learn about how this student thinks and learns? This colleague? What about the process helped you see and learn new insights or deepen understanding?
• Ask again and again: What if it were otherwise? What if I thought about this in a new way? What alternatives might there be?	• What did you learn from listening to your student/colleagues that was interesting or surprising? How could you use this to think with in the future?
• Tune in to the questions, the surprises and discomfort, and the emotional charge that the student work and your colleagues' comments might raise for you. What does this reveal about you? About possibilities perhaps suppressed?	• What new perspectives did your student/colleagues provide?
	• How can you make use of your students'/ colleagues' perspectives?
• Compare what you see and what you think about the student work with what you do in the classroom. How are they connected? How could they be more connected? What are the challenges facing students? Facing you in helping them meet the challenges? How can you best meet student needs?	• What big and small questions about teaching and assessment, reading/composing, did looking at the work raise for you?
	• How can you pursue these questions further (teacher research possibilities)?
	• Are there things you would like to try in your classroom as a result of looking at the student's work (action research possibilities)?

Exhibit 2.3. Giving Procedural Feedback

Procedural feedback generally starts with a description of what the writer (or reader/performer/problem-solver) has done, and then the meaning and effect or consequence that follows.

Describe the Accomplishment and Attribute It to Effort and Strategy Use

One could provide feedback to a student argument by saying: **The way you** used the PMI strategy **had the effect** of helping you to compose a claim that was debatable, defensible and significant.

Frames for providing this kind of feedback are things like

- The way you . . . led me to . . . .
- When you . . . it had the effect of . . .
- The move you made to . . . resulted in . . . should lead to . . . exhibited the principle of . . .
- The quote . . . made me think/consider/rethink . . . because

Anything that explores cause and effect in the writing, reading, problem-solving, etc. would constitute nonjudgmental procedural feedback.

For Future Directions: I wonder what would happen if . . . (you made this specific move, or tried this strategy) because . . . (describe the meaning and effect that you think might accrue from this move)

This leaves the authority and decision-making to the author, but is specific in suggesting a *move* or *strategy* that helps you to make a move and provides a justification for it—this requires expert readerly and writerly thinking about a toolbox or repertoire of expert strategies/threshold procedures and asks students to go back to the strategies that they have been taught in the context of this unit and in the past . . . this in turn promotes agentive thinking.

This in turn can be done for authors as readers analyze a text, the ideas it presents, about a topic, and how those are structured and situated for meaning and effect.

For Chapter 1 of *Opening Minds*, I might say: The way Johnston uses excerpts of classroom dialogue between teachers and students (e.g., Pegeen and Michael) and between students (Manny and Sergio) helps me to see how students are taking on agentive identities and how teachers are inviting and reinforcing the formation of such identities, and this in turn makes me rethink how automatically I give praise instead of describing how student growth is due to effort and the use of strategies.

Exhibit 2.4. Getting Started with Teacher Research Planning Worksheet

Team Members:

Research Question:	How does the question relate to your central concerns as a teacher, e.g., inquiry, understanding, reading comprehension, rich classroom discussion, service learning, etc.?
Rationale: Why do you want to know the answer to your question? What's the payoff?	Prior Knowledge: What do you already know (or think you know) regarding your question?
Literature Review: What has been written about your research question? How can you find the "conversation" that you are entering?	What do you want to find out that you do not yet know? How are you going to add to the conversation, and uptake or contend with current turns in the conversation?

Exhibit 2.4. Getting Started with Teacher Research Planning Worksheet *(continued)*

What information or evidence would help you answer your question?	Sources: Where could you best get this information or evidence? Where does the data reside? With students? With particular students? In their work?
Team Plan: Who will do what when?	Methods: How can you elicit the data from the data sources?

3

✿

The Dimensions of the
Reader's Response

As I tried to find windows to my students' reading activity, I asked them to try and make visible what they were doing, thinking, and feeling as they read and responded to their reading. This was a project that I pursued with all of my students throughout the school year, but most intensively with Ron, Cora, and Joanne, as well as with my other six case study students.

CLASSROOM RESEARCH METHODS

I developed three criteria for any classroom research method I used with my students:

1. that it offered a window into my students' reading processes.
2. that it fit naturally into the life and flow of the classroom, being accepted by students as something interesting and even fun to pursue.
3. that it was pedagogically useful, providing students and myself as the teacher with empowering ways of seeing, knowing, studying, and sharing ourselves as readers and learners.

These criteria inevitably led to undertaking research collaboratively with students, to sharing findings with them and with other teachers, and to asking them to share with each other. I continually asked students to display and perform what they were coming to know, and to talk about what and how they were learning. To these ends, I used the following methods.

Teacher Journal

The bedrock of my teacher research was my teaching journal. I have kept a journal and notes about my teaching experiences for the past 13 years. I record observations about particular students, assess what seemed to work or not work for the kids, tell stories, posit theories, make plans, and revise lessons that I hope will be more successful in the future. During the year described here, I recorded as many observations and conversations as I could regarding the nine students I chose as case study students. I was sometimes able to write in my journal during classes, but I usually did so during lunch, after school, or during my free period.

Literary Letters

On an average of two times a week, students exchanged literary letters (Atwell, 1987) about their reading, both with me and with other students. All letters and responses to them were kept in the students' journals. The letters concerned what students read in class and the reading they pursued on their own. I sometimes asked students to write about not only what they read, but about how they were reading—anything they noticed about what they saw, felt, did, and thought as they were reading.

Think-Aloud Protocols

Throughout the year I made use of four types of protocols: a free-response protocol, a cued-response protocol, a two-column written protocol, and eventually, as we began to study the use of art as a response to our reading, what we called a visual protocol. I modeled my use and analysis of protocols on the work of Flower and Hayes with written composition (1981) and after Newell (1984, 1990), who adapted protocols for use with both writing and reading.

Free-Response Protocols

Several years ago, I began making use of "free-response protocols." I would ask students to read something—sometimes a story I had chosen especially for them because I thought it would be challenging or offer them rich response possibilities. As they read, I would ask them to simply stop and talk into a tape recorder whenever they noticed something about how they were reading. I modeled a couple of protocol responses for the class, and began making use of them during workshop conferences.

Cued-Response Protocols

The going with free-response protocols was tough. Some students provided very rich protocol information, but most students revealed very little. Since I wanted to get a sense of how each student was reading, I began to make use of "cued protocols." I would provide students with a text and insert a caret wherever I wanted them to stop and talk into the tape recorder about what was going on with them at that point in their reading. If students were reading from a book of their choice, I asked them to stop and respond at the middle and end of pages. This technique worked much better.

One of the best things about the protocols is that "they have focused the attention of the class on *how* we read, and made this the very subject matter of what we do together" (November 1991).

Two-Column Written Protocols

Despite the success of protocols in yielding rich data and supporting student thinking about "their thinking and their reading," I was somewhat nonplussed about the amount of time it took to record protocols with each student, and then transcribe and analyze just segments of them. As a teacher, I was just too busy and tired to spend that kind of time translating data into usable forms. So I began using two strategies: asking students to tape protocols at home and transcribe segments on their own, and asking them to complete two-column written protocols. In this technique I would provide a story on one half of a sheet, leaving the other half clear for their comments, which provided a kind of gloss of their activity as they read the corresponding passages. Later, we simply recorded observations in our journals as we read.

This procedure meant that every student could complete a protocol during a single class period, and it saved me a tremendous amount of time, as the data were immediately available to me. The protocols were in a form that could easily be shared by the students with reading partners or friends. This they pursued with gusto, comparing responses to particular passages and beginning to evaluate and borrow particular strategies for making meaning. This was and continues to be tremendously exciting for everybody.

Visual Protocols

During the visualization study explored in Chapter Five, Tommy and Walter suggested that instead of writing down what they were seeing and thinking at a particular point in a story, they draw pictures of what they envisioned as they read. This was an option I made available but did not require of all students, and most used some form of artistic response on all of the protocols that followed. (On one protocol, 72 of 121 students drew pictures, without or with only a few words. With so many students indicating a preference for visual note-making, perhaps we could encourage and build on this more often in our classrooms.) Some students used a combination of writing and drawing, drawing themselves or characters with thought bubbles, or using pictures with captions. Some framed off a picture of themselves as readers engaged in their reading activity inside a larger picture depicting the world of the story; others included themselves as readers in a picture of the story world. Some just drew what they were seeing at that point in the story.

Symbolic Story Representation

In Patricia Enciso's research (1990), which catalyzed my thinking about reading and response, she developed and made use of a technique she calls the "Symbolic Representation Interview," which I adapted and made use of in my own classroom and called the "Symbolic Story Representation" (hereafter referred to as SRI so it will not be confused with the SSR of sustained silent reading). In this technique, students create cutouts or find objects to dramatize what they have read and how they have read it.

During or after their reading, the students, using an adaptation of the SRI, created cutouts symbolizing characters, character qualities, groups, or forces from the book; objects, scenes, or settings of importance; motifs, themes, or ideas that played a role in the story; and a cutout symbolizing oneself as a reader. Some readers chose to create cutouts of the author, or special props and backgrounds for particular scenes they wished to talk about, but this was something they did on their own initiative.

The cutouts could be of any shape or design the student wished. Some students used little squares, associating the size or color with the characters in question. Most students made highly stylized cutouts, sometimes realistic—being a face or including the special features and dress of a particular character; sometimes highly abstract—consisting of an object associated with the character, or symbolizing a quality of the character.

When the cutouts were complete, the reader met with the teacher, reading partner, or classroom reading club. The reader then identified the cutouts he had made, and explained why this character, quality, force, or idea was important, and how the cutout worked to suggest or symbolize that particular referent. Next, students would use the cutouts to both dramatize the story events for their audience and recount their readerly experience of these events—or in the case of a short story, to recount their experience of the story from beginning to end. I encouraged students to interview each other throughout the presentations about the nature of the cutouts, the story, and how the story was read and presented by the reader. Throughout the year the students developed and encouraged each other to meet high critical standards for the creation and presentation of an SRI.

Some readers began to use pictures from magazines as cutouts, while others began to use actual objects instead of cutouts: dice for the idea of risk-taking, a tortilla for the quality of egotism or being "all wrapped up in yourself," playing cards for the characters of a king and queen.

The reader moved the cutouts around to dramatize the story and to show the changing relationships of various characters or forces, and used the reader cutout to show where he was in relation to story events, explaining how and from what perspective he was experiencing the story.

I began by videotaping individual students using the SRI. The data were so rich and the students were so enthusiastic about the procedure that I was astounded. "I sort of knew I was doing this stuff [when I read], but this helps me bring it out, now—it's like WOW! I like totally know that this is *how* I read," one student told me excitedly.

Just as with the protocols, I brainstormed for a way to include all students on a more regular basis in the use of the SRI procedure. On four different occasions during the year, I asked all students to prepare their cutouts as homework and choose a scene or story to talk about. The next day, as part of a workshop, students would share their SRI response in triads, then discuss their various responses and reading strategies.

On the first occasion, students dramatized one of several assigned short stories for each other and were asked to make use of a reader cutout to demonstrate some of their moves as readers. Thereafter the SRIs were used with readings students chose on their own. On the second occasion, students were asked to layer in cutouts that demonstrated the importance of setting or scene to their understanding of the story. On the third occasion, students included cutouts of recurring motifs or ideas of importance to the story, including a central focus or main idea cutout that was brought into play whenever this particular thematic statement was reinforced by events in the story. In the final required SRI, students were asked to include a cutout symbolizing their idea of the story's author, and to use that cutout whenever they thought of the author during their reading and SRI performance.

Some students did not make use of these cutouts of more sophisticated story elements, but I used the SRI to make them aware of these elements and to encourage and guide their eventual attempts to use them. (For more extensive discussions of how to use symbolic story representations with students, descriptions and exhibits of student work, and findings about how SRI works for students, please see Wilhelm, 1996.)

The use of SRI as a classroom activity was incredibly beneficial to the students who were trying to become aware of their own reading strategies and to share these strategies with others. Though I had noticed this phenomenon before with the literary letters and protocols, it now became even more pronounced: Students were sharing moves and strategies, trying out the moves described by others, and supporting each other in the use of such moves. It was mind-boggling.

> In addition to accessing just huge mother lodes of data about how kids read and think about reading, something amazing has happened that I never planned or predicted: the kids are teaching each other how to read in ever more sophisticated, imaginative and creative ways! I've got a classroom of readers teaching each other all these new and powerful ways to see, to read, and, to be! (February 1993)

SRI is appealing because it captures and encourages the creative and dramatic elements of reading. It also allows students a way to objectify the very hidden processes of reading and get them out where they can talk about them, and try to understand and improve them. For classmates and for the teacher-researcher it provides a magical window into the inner world of the reader. This, in fact, is what I noted in my journal:

> Using the SRI makes the magic of reading so obvious! This is something that nearly all traditional classroom activities regarding reading seem to completely obscure and kill off! But not this! The kids are having an absolute blast with it, and learning from it. They are making the magic of reading visible and creating more magic by sharing it! (March 1993)

In another entry I write about my excitement regarding the sharing:

> I have never really structured my classroom for this sort of sharing. Students are seeing how differently they read and understand the same words, scenes, or stories. When there are differences in "readings" or

interpretation, we are asking each other "What about you, what about who you are or your background or experience is making that difference? What is it that is informing your reading?" The students, I truly believe, are seeing their lives and the lives of others as resources for learning—learning about the world, and about themselves. There is a sort of metacognitive self-awareness happening here that I've never seen before. Their reading is being used as an exploration and extrapolation of selves and their possibilities . . . as individuals and as members of a group. It's unbelievable to think that it was a book or me as the teacher that used to be the sole resources for learning. How incredibly limiting it must have been! If I could only go back and teach all those years again! (March 1993)

In addition to the data collection methods described here, I also continually conversed with students, interviewed them informally, and conferenced with them about the portfolios they put together throughout the year to document their reading activity and improvement.

THE DIMENSIONS

Through the process of analyzing the variety of information I collected about student reading, I came to think about 10 different dimensions of response that my students seemed to use as they created, experienced, and responded to literary worlds. As I worked with them, it became clear that these 10 dimensions fell into three different categories of response, which I labeled evocative, connective, and reflective.

Evocative Dimensions

1. *Entering the Story World.* On this dimension students prepared to read and started thinking about what the reading would be like. They activated prior knowledge that would help them read.
2. *Showing Interest in the Story.* Students comprehended the literal meaning of the plot and became interested in it as they read. They made predictions and formed expectations about story action.
3. *Relating to Characters.* Readers created characters and took up relationships with them. The reader often became a presence in the story and made judgments about characters.
4. *Seeing the Story World.* The readers noticed clues for creating mental images and envisioned characters, settings, and situations.

Connective Dimensions

5. *Elaborating on the Story World.* The readers built up clues from throughout the story to create meaning. The readers played detective, fleshed out clues, and filled in story gaps, often creating meaning that went well beyond that suggested by the text.
6. *Connecting Literature to Life.* The readers made explicit connections between personal experiences and character experiences, often looking for ideas that could inform how they could solve problems or think about situations in their own life.

Reflective Dimensions

7. *Considering Significance.* Students asked how the text worked to create meaning and considered the significance of various events and behavior and how this contributed to the meaning of a story.
8. *Recognizing Literary Conventions.* The readers noticed that the author made particular kinds of conventional moves that they had to respond to, and they used previous experiences with conventions from their reading, viewing, or conversing to figure out how to do so.
9. *Recognizing Reading as a Transaction.* The readers recognized an author and the choices of the author in telling the story. The author might be embraced or rejected as a person to converse and agree with. The reader recognized that they create meaning with the author and her text.
10. *Evaluating an Author, and the Self as Reader.* The readers considered the author's agenda, and their own. They thought about the author's effectiveness as a writer. They considered their own reading processes and how these related to their personal identity.

As I coded data and thought about the dimensions, I was helped very much in my thinking by Judith Langer's (1989, 1990) work on the various stances students take on in regard to created "envisionments" as they read, and especially by Jack Thomson's (1987) work on what he identified as six stages in a developmental model of response. Though I came to differ from Thomson's views in many ways, particularly with his developmental view of response, I did borrow some of his categories and I feel very indebted to his work.

I describe the 10 dimensions as a way of organizing the data, and because I believe the description of various dimensions to be pedagogically useful. I do not think that I have exhaustively described all that adolescent readers do, nor that this is the only way of organizing the information my readers provided. The data, as organized, do point out very specifically that there are many types of responses that we typically neglect when we plan classroom activities, ask questions, and discuss readings. The dimensions show that there are important readerly activities that we ignore and perhaps devalue in the typical classroom, and why responding in various media and forms is important to the development of response and literary understanding.

In the pages that follow I provide detailed examples of the kind of moves my case study readers made on each dimension. This is because if we ask what engaged readers do—and if we ask, as I do here, how less engaged readers can be helped to develop the same repertoire of reading strategies—then a detailed picture is necessary, and none is currently available. A summary of what the readers did within each dimension, as well as questions and activities that can be used to encourage and develop response on that dimension, are included in Appendix A at the back of this volume. I borrowed many of the questions listed in Appendix A from Aidan Chambers's "Tell Me . . ." framework (1985), and from Wolfgang Iser (1978), and came up with many others with the help of my students.

The response information from my readers suggests how engaged readers employ very different ways of reading in different situations. Often they have indicated that they are reading a particular text solely to be "entertained" or "enjoy" themselves. In these cases, the readers have reported making many moves to evoke and move around in story worlds, but few moves of a reflective nature. If readers indicated wishing to learn something about their "own life" or about "what to do" in parallel situations, then their readings concentrated on connections that can be made from literature to life, and from life to literature.

In this way, the dimensions point out that there are various purposes and ways of reading. When reading in different ways, readers operate on different dimensions—privileging the ones useful to them and responding less, if at all, on other dimensions. One particular way of reading may offer less rich response than another way and still fulfill the reader's purpose.

Also, some ways of reading can be seen as a way to richer and more complete readings. For example, relational readings—which Michael Smith (1992) calls "association-driven readings"—those in which the reading seems only to stimulate related memories and life details of the reader, can be seen as a necessary step in the direction of evoking complete story worlds in the reader's mind. Instead of discounting these sorts of moves on the part of less engaged readers as irrelevant or tangential, they can be seen as a starting point. Reading in richer ways, ways that involve other moves, satisfactions, possibilities, and considerations, depends upon first having built a story world that depends in large part on associating real-life experiences with textual cues. This indicates that what a teacher might at first regard as an impoverished reading is in fact a necessary building block to richer readings that may be achieved later.

All of these points are important considerations for a teacher who is encouraging, responding to, and evaluating student response, and planning what to do next with individuals and groups of students in the language arts classes.

SURPRISES

As I asked all of my students to describe their reading through interviews, literary letters, and the protocols, I was continually surprised.

Though many students, as I expected, offered very little as they described how they read, I was surprised by almost 40 of the students. They represented nearly a third of those I taught. There was a veritable explosion of articulate and often lengthy descriptions of the various moves these students made. The number of dimensions they responded upon and their response moves on these various dimensions were more sophisticated, deeper, and much more varied than I had ever expected. I was also immediately struck by how often and how far they went beyond what was explicitly suggested by the text. I was surprised by this important role of elaboration in their reading, and the data eventually led me to consider it as a separate dimension of response. I was surprised by how many readers considered the author's use of particular choices—and again decided to treat this sort of response as a separate dimension (elaboration). I was also surprised that several of my seventh-grade readers would sometimes take up active relationships with an author, and reflected on the politics of a text and their own role as a reader in shaping what they had experienced.

Perhaps most surprising was how naturally many of the students described and discussed their reading experiences. I had expected data to be sparse, like collecting flora in the desert—but they were as abundant as if I were struggling through a rain forest, having to choose what to collect and make note of. Most students knew exactly what I was talking about when I asked them about their "experience" in the "world" of the book, and were adept at considering and then describing what they were "doing" as they read. Quite a few students were initially reticent, only to become positively loquacious when they became convinced of my interest. It was almost as if they were getting to share and celebrate all of what reading really was for them for the first time, and they could not believe their good luck.

Also surprising were nearly 20 students who could offer absolutely nothing about how they read or what they lived through as they did so. The students were surprised, too. After Ron shared an SRI with his reading partner, Jon, Jon said, "I can't believe you do all that stuff when you read! Holy crap, I'm not doing . . . like nothing . . . compared to you!"

Ron responded that "I can't believe you don't do something. If you don't, you're not reading, man. . . . It's gotta be like wrestling, or watching a movie or playing a video game. . . . You've got to . . . like . . . *be* there."

Pairing students as they read and shared their readings and then asking them to share with other pairs turned out to be a powerful teaching move. Students learned from each other about ways of reading. I was also impressed by the type of student dialogue I witnessed. After videotaping groups of three sharing their symbolic story representations (SRIs), I wrote:

> I expected the students to describe the basic plot and situation of the scene they had chosen and then to describe in some way how they read it. I couldn't believe how elaborate many of the cutouts were, how many forces or ideas students included as playing a part in their reading—like Katie's bubbles for character thoughts, or Greg's cutouts of forces and feelings that they considered as they read. The descriptions of how they read were incredibly involved. Greg was a "mist who can float inside of people"; Megan was a "giant eye, like the sun, that's up in the sky and can see everything and even come down and focus in like a microscope on stuff"; Tommy was "a mouse. I can hide and like be a Peeper Tom."
>
> And best of all, students were interrupting each other to ask questions like "Where are you now?" "Are you still identifying with her? Why not with him? Because I'm identifying with him now because he's the one who's hurt." And so on. The students were having extended discussions in small groups like nothing I have ever seen before—and the discussions were about readers and the experience of reading—as well as the meaning of the reading. The SRI seems to make ways of reading into objects that can be seen and talked about, and to therefore scaffold presentation and discussion of the reading. (January 1993)

The final and most pleasant surprise was how well I was coming to know my students as individual people and readers through the project. After interviewing Theresa about her reading, I wrote:

> I felt like there was this very human bond between us. Sharing as people, and as readers. Theresa is the sort of girl I couldn't even describe physically to you in years past. Now I've looked in her face and really seen her, how her eyes express her feelings as she reads. I know how she uses her own house and friends and experiences to create worlds as she reads. As a result, I know her house, her friends, her life . . . I know her! That means that the other students know her, too. And I think she feels better about herself, the class, and her reading than she would have if she had been my student in a previous year. . . . This is the best thing about what I am doing this year, that I feel I know the students and that they are getting to know each other and that everybody is involved . . . that I can teach them better because of it, and that they know me, not just as a teacher, but as another reader. The subject of the class has become not only our reading—but who we are as people—it's about us! (October 1992)

EVOCATIVE DIMENSIONS

Readers operating on these dimensions indicated a willingness to read, even an excitement or interest in reading, and began to "think about" what the reading would be like by recalling appropriate experiences from real life and previous reading.

As they started to read, students would "enter" or "get into" the story world by comprehending literal meanings, taking an interest in the story action, and deciding to continue with the reading. They would begin to make predictions and form expectations as they recognized "the rules" and "the game" set up by the text. The reader entering the story world also began to create rudimentary mental images, often stereotypes from television or films. Some readers, at this point, could be confused or tentative. They might give up their willingness to read and their interest in the story action.

Entering the Story World

Cora, Joanne, and Ron all anticipated pleasure before they began reading. They often chose a book for themselves based on recommendations of friends, or in Ron's case on the recommendation of his father. All three also searched randomly through the library, "foraging," as Cora put it, for "tasty"-looking books. The two girls in particular often went to the library without a specific idea of the book they would check out.

Library books were chosen on the basis of topics that were interesting as indicated by the cover and book jacket. Cora indicated that "it's the title that jumps out at me. An author who has an interesting title can probably write an interesting book." These readers all indicated that they were willing to read, and that they expected to help create an aesthetic experience in concert with the text. They also considered their previous experience with similar genres and topics in order to begin creating meanings.

During an SRI, Cora said, "The author writes about something meaningful to understand it himself. Then he shares it and it's up to you to make something meaningful of it for you, to understand it in your own way, make it beautiful or whatever it's going to be."

Ron revealed that:

> When I get ready to read I always think about what kind of story it is, you know, and what I'll have to do to get into it. I kind of imagine myself in the story, even before I start reading, and what it's going to be like in there and I might kind of review stuff from other stories or from my life that I might need to know as I read. . . . If it turns out to be a different sort of story I might not want to do the things that need done, or I might not want to feel the way it makes me feel, so I'll quit. . . . I hate it when the cover or the beginning of a book sort of fakes you out and you get confused about what you should be doing. . . . You know because you're excited and ready to do some certain things and then you find out you have to do something else. Bummer!

Ron specifically points out something that was also true for the two girls: the created story world of the reader was always made up of both intratextual and extratextual references. In other words, the words of the text were used in such a way that the reader's knowledge and experience of the world was brought to bear in the creation of a "secondary world."

Ron was the sort of reader that Nell (1990) calls a "ludic reader": He entered a trancelike state as he experienced what was, for him, the intense reality of the story world. He indicated that once he entered a story world he was never able to stop. He reported reading deep into the night, through weekends, and in every spare moment once he had entered a story world. He recited to me a litany of tricks used to keep reading: flashlight in his bedroom, fake book covers, book inside a math book (though this was getting hard for him as he was reading very thick books), and even faking illness—in extreme cases—because "it was like I couldn't go on living until I had got through the story." When he was forced to stop reading, he continued to live in it. I witnessed this myself during our class reading of *The Incredible Journey*. Ron finished the book on his own, but continued to read with the class for about two weeks. Before class and in the hallway I would observe him playing the part of characters in the book or elaborating on the plot. Here is an entry from my journal:

> When Ron comes into reading class, it's like he's entering a strange admixture of the class itself and the world of the story . . . he is reading. When we were reading "The Horse Hunters" he comes in, and addresses me as Dodge and says, "We gonna rustle up some horses this class period, pardner?" While reading *The Incredible Journey*, he told me, "On my way to class I looked out the window and saw two dogs and a cat heading into the forest" [there is no forest in sight of the school]. "I told my boss but he laughed at me [and] asked if I'd seen any elves." (October 1992)

Joanne and Cora, on the other hand, were able and often chose to read several different books, and various kinds of books, at the same time. They indicated the ability to leave and re-enter stories at any time, almost immediately reorienting themselves to the story at hand. Joanne reported that:

> I might have to do something [to re-enter a story] but I can't tell you what it is. The story stays inside me and it's like as soon as I start reading again I'm right back where I was. The story stays fresh in my memory, sometimes for a long time. I just pick up where I left off. It's easy.

Cora indicated that she liked different books for different moods and needs.

> If I'm mad I sort of like to read a mystery, or something like The Secret Garden or Anne of Green Gables, stories that soothe me. Anne is always, well . . . in control of her life and makes things work out and that helps me. On the other hand if I have energy and I'm interested in something I'll read nonfiction. So I'll just pick up one of the books I've been reading that seems to fit. . . . I never really have trouble deciding which one. It seems pretty obvious.

In light of this information, it is interesting to consider that Cora and Joanne were both excellent students, earning straight A's in all subjects. Their teachers reported that they were both very conscientious, turning all work in. In contrast, Ron's grades were mediocre, and his teachers reported concerns with work habits, missing homework, and a "dreamy" or "inattentive" attitude. Cora told me that she would hate to leave off reading a book if she had homework, but she knew that she "had to, and that I could get right back to the book when I had time." Ron, on the other hand, told me that "I just can't shake a book when it's got a hold of me. It's hard to think of anything else." Ron admitted to me that his reading habits interfered with his school performance, but that he didn't "know what to do about it. . . . I don't really want to do anything about it—I mean the stuff you do in school is sort of a waste compared to a great book."

Ron and Joanne reported that they expected to be engaged in a book by the first few paragraphs. Ron said, "Maybe the first line, if it's good." Despite these expectations to be immediately engaged, they both gave a book two or three pages to engage them if necessary. Cora would give a book much longer. "I'll probably read 20 pages or more if I can't really lose myself. Maybe longer if I have reason to think it might get good . . . like a high recommendation from someone I respect."

Ron entered the story primarily through what Bruner (1986) calls the "landscape of action" and through visualization of the setting that goes along with it. "I want to know where we are and what we're doing there, then I can see the place and I know what's going on and then I'm off to the races." During an SRI, when he was retracing for me how and at what point he was fully immersed in the story, he made this comment:

> When an author explains scenes it makes it easy to see. That's what helped me get into the book. I have to see the scene—like here it's the totally cold and completely snow-covered city totally frozen and quiet and windy—I have to see it to get into the place or I can't get to know the characters. . . . I can't see the characters until I see where they are. . . . It's like walking up to a house, checking it out, figuring out what sort of people would live like this before you ring the doorbell.

Ron indicated that details about plot and the place helped him to enter the story. Though he felt that he was with other characters, "I'm really tuning in to . . . you know, to my idea of what's happening."

The two girls, on the other hand, tended to enter and participate in the story primarily through what Bruner (1986) calls the "landscape of consciousness." Cora reported that:

> I want to get to know people . . . characters, or even the author. It's like I'm not really into the story until I recognize and get inside another person. . . . I want some details of the place, but especially about the people. Just a couple of details and I feel like I know them and the whole scene just unfolds in front of my eyes and I feel like I've known them forever and what they're feeling and want and everything.

On a separate occasion, during an SRI, Cora gave this running commentary:

> I pick up this book and I want it to be very detailed at the beginning. I want to learn about the characters and where they are right away. . . . I want to learn from myself, by [comparing] my personal life to the story; I want to learn from the characters and from the author. . . . I can't learn unless the author lets me in on how he sees the world and what it looks like to him and to his characters. Otherwise you can't know them or relate to them.

Cora was adamant that getting to know other consciousnesses was the seminal part of reading.

> I can make plots up on my own. Reading is relating my life to other people and to do that you have to really know them, not just see what they did. . . . I can observe people doing things on my own and guess what it does to them. A book is to get inside people and events. That's what a good author helps you do . . . to get inside characters and inside him, the author, I mean, revealing his innermost feelings and visions and things. You have to read to understand. You can't tell someone about what you learn about people from a book and expect them to understand. They have to read and go through it themselves.

Joanne concurred. "A great book is a book with characters you really feel you know and who you have very strong feelings about."

Flynn (1987) and Bleich (1987) found that males tend to take a more detached, action-oriented stance toward stories, and that females tend to have a more intense sense of participation in the inner lives of characters, finding themselves, as Bleich says, "in the teller and the tale." This was certainly the case with these case study students.

Joanne said that she would give up reading a book that "lacked details" or that was about

> a topic I don't know much about and don't enjoy . . . like hunting. . . .
> A story about a hunting trip couldn't enthuse me. . . . I'm a vegetarian
> and I don't like meat and killing animals. I like woods and animals and
> would read a story in the wilderness, but killing for fun? I don't want to
> get involved in that. If I find out I don't want to know about a topic, I'll
> quit.

And reminiscent of Stephen King's distinction between "Gotta Read" books and "Wanna Read" books, Joanne said:

> If you have to read something for school you try to make it fun and
> interesting. But if it's a book you're reading for yourself and it's about
> something that doesn't interest you, why waste your time? There are so
> many good books. . . .

In these cases, Joanne did not wish to activate the necessary schema for understanding, nor did she have the desire to develop them. She would move on to something more naturally interesting.

Once a story had been entered, and these three readers all expressed that it was such an intense involvement that there was no mistaking their utter engagement, the readers began to engage in other dimensions of response in order to fully evoke the world of the story. Ron described the experience poetically.

> When you're not into a book yet, it's really obvious [laughs]. It's like
> you're standing in line for the diving board on a windy day and you're
> freezing your nuts off. If you'll excuse the expression [laughs]. Where was
> I? Oh yeah. It's like you're in pain and you have your arms wrapped
> around you and the concrete is scratching your feet. The first part of the
> story is the line and the ladder and the board. When everything comes
> together and you jump it's like you're in this underwater world like
> INSTANTLY and then you just stay down there and never come up until
> someone makes you.

The initial contact with a story depended upon these readers comprehending literal meaning and getting themselves into the story's sense of play and action. Expectations were formed and predictions made. Some rudimentary images were created, and the readers began to acquaint themselves in at least superficial ways with the introduced characters. These readers recognized what Rabinowitz (1987) calls "rules of notice" to get a sense of story and their roles in creating it. These readers then accepted the game devised by the author, and attempted to understand the basic conventions of it. By this point, the reader decided, if engaged, to continue with the reading—or, if the book did not meet current needs, to give it up.

Showing Interest in the Story Action

Having entered the story and been engaged by it, these readers immediately began to anticipate action and make predictions.

During a protocol analysis of a first-time reading of O'Flaherty's "The Sniper," Joanne's comments existed almost entirely of predictions based on noticed details.

"The Sniper" is a story set during the Irish Civil War. Two snipers, after discovering each other on opposite rooftops, play a cat-and-mouse game. The first sniper is wounded, but then he fools and shoots the other sniper. He then goes into the street, turns over the body, and sees that he has shot his brother.

When the sniper takes out a cigarette, Joanne said, "He'll get shot. I wouldn't take my life in my hands for a cigarette." When an old lady crosses the road to talk to the driver of an armored car, she commented, "If she reports him . . . now he'll have to kill both of them. He'll have to."

Ron indicated that when he had entered a book:

I'll have this constant urge to find out more. I totally feel the excitement and live the action. I want to see what's going on and know why they are doing it. That's the feeling I love when I get into a book. It's like your brain is a Pac-Man totally hungry with curiosity.

Once such initial contact and subsequent immersion was made, these readers made particular moves to flesh out the story world. Though the girls showed a propensity for perspective-taking, and boys, such as Ron, for visualizing, all the readers I studied engaged with both dimensions of response.

Readers who successfully entered a story world began to make new moves to relate to characters and to see the story world. They noticed cues for creating and sustaining a "secondary world" in their minds as they read. They created characters and felt emotions in relation to character activities and problems. Quite often, the readers would become a presence in the story world, and begin to move around in that world or manipulate it in some way. In this way they would project themselves and their real-world knowledge into the story world. They would also mentally create visual pictures of settings, situations, characters, and their physical features and gestures. The readers on these dimensions evoked a complete story world, and at this point the virtual world of the story had intense and comprehensive reality for them.

Relating to Characters

Having entered and become interested in the story, one of the two types of moves these readers made to fully evoke the story world was to establish contact with characters. The case study readers typically took on a variety of perspectives, often switching during the course of a single story. Nonetheless, they tended to have a favored perspective in any particular story. As reported by Enciso (1990), these readers often took on the perspective of a main character, sometimes becoming the character, merging with him or her for short or extended periods, or becoming a friend. Sometimes the readers established a more distanced relationship, observing characters from outside, either from close in or afar, sometimes part of the story, sometimes "above" or "outside" it, as a "spy" hiding somewhere using cameras or "see-through" devices (Ron), or as an object such as a wall, a piece of furniture, a ship (Cora), or, in one case, a "fish." When outside the story, sometimes these readers still felt that they had a friendly relationship with a character, despite their inability to communicate. Joanne was a reader who often expressed what Enciso (1990) calls a "parallel focus," referring to characters as friends, and to her friends as characters in a story! As such, she imagined scenarios that seemed parallel to story events. Joanne also often took on the role of "agent" (Enciso, 1990), expressing the desire to act on behalf of the character, or feeling that she was actually doing so.

Joanne tended, at some point, to "become" the main character in whatever book she was reading. She professed that she liked to read about "girls, about my age . . . it helps me to become them and understand them . . . though I can become characters really different from me—even a boy or an older woman—if I know where I am in the story and have some similarity with them." She indicated that though at times she "really was the character—it's like Joanne herself is totally lost," at other times she "merged" (Enciso, 1990) with a character: "It's like we're Siamese twins in one body, both Joanne and whoever the character is all at the same time." At other times, characters were just too different from her and she became their friend; or the protagonist was too unsavory, and she became a minor character, or made herself, as Joanne, a presence in the book, sometimes resisting the main character and his agenda.

When Cora completed a protocol during a reading of a poem called "The Wreck of the Hesperus" (Longfellow, 1952), she said:

> I took the place of the ship. I could mostly hear the waves and the wind and the captain and his daughter talking through it. . . . I really felt like I was there. I didn't relate to characters as much as I usually do, but I mostly watched and judged them.

Later in her reading she revealed, "Now I'm sitting in a chair down [on] the deck, but I still sort of feel like I'm the ship. Every now and then I've felt like I was the daughter and felt really afraid. As the ship I'm like an unfeeling observer." During a separate interview she said, "I'd rather follow characters around and watch them than become them, but sometimes I become them anyway, for a short time like a scene or situation, or a longer time and it happens almost automatically."

In her first self-evaluation, she wrote:

> I learn about the way others live[d] by putting myself into their lives, by watching them or putting myself into their characters. When I read I put myself in that person's position and sometimes really become them and that's really what I do best when reading. I don't want to sound snooty but if you can't read in a way to be a character then I don't see that you're reading. A lot of people don't realize that about reading and it's really too bad.

However, when reading *A Gathering of Days*, Cora revealed that "I'm more of an observer in this book. I feel what she feels, and it feels to me like the story is taking place now, even though it took place a long time ago." When pressed about why she was an observer in this book, Cora explained that:

because it's told like a diary, it's like I'm always looking in, like over someone's shoulder. There's something about the way it's written that is always reminding me that I'm a reader. . . . I mean, I liked the book a lot and was really involved in it, and sometimes, for a situation or a scene, I sort of became the character, but only for a while and then I was just watching again.

Ron usually found himself in the thick of a story, as an unmentioned confidante or sidekick. When reading through a sequence of Tom Clancy novels, he began by being a CIA colleague of Jack Ryan, but quickly took on the persona of Jack himself for the duration of the books. When reading De Marino's *The Odyssey Project* (1989), he became a friend of the main character, Ted Amundsen, "shadowing him around, looking around him or through him." This was one of Ron's typical positions, "almost like a bodyguard," but he occasionally found himself "above the story, like high in the sky looking down on it."

Joanne described her relationship with the character of Nancy Drew as

understanding her completely, and following her every move, and it was like I was living [right next] to her, but we were separated by this wall of glass and I could see and hear everything from her world but she couldn't see or hear anything of mine. And sometimes she would be in danger or ready to make a stupid decision and I was just screaming at her—in my mind I mean—but she couldn't hear me and I was so upset. It was like I really wanted to contact her and save her and it was terrible that I couldn't. In my mind I would write letters of advice to her and send them off. . . .

Perspective-taking, as pointed out by Enciso (1990), is a highly complex social-cognitive process that entails considering what someone else might be seeing, thinking, or feeling. It requires, in conjunction with this, the recalling of the reader's own experiences and the relating of these to another person, and considering the most likely experiences and interpretations the other might have in a situation.

In nearly everything that they read, these case study readers indicated, they had a preferred perspective, but they also took on multiple perspectives, continually shifting, if only briefly, throughout a reading. Benton and Fox (1985) argue that this experience of taking multiple perspectives and of shifting viewpoints is critical to the development of more sensitive and powerful readings that lead to greater understanding of self and other.

All three readers also indicated at times the use of "mutual perspective taking" (Selman & Byrne, 1974), in which they eschewed the switching of perspectives, adopting instead a third-party view as an attempt to reconcile two other perspectives. As Joanne reported about her reading of *Just as Long as We're Together*:

> I'm really most strongly relating to Stephanie. But there's this other girl who really likes the same guy and I sort of related to the other girl and how she must feel, and to Jeremy and how he would feel when he found out and what he would do and I sort of saw that everyone had the same sort of problem of working things out in a situation, I guess, that involved other people in ways they really cared about, you know? Like I said, it helps you to see that love is crazy—for everybody!

The students' alignments with characters were very important to their reading experience, contributing in important ways to their creation of the experience, and in their location of the conflict and interpretations of theme, as will be seen later. This, too, is consistent with research in the field (Golden & Guthrie, 1986; Rogers, 1988; Tierney & Pearson, 1983). I think that it is important for teachers to note that differing student understandings and interpretations might be the result of how they have matched up with characters in the story.

The case study readers often felt intense emotions about characters and their actions, and often evaluated characters and their activities and situations. They began to elaborate a character's personality and life history, implicitly connecting what they knew from the text to what they extrapolated from what they knew. As they related to and elaborated a character, they would often begin to critique the elaborated character.

Joanne described her relationship with Stephanie in *Just as Long as We're Together* as follows:

> Stephanie is sort of like me—gets good grades—quiet—not the most popular. I feel like I'm her and I can feel what she's feeling. . . . Like when Jeremy Kravitz is in the same room, I'm totally surprised and delighted and I could feel my heart beating faster. I can imagine how she would try to dress and where she would try to be to catch his attention.

Even when filling the role of his hero Jack Ryan, Ron would be critical of certain activities:

Jack likes to work out, and I felt proud about my power and strength and stuff when I was Jack. But Jack, like my dad, is really outspoken and doesn't hold anything back. It was like I could hear myself [as Jack] saying something that I shouldn't and I'm thinking, Uh-oh, man, I shouldn't have said that, but I just couldn't help it and now I'm gonna pay for it you stupid klutz.

During Joanne's symbolic story representation of "The Sniper," she revealed that it took her about a paragraph to enter the story. "Now I'm in it and I'm on the rooftop. . . . I'm sort of an extra unmentioned detail of the story. I'm there and I've jumped into it. The author didn't know that it would be me or where I'd be, but I'm there and I can tell I'm there though I can't affect anything, only watch." She immediately began to elaborate and evaluate character. "Boy! I'm thinking, you sure are stupid!" Joanne reported after the sniper was shot while lighting a cigarette.

He should have used the lighter as a trick for an ambush or something. It was stupid of the other guy to miss too. You can't blow a chance like that. Not in a war. I'm thinking that the other guy is nervous, he's probably not a real soldier, he's probably been drafted or fighting against his will or something.

When the armored car enters the scene, Joanne switches perspectives:

I felt I was down in the street then [instead of on the roof]. . . . I could hear the car putting and feel how big it was and could see it rumbling down the road and I felt fear and disappointment that the scene was interrupted and keeps him from solving the problem. . . . I thought the old lady was helping the sniper's side but then I realized she wasn't. I felt for an instant like I was the sniper, and I was angry, but then I was scared for everybody. When the tank driver looks up I thought, Stupid! don't stick your head out!

Her feeling for the sniper is different when he dresses his own wound.

Wow, I'm thinking, he was careless not to pay attention to the other sniper, but I'm impressed with him. I'm watching in wonder. He's bleeding [this detail is not stated in the story] and his shirt is soaked and I don't know what he'll do. I wouldn't have planned for this. But he did. And he did what he had to.

Cora, too, evaluated the characters that she elaborated. In response to the scene in *Roll of Thunder, Hear My Cry* when Cassie unwisely tells the temperamental Uncle Hammer about being harassed by Mr. Simms, she wrote this spontaneous literary letter in the persona of Cassie:

Dear Mama,

It's just been one big learning experience this week. When Stacey and I saw that ole shiny silver Packard in the barn I thought for sure that ole Harlan Granger was here, and boy was I happy and surprised to see Uncle Hammer.

Mama, I just had too much hurt inside to keep it in. I know it was wrong, but I just ain't never been treated that way. It got scary when he [Uncle Hammer] got so angry and his eyes started bulging and I knew I should stop and I just couldn't. I know it's all my fault. I should of listened to Big ma's gestures for me to shut up but I was so steamed up and all. I just hate myself for being such a blabbermouth!

Now I'm thinking back to all the good times and how safe we all is all together and now here I am gettin us all in trouble, good and deep. I'm just scared. I feel like I'm even jeperdizing [sic] your life, Mama.

Oh, please forgive me if something bad were to happen!

Love,
Cassie

Here Cora becomes Cassie, infers and elaborates her character, and then critiques this elaborated character. She told me, in regard to this letter, that

As much as I feel like a character sometimes, I guess I'm always aware of myself, too, and that I'm reading. I really related to Cassie in the scene in Strawberry and when she told Uncle Hammer about it but at the same time that I felt her anger and frustration I also was watching what was happening [telling her story to the volatile Uncle Hammer] and I knew it was stupid and wrong [for her to do].

In this letter, Cora continues to relate to character by making inferences about how Cassie must be feeling, and what she must be thinking about. The letter and her discussion of it show an understanding of the greater context of the story, and the situation that the Logan family will eventually find itself in. During the same conversation, Cora told me,

I read to understand myself and others. I associate very closely with Cassie. I learned by being associated with her that it would be hard to live during that time. I read to understand people, their atmosphere, their emotion, their place, so I can feel like I am them or I am there with them.

Seeing the Story World

Once inside the story world, the other move the readers continued to make to fully evoke and flesh out that world was to create mental images of the story landscape.

These readers began by noticing cues for visualizing a "secondary world." All three repeatedly told me that they consciously looked for such visual clues as they first began to read a story. Once such cues were found and interpreted, these readers created and sustained a secondary world in their minds, creating visual pictures of characters, settings, and situations and mental images of affect. As more clues were processed, these visualizations were revised and deepened, or completely new visualizations were created. The visualization was typically achieved through the reader scanning a setting, sometimes from "on top of the world," as Ron put it, and relating extratextual real-world information about settings to the details of the text. On occasion, the readers immediately related to a particular character and created the setting through the eyes of that character.

Very early in the reading of any particular text, it was already clear that decoding words and making verbal sense of a text was only a fraction of the larger picture of how readers transacted with text. These readers' visualizations were related in many ways to their own real-life experiences, and sometimes built upon them. Cora speaks of the pictures she sees while reading:

When I read a book that takes place in a house, and it isn't really described in great detail, then I always see the same house in my mind. The house is a mixture of all of the houses I've been in. But if there are details that don't fit my idea of a house then I have to change the house. Once I do, it stays changed for the story. If too many things are different, I have to imagine a completely new house, but I'm sure that's based on what houses I've seen in my life, too.

It's kind of an odd thing because whenever I'm reading these pictures just pop into my mind, and it's almost as though I don't control it. It happens the minute I open a book and find a detail that helps me to see. When I'm reading a book with mountains in it I always see the exact same mountains, unless, like this book I read about this boy in the Andes, the mountains are specifically described and then I'll like reshape things in my mind and that's the way it will be. . . .

When I asked Cora about recalling what the original house or mountains were like, before she revised her idea of them, she said,

I can't really, because once you change your picture of something you change it back all the way through the things you can remember from before. I might know that it looked different, but I can't see it that way anymore when I'm thinking about the book.

Cora constantly confirmed her mental images against new information, and made necessary adjustments. In one book:

I got the idea that the Barkers were black. . . . But then she [Celine] could see Mr. Barker's black hair on the skin of his white hand and all of a sudden I know he's white and it really confused me because then I had to rethink how his wife looked and his son and I started to think about how I got the idea of their color anyway and if it was important or even if I was being racist or something, do you know what I mean?

One or two clues was all that was needed for Cora to create the rest of an object or scene in her mind.

When I was reading Come a Stranger *she was at ballet camp and the author mentioned that it was like an estate or something and immediately I imagined that it was Elvis's house—I think it's called Graceland, but I put it on a hill because it was on a hill in the book. When she went home, I'd already imagined the sort of neighborhood where a girl like this would live and then the author mentions the color of the house, I think, and suddenly I knew it and pictured it as my old neighbor's house. And that really worked for the whole story.*

Both Cora and Joanne compared reading a book to watching a movie. Cora was able, she said, to "use slow motion, or flashback" as well as being able to speed up certain sequences, "especially if it's really exciting and I want to know what happens." She described this sensation even when she felt like a character in the story. Joanne reported that she saw some books in black and white, if they were set in a far-off time or if the story was sad or told "in a cold way." Most of the time what she visualized was in color, "just like you were seeing it in real life."

Ron, during an SRI, told me that "The only time a book is hard to read is where there's no scenery, only action. I like to feel the book was made for me, and that the author has given a way to see it." When reading a section of *The Odyssey Project*, Ron said:

> The story is in Wisconsin and it's like a new Ice Age. So I just imagine scenes from Madison or other places I've been totally covered in ice and snow, like it goes halfway up to roofs. I needed to know a couple of things but not much in order to imagine the rest of it. You get those first clues and the rest is automatic. . . . It [the book] says that Torrance is big and has a beard. That's all I needed to see him. I know it's winter and he's going to help Amundsen so I see him in a coat, but it's white camouflage clothing so no one can see them. If he's a friend of Amundsen he's smart and won't give himself away. My dad has a book about the Battle of the Bulge and I flip through it sometimes. The battle was in snow and the troops wore all white, even white pants and so that's what I see Amundsen wearing . . . his face is sort of fat and red from the cold. I feel like he's a good guy, and dependable, and smiles a lot. I got all that, I guess, from those two details.

Both Joanne and Cora spoke at various times about the different experience of visualization when they reread a story. (Ron rarely read short stories, nor did he reread, a phenomenon tied, I think, to his style of reading and preoccupation with the landscape of action.) Cora reread the story "High Beams," about an assailant hiding in the back seat of a woman's car who is foiled by the flashing high beams of a following truck driver.

> It was different when I re-read because I could see more details, like especially around the edges, and I noticed more clues . . . like I could see flitting shadows that could be the man . . . that I know are the man on one level because I already read the story, but I act like I haven't so it's just a shadow that could be a man. I have the feeling there's more color when I re-read.

These descriptions from highly engaged readers suggest both the value of encouraging active imaging and the value of rereading as a separate reading experience from a first reading. It also suggests the necessity of providing time for reading, rereading, and response activities. I had the experience of asking Ron one day what he was doing as he sat staring into space. "I'm thinking!" he hissed, in an obvious reaction to the "teacher tone" in my voice and the implicit suggestion that he was doing nothing of value. He then told me that he was thinking about a story, what it looked like "in there. I can't quite get it. There's a building and passageways and I need to get it straight." A story world and the experience of it are clearly highly complex, dynamic, and developing. This requires the deployment of strategies many readers may not naturally use, and in any case, time and energy for the construction of characters, settings, and situations. It shows, I think, that teachers might provide not only guidance and support for visualizing activities, but also allow more support and time for this to occur.

During the first 12 weeks of the study, many of the less proficient readers and all of the LD readers failed to reveal a single move on the dimension of visualizing or seeing what they read. For these readers there were no indications that they made personal associations as they read. Many expressed incredulity when I asked questions about what they were "seeing" or when other students described what they saw while reading. They seemed to be entirely unable to visualize a secondary world without some sort of artistic aid such as photos or drawings—or the chance to draw, make a collage, or flip through a magazine to identify what a character or a place probably looked like. Once these students were given the support to create a concrete visualization of a story, then they often became excited about reading that particular piece, and became capable of empathizing, connecting, and reflecting upon the literary experience (see Chapter Five). It became clear, in repeated instances throughout the school year, that these students had great difficulty in spontaneously visualizing the story world. And if the visualization did not occur, they were unable to respond in any of the other response dimensions.

CONNECTIVE DIMENSIONS

These next two dimensions, of elaborating and connecting, were a kind of transition between the moves students used to evoke and experience story worlds, and the moves used to step back and reflect on that experience. One set of moves was used to elaborate on and extend the story world beyond what was explicitly described in the text and to set up and explore alternatives to the written story. The second set of moves was used to explicitly connect personal experiences to those of characters, and to consider how the reading experience might inform choices and actions the reader might take in his or her own life.

Elaborating on the Story World

In this dimension, the case study readers used their real-world knowledge by applying it to the virtual world of the reading, not in an automatic or naturally occurring way as in the previously discussed dimensions in which they entered and evoked a story world, but by actively and often quite consciously playing detective to go beyond and extend cues and fill textual gaps. Scenes, events, and characters were elaborated in ways not required by the story and that went beyond the story, but made the meaning more powerful and personal to these readers.

Reading on this dimension was extratextual, going beyond what was stated or even suggested by the book. The story world became, in effect, what could be called a "reader's world." Response on this dimension included the conscious use of intertextual links, in which the readers sometimes drew on previous story experiences to create or augment the meaning of the current reading and to sharpen their understanding of it.

These readers were guided by the text and its conventions, but incorporated and added significant personally elaborated details into the creation of a secondary world. The readers sometimes began to imagine extra events not mentioned in the text, alternate events or consequences for story events, or parallel events to the story world as they might occur in real life. They seem to ask and answer many "What If?" questions, playing with possibilities and suggested potentialities of character, motivation, and consequence. (When these "What If?" questions were also posed in regard to real life, the students were connecting literature to life, which is the next dimension to be described.) Elaborations were sometimes subject to revision if later textual information made them unlikely or impossible to sustain.

These readers' elaborations infused extratextual life into the text, enlivening it with personal meaning, which the readers brought to the dimension of connecting as they expressed personal principles of living explored through the text, and more global ideas about human experience.

Intertextual Elaborations

Here Cora not only elaborates on character and extends the text of a story, but combines knowledge of different texts together in an elaboration.

Roll of Thunder reminded me of some things I read about Spike Lee, and I began to imagine Cassie and Spike meeting, and what they would do together. Because if Cassie was 9 [years old] in 1933 then she would be . . . [calculates] . . . 69 in 1993. She would have lived through all the civil rights marches and things down south. She's smart and she becomes tough in the book and I think she will probably become a lawyer or someone . . . someone who is ready to go out in the world to fight. I know she liked Mr. Jamison, so maybe that's why . . . a reason to become a lawyer. . . . Spike spent his summers in the sixties down South, so they would have that in common [civil rights struggle] but Cassie would know a much bigger history of it. I imagined them meeting at some awards banquet or meeting, because Cassie certainly had become a strong supporter of civil rights and Spike would be interested in her story and probably . . . he'd consider making a movie of it.

Both Ron and Joanne often used their knowledge not only of other books, but of movies and television shows to make intertextual links. While reading "The Sniper," Joanne commented:

In the beginning I thought it would be like an Arnold Schwarzenegger movie. But then as I was comparing like Terminator *movies to this I was thinking how this [*"The Sniper"*] was so much more about real people and real consequences that you never really get to feel in a movie because it's [the movie] so thin and . . . like glamorized or something.*

In comparison to Cora and Joanne, who disliked seeing movies about books they had read ("They never compare," Joanne said), Ron looked forward zealously to the release of movies such as *The Firm.* "I can't wait to see what they make of it and how it compares to the book. It'll be great . . . it will be something to talk about." Upon further questioning, Ron revealed that "reading a book and seeing the movie are different experiences but they sort of build on each other. I use the movie to rethink the book and the book to understand the movie more."

Filling Gaps

In *Roll of Thunder, Hear My Cry* (Taylor, 1976), which we read as a class, there is an important scene between Uncle Hammer and Mr. Morrison that is completely left out of the book. Uncle Hammer is enraged that Charlie Simms, a white adult, has humiliated his niece Cassie, "a colored girl," by twisting her arm, pushing her off the sidewalk, and making her apologize for not kowtowing to his daughter Lillian Jean. Hammer, upon hearing the story and over the protests and pleas of Big Ma (his mother) and Mary (his sister-in-law and Cassie's mother), jumps into his car, ready to use his rifle to wreak revenge. Mr. Morrison jumps into the car as well in an attempt to stop him, knowing that certainly Hammer, and perhaps the whole family, will be lynched if Hammer goes through with his plan. The next morning the two men show up at the family breakfast table, tired and bleary-eyed. One brief reference is later made to what had happened in the night.

I have documented elsewhere (Wilhelm, 1992) how very few of my students recognized or filled in this quite obvious textual gap. Highly engaged readers, however, such as the case study students, immediately did so. This excerpt shows how textual gaps can be filled in a way that makes them an organic part of the story. It also shows how story details or events, even those that are just suggested, are elaborated by readers. Joanne reported:

> As soon as Mr. Morrison jumps in the car and they roar away it was like I was inside the car with them, I could even hear the car [sic] slam. It's dark in the car, but I can see their faces in the light from the dashboard. I can see the dashboard because it was described earlier . . . walnut, and I'm in the back seat leaning into the front. The seats are plush red and comfortable. It's almost like I've stopped reading and I'm dreaming, I guess . . . [laughs] . . . but anyway Hammer says, "What you here for? If you ain't gonna help me just get out, right now!" and Mr. Morrison, real quiet like, says, "You're bad as them, you do this thing." And then they just keep on arguing like that and it's like I'm right there with them . . . then I'm reading again but when I find out what happened I'm right back in that scene and I know what happened to them.

During an SRI regarding his reading of *The Odyssey Project*, Ron began to fill gaps in a similar fashion, elaborating on both event and character. He was moving character cutouts around and discussing their relationships during a climactic scene when Amundsen and Torrance pick off four enemy soldiers.

> The author didn't really describe these guys [enemy soldiers] at all. That's why I made them stick figures [points to symbolic representation cutouts]. But I guess I get to know them. I'm sort of imagining they're

like Nazis with the same sort of helmets and long gray coats and stuff.
. . . Now I'm pretty excited. . . . I'm starting to think that it was a trap,
that these soldiers [points to stick figures] wouldn't be so stupid to be
standing around, that they must be like bait. So I'm feeling worried.
And like for a minute I'm over there with them and [none of the following details are suggested by the text] they're just standing around talking
and smoking cigarettes and one guy stamps on the ground and another
one spits and they all laugh. Their faces are pink from the cold and one
guy blows on his hands. I feel like a spy, I guess, and I'm feeling relieved
because I'm convinced that it's not a trap, but I'm also thinking how
these are regular guys and they're in the army and probably didn't vol-
unteer. All of this is going through my mind, I think, both before the
shooting and during it and after they are all shot. . . . Maybe it was
afterwards but I think it was all happening as I was reading. They were
still the enemy and I didn't feel too sorry when they got shot, but there
was like this instant. . . .

Extratextual, Imagined Events

All three readers explored the possibilities of extratextual events they
imagined in their minds. Cora said that she often imagined what:

Anne [of Green Gables] would do if things hadn't worked out, or if she
was in our school right now, how would she dress and deal with things,
what teachers would she like . . . sometimes I like to think that I'm her
and I try to deal with difficulties like I think she would.

After a rereading of "The Sniper," Joanne spoke at length about what
would happen after the story's end, when:

he [the sniper] has to go home. He'll have to tell his mother what happened. She'll be worried about his brother and he'll know what happened. . . . He could lie about it, say he just saw it happen. . . . No,
he's going to have to tell the truth, and his mother will really weep but
she'll forgive him. . . . Oh, it's just so horrible!

At the end of Roll of Thunder, Ron reported:

I'm like, wow, man, what if things hadn't turned out this way? What if
Mr. Jamison hadn't got there in time? What if Papa hadn't started the
fire? Would the night riders have really lynched Papa and Mr. Morrison? I
just had this scene in my mind where they come up to the house and they

try to get Papa and Mr. Morrison and they [the Logans] have guns and booby traps and they just kill them! And Mr. Jamison is there watching and he knows that the whites were just asking for it and that the Logans were just protecting themselves and so they don't get in trouble for it. I can see why the author wrote the ending the way she did, and maybe it's better . . . more believable, I know, but I like my ending. . . . It makes . . . it relieves me somehow, makes me feel better, like those night riders never get what they deserve and I really want them to.

This study confirmed what Enciso (1992) has pointed out, that elaboration becomes a key indicator of, and in fact a prerequisite to, the link between participating in a story world and moving along a continuum toward a more reflective exploration of those experiences as a spectator. Iser (1978), as well, has pointed out that elaboration is the key to personal understanding gained through reading. Bruner (1986) goes so far as to argue that the elaborations can be interpreted as the most vital element of the story world: "Literary experiences invite the reader to consider implicit meanings, multiple perspectives and the subjectification of reality." This operation of the "subjunctive mode" is what constitutes the power of literature, "the trafficking in human possibilities versus settled certainties" (p. 35). Elaboration is the exploration of possibilities, of extending what is known, of probing character thought and attitude.

Connecting Literature to Life

As was seen in both the dimensions of relating to characters (stance/perspective taking) and seeing the story world (mental imaging), readers naturally brought their knowledge of the world to bear, adding it to textual clues to build a secondary world with characters and places they felt they knew. As could be seen in the case of Cora, this sort of connecting occurred as she visualized "houses" by bringing her personal knowledge of houses to the text. She was bringing her life to literature.

Highly engaged readers, such as the case study students, seemed to naturally use actual-world knowledge, in ways invited by textual cues, to build a virtual world. The less engaged readers in my classes did not automatically do this, and seemed at a loss unless such strategies were scaffolded for them.

The data suggested that *without the bringing of personally lived experience to literature, the reverse operation, bringing literature back to life, did not occur.* This, I think, is a key finding.

In this dimension of response, the readers went beyond drawing on their repertoires of personal knowledge as readers and people, and the bringing of their personal experience to bear on the understanding of literature. Here a reverse process occurred: The readers made conscious connections from the fictional world that helped them to gain heightened awareness of their personal identities and to formulate guidelines for personal ways of living. These readers did not just apply knowledge of life to the reading transaction, but consciously derived implications for living their own lives from the transaction. These readers activated personal comparisons the text seemed to invite for them. On occasion, these students mentally or physically role-played what they would do in a character's situation should it occur in their own lives. Literature was related to life and brought back to it.

This sort of conscious relating or connecting seemed to depend on the reader first bringing a great deal of his or her life to literature, not only to take a perspective and to visualize, but to elaborate on the story world to infuse some personal extratextual life into the reading experience. Once this was done, the readers seemed enabled to draw comparisons from the literary experience to their own lives.

Learning from Characters and Events

Ron spoke in general terms about making personal comparisons to characters that helped him consider issues in his own life.

> I guess I'm comparing myself to Jack Ryan a lot when I read stories with him. When he's in a jam, I think, what would I do if I were him? Could I do it? And then when I'm in a jam, I think about the stories and think, "What would Jack Ryan do if he were me?" What if I were like the "young Jack Ryan," you know, like the "young Indiana Jones," what would I do then?

Cora, discussing her reading of *Roll of Thunder* during an interview, had this to say:

> After I read it anyway, I thought a lot about what Cassie had to teach me. I was especially impressed about how she handled Lillian Jean. She was in control even when it looked to everyone else that she wasn't. I learned that . . . it's hard to express . . . like if someone is using you, and you know they're using you, then they're not—because you have a choice about them using you then and where it's going to lead and what

you will do about it. Knowing—knowing what's happening puts you in control and it's better to use that control and not get angry.

After her reading of *Just as Long as We're Together,* Joanne explained that:

a book might not give you an answer of what to do in your own life, but it helps you think about it. This [book] made me think about what I would do if my friend and I both really liked the same boy. I mean, is friendship or love more important? What's more lasting? Would I want to risk what I already have for something I might not get? I don't know. . . .

During her SRI with "The Sniper," notice how Joanne initially brings life to literature by making a personal comparison, and then makes a connection, bringing literature back to life as she formulates an idea about living.

[When the sniper was wounded] I felt the pain of the iodine. I even clenched my teeth and shook. I had something like that happen to me— [laughs]—it didn't feel good. I could remember that so well. . . . When the other sniper he shot fell over the side of the building, that really affected me. I pushed my sister down once and she started crying so piti- fully. I felt so terrible. It was the crying that got to me, just like the guy falling and his bones being smashed when he hit the street [last detail was elaborated]. You know, I'm thinking that it's when you see the . . . consequences of what you do, that's when it gets you. It makes me think that we should always imagine the unseen consequences of what we do . . . that we should think, like what is it? The golden rule . . . that we should imagine what it would be like from the receiving end before we do anything.

When the sniper kills his enemy, he is repulsed and throws down his revolver, which then discharges. Joanne elaborates on the scene and indi- cates heightened personal awareness, which in turn leads to the formu- lation of a personal guideline.

He almost killed himself! It's ridiculous! [Laughs] I felt like he almost killed himself for no reason. All of a sudden I feel like I'm there with him again and it's cold and damp up on the roof like just before the sun rises and I'm shivering and the gun goes off and about blows out my ear-

drums and the bullet whizzes by me . . . and it makes me think how you have to be careful . . . especially when you're angry about something or upset, not to do something stupid. It's like when I'm really upset I'll do something wild—oh, I'm seeing myself so well right now and how I could do the exact same stupid thing, out of control, and it could really ruin things and that shocks you back to reality, and I'm thinking the being upset has to be enough to shock you back so you don't screw things up even more. You have to know yourself well enough that you know you might do something like that and that is what has to stop you.

Role-Playing

Both Joanne and Cora reported mental "role-plays" in which they would be the character in the story world acting out a scene as it was played out, might be played out, or could have been alternately played out. Apropos to the dimension of connecting and relating literature to life, they reported that they would also role-play scenes in which they might find themselves, in the context of their own lives, in a similar situation to the characters. They would then role-play the scene, often revising the role-play, and rehearsing over and over a particular enactment that pleased them, or, as Joanne put it, "You might find really happening to you and you want to make sure you get it right. So you can automatically do and say the things you want right away instead of saying later, ohmygod I missed my chance!"

Ron was the only one of the three given to overt, physical role-plays. He would sometimes enact a scene by himself as a single character, and sometimes play multiple roles. At other times he would begin a role-play hoping that others would play along, or he would actively enlist friends to try out a particular scene. His success in such schemes was erratic, especially when he had to explain a scene from a book others had not read and they quickly became uninterested. He was more successful role-playing scenes from texts the class had read as a group.

This highlights the importance of balancing shared and individualized readings. When students read individually, they can exercise their individual taste and response, and they can encourage others to read the books they have enjoyed. When readings are shared, students have the opportunity to create response together, to compare response and ways of reading, and to learn from each other about these ways of reading.

Ron's overt role-playing is not common, but neither is it unique. I have written several journal entries over the years about students spontaneously role-playing scenes or elaborations from their reading, and once I observed several remedial reading students enacting the tiger hunt we had read about that day (from Jim Corbett's *Man-Eaters of Kumaon*) on their way home from school.

Drama is a natural way of making meaning for children, yet it is a terribly underused part of American teachers' repertoires. Students, I think, lose their propensity for learning and exploring through drama partly because of school. But this propensity can be recovered and can work to support better reading, as we will see in the next chapter.

Telling Others

Students who analogized principles or ideas from literature seemed to have a special urge to share their understandings with others. Cora indicated to me that she and Joanne were "reading friends," and that they enjoyed "sharing what we get out of books, what they mean to us," although they were not friendly in any other social sense. "Some books I don't need to talk about, only if, you know, there were things I learned from it about myself." Joanne said:

> I share and trade books with a lot of girls, mostly Christie and Cora. We have the same taste. You have to find people with your own reading style, who know what you like to see and feel when you read. . . . One of the really nice things about reading a book someone gives you is that you can see what they learned from it and how it, well, not just what they thought about it but how it will change how they act. It's so much fun to talk about when and how we might have the chance to act like the characters, or what we would do differently in their situation because of what happened to them.

Ron expressed on several occasions that he loved to talk with his father about what he read, and that he actively enlisted friends to read certain books so "we can talk about them." He loved it "when people borrow me books [*sic*—this is a Wisconsinism]. Then I know if I read it we can talk about it."

REFLECTIVE DIMENSIONS

In this last set of response dimensions, the case study students seemed to have separated themselves from their participation in the story and were looking at that experience in a more detached and objective manner. They seemed to be spectating on the reading experience and reflecting on it. Often this reflection would occur while they read, and it seemed to almost always occur after a reading. In fact, this reflecting on the textual experience seemed to be an organic and highly enjoyable part of the reading act for these students.

Considering Significance

In this dimension, the readers asked various forms of Galda's (1982) analytic evaluation question: "How did/does the text work?" and "How does this particular detail or rhetorical move contribute to its working?"

Operating on this dimension, these readers vigorously interrogated the text, continuing to fill in gaps but consciously recognizing not only details but the openness of the text—of what is not told, of what is left for the reader—and considering the significance of such openness.

These readers became consciously concerned with what could be termed "a narrative world," or the way the story is told. Narrative conventions for interpreting text (cf. Rabinowitz's rules of signification, 1987) were applied, and the significance of certain details was considered. The implications of character behavior were considered and evaluated. These readers continued to reflect and elaborate on possible meanings that such details might convey. Story events were considered in relationship to possible themes and complex authorial generalizations that readers recognized the literature was attempting to make.

These readers formulated puzzles and enigmas and consciously welcomed, accepted, or rejected what Iser (1978) calls "hermeneutic challenges" to their interpretive, meaning-making abilities. In other words, the readers would set up detective games for themselves, posing sophisticated mysteries for themselves and then trying to solve them.

Details were considered in relation to previous details; these readers read along what Barthes (1986) calls "textual indices," building up meaning by adding together an accumulation of various details considered to be significant that were presented at different places in the text. These readers actively looked for patterns that evolved through a reading and considered matters of coherence and how separate elements fit together to indicate meanings. In contrast to extracting personal principles and guidelines from isolated events and details, as in the dimension of connecting, when operating on reflective dimensions the readers knew that the author was making a complex statement about life that could be understood only by considering the experience of the literary work as an organic whole.

As Ron commented: "Sometimes I'll be reading and something will just knock my socks off and I'll say, 'Whoa! How'd he [the author] do that to me?' I mean, how did he shock me like that or make me feel that way?"

Interrogating the Text

Throughout the reading of "The Sniper," Joanne interrogated the text. When the sniper puts his hat on top of his rifle to fool the other sniper into shooting it, Joanne asked:

Could he really trick the other sniper that way? It seems so obvious. . . . I guess it was dark, but it wouldn't fool me . . . and why drop your rifle? It has his fingerprints on it and he just killed the driver and the old lady! Does he really have to do it to make the trick work? Now he doesn't have a rifle! He's laying everything on escaping and on his side winning. . . . I'm asking why are they all doing this? It makes me shiver. How can war be pushing them to do this when you see that they hate it [the killing]? I'm asking what it is they are fighting for that can be this important, especially when none of them really seem like soldiers who really know about fighting.

At the end of the story, Joanne recognizes and considers the openness of the text.

I felt total awe at the ending. . . . The author doesn't tell what he felt so I could fill it in and feel it myself. That was a good thing to leave to me. I would have gone nuts, blown my cover totally, it's so terrible! So now I sort of take over the story and I'm asking "How could you have done this?" and "What will your life be like now?" and I'm thinking. . . . Now he doesn't know why he did it himself or why he's fighting and how he ever could have done such a thing.

Interestingly, Joanne first thought that the story took place in Central America, "between the contras and the other people," but later thought, "It must be in Europe, I think because of the city rooftops and chimneys and stuff." At the end of the story, she said, "It doesn't really matter where, maybe the author doesn't want you to know where because it [the theme] applies anywhere people fight each other."

Cora considers how endings contribute to a story's workings and meanings at the same time that she shows that she has added together various pieces of information from throughout the story.

Like at the end of "High Beams" there's that twist, that it's not the truck driver who's the . . . danger. He's the hero who saved the girl [from the guy trying to kill her from the back seat of her car] by flashing the high beams whenever he saw the guy getting ready to hurt her. I was really surprised by the ending and . . . I think, "What did the author do to make me expect another ending?" and then I'll ask if there was a point to the twist or if it's just to surprise me.

Later during the same discussion, Cora considers not only how details work, but also shows pleasure in the challenges she and the text set for her as the reader.

Then at the end I imagine what happens after the ending . . . I see the police grabbing the guy and dragging him away and he has this evil smile on his face. And I think, "What did he want?" "Why did he do this? "He must have had something, some relationship with the girl, or she must remind him of someone. I keep imagining—it's part of the fun of the way the story was written—but I never really want to come up with a final answer like some people do.

Cora then considers the text as a whole as she considers its meaning.

When you consider all the clues you see there's a message, like . . . things aren't always what they seem. Yes . . . because it seemed like she was safe in the car . . . and that the truck driver was evil instead of good.

Revising Interpretations

All of these readers often expressed confusion when operating on this dimension. Often they were troubled about the meaning of a detail, or their particular interpretation of it. Nonetheless, these readers were quite adept at acknowledging a lack of clarity, or realizing that they lacked essential information: either background information, or essential information that, as Ron put it, "I must have missed. I had to have missed something. Damn!"

Sometimes they acknowledged that previous responses were too narrow or incorrect and needed revision. Cora, responding to the end of "Lob's Girl," said:

You see I thought the dog was still alive [when he came to the hospital to wake his owner, Sandy, from her coma], but when I found out he was dead then I went back and I saw lots of clues that showed he was dead. And I had to, well, rethink the story from that point [where Lob died] . . . and I was thinking how much he loved her, but then I thought how she came out of the coma because she thought he was there and I thought about how much she loved him and how she really had come back from the dead too! It's more than about the power of love and how it goes beyond the grave . . . I think it has something to do with memory.

This is exactly the sort of attention to detail and consequent revising activity that most of my student readers rarely engaged in. I think that this building and revising of understanding based on accumulating and adding together details from throughout a text should be a reading activity that is modeled and encouraged. Another lesson for me as a teacher is to tolerate, or perhaps even contribute to, student confusion by pointing out details they might not have considered. Then time needs to be given to consider and work through the confusion. A further implication is for assessment and evaluation of student reading: Confusion and the inability to answer certain questions may indicate growth, that is, that the student has taken on a new challenge that she is still struggling to meet. This kind of move needs to be applauded and encouraged. Error and failure may be a great indication of growth.

Recognizing Literary Conventions

On this dimension, the case study readers exhibited an awareness that the literary event is a highly conventionalized and socially constructed experience. As such, the readers recognized highly sophisticated rules of signification that often undercut literal or usual expression. On occasion, I noticed that they considered irony, story inversions, narrator and author reliability, and symbolism. To interpret and construct the meaning such conventions implied, they drew on their previous experiences as readers and people, and upon the literary and cultural repertoires these experiences had developed.

We have already seen how these readers considered the constructedness of a text, the meanings of its revealed and withheld details. In this excerpt from a discussion of *Just as Long as We're Together,* Joanne considers the issues of withheld information and a narrator's reliability: "I know she's [the author] withholding information about Jeremy and I wonder why. I wonder if I can believe her, if there's a story behind the story. And whether, you know, I'm actually supposed to guess at that story behind the story."

Ron spoke in general terms about irony.

Sometimes I know I've read a story and you know you've understood all the words but the story just . . . doesn't make any sense. You just know you've missed something. And I'm racking my brain and all of a sudden I'll get it! Like, you know, maybe people weren't saying what they meant, but the opposite of it . . . like you weren't supposed to believe something or take it seriously . . . you know, like real people do all the time . . . and presto! The story makes sense.

I took this opportunity to explain and illustrate verbal, situational, and dramatic irony to Ron. It was a lesson he was ready for, and he identified several instances of each kind of irony from his recent reading. Recognizing irony was becoming part of his repertoire; being able to name it helped him recognize and understand it more powerfully.

Ron showed the importance of activating a cultural and literary repertoire as he discussed his reading of spy novels.

You know, you're always looking for the mole. You know there's somebody you can't trust and you try to figure out who. [In response to a teacher's question, he added] You just know, because you've read a lot of books and a lot of movies and it always happens and usually there's been some clues of some sort . . . so you're on the lookout.

Though these students showed some awareness of sophisticated literary conventions, like most other readers in their seventh-grade classes they continued to have difficulty with such conventions and would sometimes completely misread a story despite many clues contrary to their reading. The most engaged readers, such as the three profiled here, did tend to recognize a misreading more readily than their peers, even if they had difficulty revising that reading.

I found Michael Smith's (1989, 1991) work on teaching such sophisticated conventions through sequences of textual experiences very useful for helping my own students. Smith suggests providing students with repeated exposure to particular conventions like irony, starting with simple texts such as cartoons and moving through shorter and simpler examples to longer and more subtle forms. The students build up the experience necessary to formulate heuristics, or problem-solving strategies, for reading and interpreting such conventions. I think that such direct instruction is probably necessary for students to understand texts that make use of complex conventions, since even the case study students struggled to recognize and make use of these.

Recognizing Reading as a Transaction

On the reflective dimensions, the readers consciously recognized that the text was constructed by a human and fallible author. Moreover, they expressed recognition that the author, through the textual construction, and they themselves as readers had to work together to create meanings. The author of the work was considered as an individual who created the work through artifice and the weaving of patterns to communicate a feeling or interpretation of some aspects of the human condition. In addition, the students recognized that they had a role in responding to the details and patterns.

The readers sometimes recognized an implied author and interrogated that author, evaluating the techniques used by that author to construct the story. An attempt was made by them to understand the story's expressed vision in terms of the constructed nature of the text. The author's representation of the world was matched with their own, and that representation might be accepted, rejected, resisted, or revised.

The readers sometimes recognized and reflected on their own contributions to the literary event, and began to consider if the role they played matched the expectation of the author and the text.

Many of the data reported previously show how these readers considered these issues, demonstrating that the dimensions discussed here are not really separable in practice. Nonetheless, I will cite some examples that do seem to highlight how readers considered their role vis-à-vis that of the text and the author behind the text.

Cora was one reader who almost always considered herself in conversation or communion with an author. After reading *The Incredible Journey*, she noted, "This author must really love and understand animals." And in regard to several Katherine Paterson novels: "When I read her books I feel like I'm getting to know a very kind and sensitive person who has a powerful heart and . . . an ability to understand people."

As Thomson (1987) noted in his study, readers who read several works of a particular type, or especially by a particular author, are much more likely to consciously consider the notion of an author with an individual agenda, and individual interests, styles, and techniques for constructing a literary work of art. Students choosing their own reading frequently read several or all of the works by a particular author they have come to like. Yet this opportunity to know an author through multiple works is very rare in classes that are directed by a teacher or a planned curriculum. And then these kinds of moves will be much more difficult for students to make.

As Cora continued this train of thought, she said of Paterson:

Sometimes she lets me down and I'm a little disappointed . . . not in her so much I guess as the way she wrote something because I still think a lot of her. I was disappointed by the end of Gilly Hopkins and by the whole book Park's Quest. It just wasn't up to her standards. But then Liddy [sic] restored my confidence and put things back on an even keel.

Ron, who would plow through several books by the same author on great binges, had similar reactions. "*The Firm* [by John Grisham] was great and I was thinking what a great author he is. Then *The Pelican Brief* was good too, but not as good."

These readers would sometimes compare the representation of the author with their own views of the world. Ron said,

I like Clancy a lot, but he has a really negative view of the world. When I read a couple of his books it wears me out. I need to read a fantasy as a relief from being dragged down by all the problems he sees in the world. I guess I just don't see the world as being that bad. Some authors just concentrate on the bad stuff and they don't give a complete picture and that can really get you down.

Joanne recognizes and evaluates the constructedness of "The Sniper" at the same time she mildly interrogates the author:

I knew as soon as the author tells me he's going to check the body that he would know the guy. Why else would the author have him look? When he did that I thought, the author has to have a good ending. The guy who was shot . . . family member, definitely. It was still a shock to find out it was his brother. . . . I don't know if it's good, maybe the same point could have been made in a more believable way. But maybe it has to be the brother to have that force.

Joanne also recognizes and reflects on her own contribution to the story:

Sometimes I'll read something and I'll think, "I just didn't get enough out of that. I wasn't up to it. I know there's more there." What's nice about this story is that I think I really . . . you know, thought and felt along with it. I think I did a good job. At the end I feel like I really related to the story.

Toward the end of *The Great Gilly Hopkins,* Cora considers the role of a particular character. She related:

I'm thinking about her [Gilly's] grandma and why she's even been put into the story. I thought about it a lot and I guess it's for the plot, so Gilly will have a place she'll have to stay . . . but much more important than that is that the grandmother is suffering too and it's the first time Gilly has the opportunity to really understand someone else and help them from the very start.

All three readers indicated that when they were confused about something they just simply read on, trusting that the author would eventually reveal enough for them to resolve the confusion. Often, as Ron said, "You just have to like get the problem straight in your head, so you can solve it when the chance comes. . . . You have to trust that the guy writing it knew what he was doing." This is reminiscent of Iser's view of the reader's setting up and solving "hermeneutic puzzles" (1978), and of Meek's (Meek et al., 1983) view that the practiced reader can tolerate uncertainty because she knows that if she continues to read, "the puzzles and suspense built by the author will be resolved."

However, this kind of ambiguity was difficult for my less engaged readers to tolerate and often caused them to give up their reading. Interesting, too, in this regard was the universal desire of the three case study students for "surprise." This desire was not shared by lower-level students, who were disconcerted by surprise, and who felt, as Walter told me, "screwed over" in their attempts to figure out the text.

Not only did the case study readers desire surprise, they desired different types: not only of event, but of style and metaphor. And they relished the opportunity to realign their readings with new revelations about the story world.

I interpreted this desire for surprise as a desire for new challenges as they outgrew the demands of formulaic fiction. Joanne, who read more formulaic fiction than the other two case study students, had this to say:

Like a Nancy Drew book is sort of comforting and relaxing. Every book is like an old friend, you can almost tell what's going to happen and when. It's predictable and easy. But it gets boring too and it's like having ate too much candy. You just get sick of it and you want a book that will really throw you for a loop.

Evaluating an Author, and the Self as Reader

The case study readers would occasionally seem to recognize the reader implied by the text (the reader imagined by the author as she wrote), and Cora, especially, might even critique the role of the implied reader, or her own performance of the implied role. She would comment on the acceptance/resistance/rejection of the assigned role as implied reader, or the interpretive moves she made because it was expected of her, perhaps because she was a member of what Fish (1980) regards as a particular reading community.

These readers, when operating on this dimension, exercised reflexiveness, considering what the processes of reading and making interpretations revealed about their personal identities. A personal interpretation was sometimes compared to another reader's interpretation in a way that revealed a personally characteristic way of being in and making sense of the world.

Finally, these readers very occasionally seemed to consider the ideology or political agenda of the author and text, and the implications of such an ideology.

I gathered data about this dimension when these readers were sharing interpretations, comparing these to reveal their personal characteristics as readers and as people.

Ron would often enlist friends to read the books he was reading.

I like sharing. If you agree [about a book's meaning], then you share this excitement about thinking the same way, like being fans of the same winning team. If you disagree you get to see it in a new way and that's interesting. I think there's lots of ways to see a book and how you see it tells a lot about you.

Ron believed that he learned about himself by comparing his literary interpretations to those of others.

For a period of time during the school year, Ron enlisted his friend Chris to read some Tom Clancy novels along with him. They would sometimes read aloud together, and did several cooperative projects together: a radio show, a story drama, a video newscast.

You know, Chris really likes sports and humor and action and stuff like that. When he read these books he was into the big climactic scenes. He always wanted to reenact these assassinations and big explosions and things. . . . Me, I was more interested in like the good and evil part of it, and could Jack Ryan save his family or friends. I guess how we read the books just showed what we care and think about.

Joanne told me that she and Cora often shared books "to compare how we feel about them. We like talking about that. Sometimes I'll read a book and I'll want to know what she will think about it. Sometimes we think alike but there's always something different too. It's fun to think about what that shows about us."

Joanne often indicated that she had stepped back and was evaluating the author, the text, herself, and her own reading. When researching for her learning group's production of a video documentary on women in the workplace, Joanne wrote in her journal:

The author of this really thinks women are always mistreated. But some females I know actually say that they aren't being treated unfairly. Is the author wrong? Has she really considered everyone's point of view, which she should if she's an author, or only her own? I think we should take a poll, because this is very weird, because I see both points of view. What I think is that females are just as prejudice to males as they are to us! Like maybe many of us prejudge them and lump them all together. Neat but disturbing thought!

When Cora completed her reading of Katherine Paterson's *The Great Gilly Hopkins*, she was irate with the ideology of the text and the text's implied reader role. Here, as on other occasions, she perceives a shift in her reading experience. Often these changes are in character, plot direction, style, or tone. Here it is in regard to the role she feels the text wishes her to perform. After referring to Paterson's Christian orientation, Cora irately reported that

The end of the book CLEARLY wants me to read it a certain way, and I don't want to read it that way. I mean, at the end, it's different than the rest of the book! It's like we get to like Gilly and get excited about how

she's growing and then . . . at the end of the book, she [the author] wants me to be sad, and I am, but I don't want to be, but then I'm mostly angry. She also wants me to buy into what happens, that it's the way it has to be. . . . I feel manipulated by that. She wants me to think that Gilly should bear her cross, that this is what she asked for and now that she has it she has to . . . well, endure it, I guess. . . . I resent that sort of ending. . . . I mean, why can't Gilly go back to her foster home? What would be wrong with that? Why couldn't we have an ending like that? They're [the foster family] her family, not this mother and grandmother. Doesn't Gilly have any rights? Is it Christian to believe that she has to be unhappy because she's made mistakes and she has to live with those mistakes? What about Gilly being forgiven and having learned from her mistakes? Why can't she just admit she made a mistake and say she wants to go where she found love? Where's the Christianity in beating up on a kid? . . . I liked the book a lot until the end. I just . . . I just can't live with that ending and what the author is trying to feed me with it.

Joanne, responding to the end of *Roll of Thunder, Hear My Cry,* had this to say.

One reason I really liked this book is that the author obviously had a lot of respect for me. I mean, I've read books like this that beat you over the head kind of [laughs] . . . like a fable with a big moral written all over it. In this [book] there's a moral too, like that blacks were really mistreated, and everybody . . . well lots of people accepted it. And that's bad because people like Mr. Jamison and Papa showed that you do have the power to change things and make them better. The story, I guess, is about people being treated equally . . . deserving to be treated equally . . . but the author, she doesn't beat you over the head with it, she lets you in on their life so you can feel their problems . . . see for yourself, well . . . their dignity, and you believe it and really feel it because you were allowed to come to it yourself. You know, I really believe people will only change if they are helped to see things for themselves. They won't change by someone telling them what to see. . . . Another thing I liked was how not all the whites were evil. Mr. Jamison helped them, even the Simmses [during the cotton fire] . . . Jeremy was nice, and Lillian Jean was . . . well, she changed. And they [the Logans] fought back. I read another book [about discrimination] and the people just took everything and I couldn't believe that, or that the author would want them to do that. . . .

EPILOGUE:
WHAT WE LEARNED TOGETHER
ABOUT READING

I pursued this study not only with Cora, Joanne, and Ron but also (to a much less formal degree) with all of my students for the whole of the school year. It became what we did together: sharing how we read, discussing it, trying new things. It was a giant reading experiment.

Studying how my students read helped me as a teacher, helping me to see that I had previously neglected how readers evoke and experience their reading, and how they connect and relate personally to that experience. I saw how I had privileged particular kinds of interpretive and reflective response through my past teaching and I saw ways to take a new tack.

The process allowed me to see what my most engaged readers were doing, and to begin considering how I might help less engaged readers to begin making the same sorts of moves.

Our focus on the process of reading helped my students as they learned new moves from each other, trying on other readers' strategies and perspectives. Their personal experience of reading, whether relatively impoverished or highly engaged, was validated and expanded. Because of the way we ran the class, they were not told that they were "wrong," but that they were readers doing what readers did, and that they could be better readers by doing new and different things.

The students noticed and spoke often about how differently they would experience and understand the same text—discussing why this was so and if a particular reading was richer than another. They came to value different readings and different ways of reading.

Many students reconceived the reading act in a way that empowered them because it gave them a sense of their own agency as meaning-makers. They came to see reading as something they did, that they controlled, that they could talk about, think about, manipulate, and change.

Throughout the process, students were given a metacognitive vocabulary, frame, and voice. This is important because readers must become aware of and alert to their behaviors to be in control of them. Becoming aware of reading processes creates the possibility of changing and improving one's use of these strategic processes. As a result, I believe that students began to set about the business of learning how to learn and learning how to read in creative and productive ways.

What I learned from my students helped me to explore classroom activities and questions that would help elicit and develop evocative and connective response moves, helping many students to develop powerful and necessary response strategies that they previously knew little if anything about.

As I saw the intense visual experience of my engaged readers, and how vitally they related to or became characters during their reading, I was led to develop response activities including drama and art. Drama and art, I believed, could help to develop response and awareness of readerly activity in my many less engaged readers. It was a way of bringing the invisible secrets of engaged readers out into the open, where they could be observed and shared and tried on by other readers. Drama and art naturally engender involvement and a sense of ownership, which I wished to develop in my less engaged readers.

At the same time, I developed a new attitude toward how my less engaged readers were reading. I became aware that many readings that I had considered invalid or impoverished often served student purposes, and at other times provided a springboard to richer readings. This made me more accepting and less goal-driven, monolithic, and judgmental of variant readings. My new attitude helped me become a listener instead of a teller.

Through my research, I was helped to see that I needed to be more open and student-centered as a teacher, getting to know each student and what they could do so that I could teach them "where they were," responding to them personally and offering more opportunities for descriptive and artistic response, for free reading and sharing. The research methods themselves helped me to get to know my students as readers.

I expanded my notions of the types of moves and activities readers engage in. I developed a vocabulary to describe reading and discuss it with readers. My teaching became more informed, and new directions I could take as a teacher to develop and extend my student readers became clearer. I have become more forward-looking—toward the ultimate goals of the individual reader. My classroom, in a way, became "de-schooled," more personal and individual, more like a studio.

What I found helped me as a teacher because I asked and found answers to the question, How can I change my teaching to account for this or encourage that? How, as a teacher, can I build on what this student is doing so that she will start doing these other things as well?

In the following two chapters, I will describe two studies that made use of the response dimensions gleaned from the practices of these readers as a benchmark for rich and engaged reading. This rubric of response dimensions became the basis for shaping instruction that would help other, less engaged readers develop the strategies, stances, and attitudes exhibited by Cora, Joanne, and Ron. It also served as a benchmark to measure the growth of these less engaged readers in experiencing stories throughout the school year.

Perhaps my biggest surprise while studying the engaged readers was how much more sophisticated their involvement was than I had ever imagined. It made me ask how many students I had sold short over the years, not imagining they were "ready" for particular books or "capable" of participating in particular activities or discussions.

Seeing over and over again just how many different dimensions of response the students operated on, and how many moves they made on these dimensions, and how deeply they engaged with literature and with others whom they considered reading partners, I was left with a challenge: How could I help my many less engaged readers to have these same sorts of rich experiences with literature? This was a mission I had failed to complete with many students through my years of teaching.

A third of the way through the school year, I began to use drama as a vehicle for letting less engaged readers into the secrets of engaged reading. When this approach showed promise for some and not as much for others, I pursued a second project—encouraging students to use visual art as a response to literature.

COMMENTARY

LITERARY THEORISTS, HEAR MY CRY!

Another of my favorite jokes involves a professor who, after many years in academia, visits a school. While there he sees many radical innovations and progressive practices. Students are engaged, learning deeply, designing knowledge artifacts on video and with hypermedia. At the end of the day he is asked what he thinks of what he has seen at the school. After a pause he replies, "I have to admit, it looks really good—*in practice*. But my question is: will it work—*in theory*?"

As Michael Smith noted in the Foreword to the First Edition, teachers are often impatient with theory. But we make hundreds upon hundreds of decisions a day that are based on our beliefs—that is, our theories—about what will work at this moment with these students to promote their learning. Theory is involved in all that we do; theory can inform all that we plan to do so that we can do it better. Experts think theoretically and heuristically, with generative and transferable and extensible and revisable principles of practice. Theories are part and parcel of threshold knowledge. Only novices think algorithmically and in formulas.

For example, expert readers and writers of nonfiction (Wilhelm & Smith, 2016) think about how nonfiction texts work as arguments, to make points and create takeaways. They think heuristically, in generative and flexible ways, about how evidence is creatively chosen and how much is needed for this audience and this topic and this text structure. For cause and effect, experts think about how multiple causes and multiple effects relate and how this differs with situations. It is only a novice who uses formulas—who thinks in a simple unidirectional one-cause-for-one-effect manner, or who uses a five-paragraph essay limiting evidence to three examples to guide one's writing or reading.

So it is of vital importance to articulate our theories, to test them against our classroom experiences, to revise and use them in wide-awake ways. Otherwise, we, as teachers, and our students are slaves to unquestioned formulaic habits of our teaching practice, to the salience of various kinds of tradition. Teaching is too important to pursue as a somnambulist!

The Teaching of Literature

In the previous chapters I explored several theories and many studies that helped me think about my classroom and my teaching. But I'll admit that certain kinds of theory, and a lot of what is called research, don't speak to me as a teacher and seem dissociated from the realities of the everyday classroom.

At the time when I was composing the First Edition of *YGBB*, I was fully enamored with the transactional theories of Louise Rosenblatt (1978) and Wolfgang Iser (1978). But over time, I've been persuaded that they didn't go far enough, weren't explicit enough, and didn't do enough to promote the social action projects that literary reading can contribute to. As a teacher, I've become interested in the authors of the texts we read, their agency, and how they construct and code these texts for their readers, and the challenges they provide to change our thinking and behavior. This focus on the author has allowed my teaching of reading to serve my teaching of composing, as anything we notice in a text can be understood as a move made by its author to create meaning and effect, and this in turn is something we can learn to do when we compose our own texts. This noticing and unpacking of authorial moves is a necessary prerequisite to providing precise procedural feedback, which in turn allows us to become better peer editors and thinking partners for each other, and become more metacognitive and self-regulating as readers and composers (see Wilhelm & Smith, 2016).

How I think about and use the dimensions of response I report on here works against some of how Rosenblatt is typically used in schools, namely to foster a pedagogy of personal response, of student-centeredness celebrating what the student thinks and feels.

In stark contrast, it's clear to me that I privilege the higher end of the dimensions, the connective and particularly reflective dimensions, because these are the dimensions used to learn something new about oneself, about reading, or about the text and the world. Though I work very hard with my students on the visual and participatory dimensions, this is because they are struggling readers and I recognize that seeing and participating are necessary to and in service of reading on the higher dimensions.

I don't see reading as personal, but as social. I don't see it as student-centered or idiosyncratic, but as relational, transactional, conventional, and teachable. I believe that there is a definable reading repertoire that can be called expertise and that it is our job to promote this expertise in our students.

Grounded Theory

What I worked to achieve in the *YGBB* study was what can be called *grounded theory*—theory that explains a corpus of data and the experiences and situations from those data.

Many theories and studies don't explain the backstory, that is, how we might explain or understand the reasons behind these findings (why are more readers struggling; why are test scores down?), nor do they suggest what I can do about it (how can I engage my students in ways that will improve their performance?). These are my concerns as a teacher: why and how.

Reflective teaching, as I explored in the last two chapters, focuses directly on real students in real situations and how to help them. As I have articulated in this chapter and want to reinforce, the daily practice of reflective teaching and teacher research shouldn't be something extra (who has the time?) but should be infused in our natural way of teaching and reflecting every day. It should directly serve our own needs and those of our students. It should be part of the everyday agenda. *It should also involve the students in researching and reflecting on their own reading, composing, and learning, as this is what self-regulation and the goal of all democratic education are about* (Wilhelm, Fry, & Douglas, 2014; Wilhelm & Novak, 2011).

When analyzing the data reported here, I developed a theory of engagement to explain expert adolescent literary reading and response. I also developed a theory of teaching for engagement involving the development of interventions to support engagement and expert activity (experimenting with methods that I thought might help less engaged readers take on the stances and strategies of more expert ones, i.e., to meet the correspondence concept). The first theory was based on what my expert adolescent readers did as they read; the second is grounded in the intervention work with the less expert readers and what I found out from these forays of the "tomorrow mind" (see Chapters 4 and 5).

I continue to be astonished when I ask middle schoolers what good readers must be able to do. Like Kevin in Chapter 1, they respond that good readers can answer the questions at the end of their readings, or can pronounce all the words, or can read fast. This is a far and very impoverished cry from what I found that real engaged and expert adolescents do when they read. Certainly, we need to reorient teaching to promote a richer conception of reading, a way of teaching that fits the "correspondence concept," (see p. 136) and one that will lead to enthusiasm and a sense of purpose.

Over the years I have tested and retested my theory of engagement and the construct of the interdependent dimensions of response that comprise literary engagement by constantly comparing the theory to new data and situations. Most recently I've been researching how adults and students make meaning from nonfiction texts, what they notice, how they know to notice those things, and what meaning they make from what they notice (Wilhelm & Smith, 2016). Though I gained many new insights, it was also clear that nonfiction readers go through all the interdependent dimensions of response: orienting themselves to a text and task, participating and visualizing, connecting and reflecting. Though there were some finer differences, the findings and theory remained explanatory to me in regard to what good readers do with complex texts, nonfiction texts, and even multimodal texts of all kinds, and it continues to be informative to me in regard to the kinds of activity I need to promote for those readers who are less expert and engaged, and the kinds of teaching that might promote it. I've found the theory helpful in considering how to promote the growth mindset and engage students in practicing expert strategies.

In other words, theories of sociocultural inquiry teaching and learning, and the theory of engaged reading expressed here, continue to do their jobs for me and for my students. The theories help me to teach students, and they help students to learn. They help me to practice cognitive apprenticeship. They are *grounded theories* that *do work*.

These theories are also generative, and I've continued to consider some instructional dilemmas around promoting engagement along the various response dimensions. Literary theory of various kinds has continued to help me navigate my way through these as a teacher. This has been particularly true for issues implicated in the 10th dimension (evaluating the author and the self as a reader), and how these relate to the 8th and 9th dimensions (recognizing literary conventions and reading as a transaction, respectively). Whenever an author composes, just as I am doing now, there is an attempt to communicate through the text. The author expects a reader who is both willing to read in the way the text is constructed to be read, and the capacity to read in that way. A centerpiece of my teaching and research agendas since writing YGBB has been about developing this willingness and this capacity. As such, I've been concerned by the tension between the freedom of the reader versus the constraints offered by texts, textuality, and textual conventions used by an author to communicate meaning. This tension plays out even more obviously in the reading of nonfiction texts, which tend to be less open than fiction, and do more to highlight specific messages and meanings.

Thinking about Engagement: The Toolish, Not the Schoolish

In the teaching and research that led to the writing of YGBB, a primary concern was with *engaging* my reluctant readers. Engagement certainly includes motivation and my desire to help my struggling students see that in fact reading is something worth doing, because of both personal satisfactions and ways of working socially in the world. But engagement, in my conception, is something much more: It is about helping students to see that they have the capacity to read in powerful ways; it is about knowing how to construct meanings with texts; it is about developing and using a wide and flexible repertoire of strategies that help the reader engage with meanings and the authors who construct these.

Therein lies the dilemma. Much of what might motivate in the near term can undermine the second goal of becoming more expert. For example, providing choice is motivating. It means you can stake your identity as a reader and a person as you pursue personally meaningful and accessible readings. But my students often choose the kinds of texts they already like and know how to read, and they tend to read them in habitual and comfortable ways. I conceive of teaching as apprenticeship, and my job as a teacher as nudging and pushing my students toward greater motivation and expertise, as helping them outgrow their current selves to become and do and be something more. I therefore need to value and celebrate their choices and how these help them express and enjoy their current state of being. At the same time, I also need to motivate them and assist them in finding and reading books they would not necessarily read on their own, and to develop new levels of strategic facility.

Cognitive science offers us a powerful tool for thinking about our teaching called the *correspondence concept*. The correspondence concept simply means that at the end of any instructional activity, reading, lesson, or unit, the learner should have something in her head that more nearly and identifiably approaches what an expert has in hers, or learning and competence have not been promoted (Bereiter, 2004; Nickerson, 1985). Edgar Schuster (2003) argues that much of what we teach in school consists of "mythrules," that is, ideas or processes that only count in school, but not in real expert activity. For example, much of what we teach in school does not fit what real readers and writers actually do (see Smith & Wilhelm, 2007, for a full discussion of this idea as it applies to writing). Schuster urges teachers to apply the "real writer test" or the "real reader test" to any instruction. If our teaching does not directly mirror what real writers or readers (or ethicists, social scientists, mathematicians, et al.) actually do, then our instruction is moving our students away from expertise; it is in fact making them stupider.

So how do we promote engagement and develop new repertoires that more closely match what experts know and do? We certainly can't use the information-transmission teaching that dominates American education. We do need to collaborate with students as real readers and writers. One salient insight from our boys research studies (Smith & Wilhelm, 2002; 2006) is that all of the studied boys *wanted* a significant challenge, but they also wanted the assistance needed to successfully address it. They complained more that school was too easy than that it was too hard. And when it was hard, they didn't complain about the hardness, but about the lack of help in meeting the challenge. Above all else, they privileged the development of new and usable competence, which they could immediately apply to their lives and current work. Their bitterest complaints about school were reserved for "busywork" and what we came to call the "schoolish"—work, like mythrules, that only counts in school.

Accomplished literary reading is hard and complex work, but it is work that can provide immediate pleasures and unique, powerful ways of knowing that can lead to new ways of being and doing, if only we teach in ways that promote this. I have been immeasurably helped in my thinking about how to do this by the theory of authorial reading (Rabinowitz & Smith, 1998).

Authorial Reading

According to the theory of authorial reading, the reader's first job is to comprehend the text the way it was constructed to be understood (Rabinowitz & Smith, 1998). That is, authorial reading requires us to first consider what is directly stated and implied through conventional ways of coding and structuring texts, to take on and fulfill the reading role the text asks us to play. This is about respecting the text that has been constructed, about working to understand it in the terms laid out by the author who wrote it.

Writers engage in an implicit contract with readers, and vice versa. Authors expect readers to know what to notice in the kind of text they are writing, and how to interpret these noticings (Wilhelm & Smith, 2016). Narrative fiction works in particular ways that need to be understood, honored, and used by readers and writers of narrative fiction (Wilhelm, Smith, & Fredricksen, 2013). Nonfiction text structures have specific features and demands that differ greatly from narrative, and readers who want to understand how authors create nonfiction texts for meaning and effect need to understand these conventions (operating on dimension 8: Understanding conventions and 9: How to use these to transact with the text; see Wilhelm, Smith, & Fredricksen, 2013 and Wilhelm & Smith, 2016 for a full discussion involving nonfiction text structures).

This kind of respectful attention can be powerfully modeled and then mentored through various means, and my preferred means is the think-aloud (see the guidelines for thinking aloud in Exhibit 3.1). When students are faced with a new kind of textual structure or genre (e.g., a nonfiction essay embedding definition and comparison in service of classification, as is the case in much creative nonfictional science writing like that of David Quammen), thinking aloud will be a powerful technique for noticing the text features and conventions, making meaning of them, and then being mentored to do so with others and then on one's own. Thinking aloud models *how* to notice and interpret specific textual features and moves in a context of reading a real text for a real purpose. And think-alouds quickly become collaborative forms of mentoring (as students help us to think aloud and then help one another), and then a way to monitor what students are doing so the teacher can provide procedural feedback or intervene to provide needed assistance. Later the reader should explore ramifications, silences, other perspectives, and one's own sensibilities to construct an understanding that goes around and beyond the text in a move toward critical literacy and evaluative understanding. This can involve resistance to the text and its construction and message, as well as accepting and adapting that message for oneself. This too can be modeled and mentored through thinking aloud.

Texts are always about *something*, and they always work to communicate and convince us to know, believe, and even do things regarding that something. My own work in *YGBB* promotes the notion that the reader is a creative producer of meanings who must bring her own interests and background experiences to bear, but I would argue also that expert readers create meaning in partnership with a text—and therefore with the author who constructed it—and that the reader's meaning-making is constrained by the rules and conventions that govern how texts are constructed and communicate meaning.

Texts constrain meaning in many ways. For example, texts constrain meaning by their very partiality. They offer us a "secondary world" that seems to stand in for the whole world. But in fact it is not the whole world; it is only a small slice of the world offered from a very particular perspective. And what is offered through that small slice is a unique way of seeing and understanding that is provided by the perspective. We are given a new way of perceiving, but only if we can leave our own worldview behind and read in the way and from the perspective that the text asks us to take on.

The writer composing a text works with a knowledge base that he shares with readers. He positions his work in regard to other texts in that genre that use particular text structures and conventions that he will expect his reader to interpret, use, and understand in a particular way. Whereas authors of literary fiction may focus on irony, unreliable narrators, symbolism, and the like, nonfiction authors might use comparisons, definitions, grouping, and cause-effect in order to create meaning and effect. Narrative always works on the logic of chronology and causality, but every nonfiction text using informational text structures will work with categories (by comparing and contrasting categories, or grouping them in a classification, for instance) in radically different and usually combined and embedded ways (for a thorough discussion, see Wilhelm, Smith, & Fredricksen, 2013).

Because of this, all texts are political—they *position* us to see this partial slice of the world in a socially or culturally constructed way that may not match our own and that will serve particular ends. This is not a bad thing. Even if we reject the projected view, we will have deepened our understanding and seen things from a different point of view. This is necessary to the process of growth, learning, and understanding and to creating an informed worldview.

In other words, authorial reading asks us to do our best to comprehend what an author is attempting to communicate and convince us of through the text she has purposefully constructed, and *then* to exercise the additional responsibility to interrogate and elaborate those messages; consider ramifications and consequences; evaluate and judge these; and eventually to embrace, adapt, offer alternatives to, or resist the messages in some way, and perhaps to take some kind of action based on that decision. I've been experimenting with Questioning the Author (QtA) (Beck & McKeown, 2006) as a way to help students go through this authorial reading process, as you will see in Exhibit 3.2.

Authorial reading resonates with Bakhtin's concept of "reciprocity." As Nystrand (1997) puts it:

> At the heart of Bakhtin's social logic is a reciprocity of roles: that is, the roles of teacher and learner (and parent and child, writer and reader, cop and speeder, lover and loved, etc.) each respectively and mutually entails those of the other, the one in effect defining the parameters of meaning and communication of the other. (p. 10)

Nystrand goes on to explain that acts we might consider to be "individual," like mailing a letter, reading, or any kind of learning, are in fact social, since "each is premised on appropriate and respective acts by reciprocal others" (p. 10). For example, mailing a letter assumes postal workers and the letter's recipient and assumes particular expectations of these parties; writers likewise assume a reader who will know how to read their text.

Reading, in these terms, is the evolution of understanding through the co-construction of meaning that occurs in "the unique interaction between author and reader, the play of two consciousnesses" (Bakhtin/Medvedev, 1985, p. 128, as cited in Nystrand, 1997).

Vygotskians call this kind of interplay the achievement of "intersubjectivity," in which we take on the understandings of another and make this understanding our own, however tentatively. In effect, we try on other perspectives and ways of knowing before taking them on or appropriating them in some form for ourselves.

In his wonderful book on the ethics of reading, *The Company We Keep*, Wayne Booth (1988) famously proclaims that we can and do learn from texts and one another, but *only if* we learn how to listen carefully and respectfully before judging and using what we learn.

The religious scholar Karen Armstrong maintains that we can only have peace and justice when we create "dialogic spaces" where "we deeply consider the concerns and anxieties of others—of people who are truly different from us" (Armstrong, 2005). She argues that this kind of dialogue is essential to democracy and to modernity. Think how many challenges of the current world are exacerbated by retaining monologic worldviews instead of engaging the dialogic.

Goodlad, Mantle-Bromley, and Goodlad emphasize:

> Meaningful interactions with others are an essential element of learning. Part of our apprenticeship to liberty must be to learn to listen to and understand the views of others, and to appreciate the values inherent in those views—even if, in the end, we may disagree with them. (1994, p. 82)

These comments remind me of Vygotsky's (1978) contention that the self is the self only in relationship. It follows that we can only become a "new self" through new relationships—relationships with texts, the world, each other—by achieving intersubjectivity with another consciousness by taking on, however tentatively, a different point of view. It also follows that we need to communicate with others to be part of a community. But this kind of communal conversation and dialogue can be difficult to achieve in a classroom, or elsewhere. Teachers and students will need to be assisted in learning the skills and using the structures that lead to rich transaction and the learning that can be achieved through dialogue. Providing such assistance and structures is the subject of the next two chapters.

This is the point of authorial reading, to respect the author and her text, and after comprehending it to grant it the seriousness of reflection and evaluation so we make what we learn from that conversation our own, and also part of a continuing and ongoing social dialogue. I hope that I've made the point that this kind of reading is not only important to expert reading, but also to all learning, to critical literacy, and to democratic interaction and living (see Wilhelm, Fry, & Douglass, 2014; Wilhelm & Novak, 2011). As such, authorial reading is at the heart of any project I pursue in my classroom.

Exhibit 3.1. General Steps for Modeling a Think-Aloud

Step 1: Choose a short text (or section of text).
- If the text and think-aloud are used to teach a particular strategy or strategies (a cued think-aloud), then this excerpt should be a "concentrated sample" (i.e., one that requires and rewards using that strategy/ies more than once).

Step 2: In a cued think-aloud for teaching specific strategies, choose one or two strategies to highlight. (You can also do a free response think-aloud, in which you can report on everything you are noticing, thinking, feeling and doing as you read, but this is less assistive in teaching students new strategies.)

Step 3: State your purpose(s) in using the strategy/ies to understand meaning and effect.

Step 4: Read the text aloud to students and think aloud as you do so. Talk off the top of your head to model what you notice, how and why you knew to notice it, and how you interpreted what you noticed.

Step 5: Underline the words and phrases that helped tip you off to use a particular strategy. Use a projection device to show how you mark and annotate the text.

Step 6: Name the strategies used to notice and interpret.

Step 7: Provide procedural feedback to the author that specifically identifies and describes the move/strategy used, and the meaning and effect achieved through it.

Step 8: Identify other situations (other texts they will soon read or compose, as well as real-world situations) in which students could use these strategies. This is a significant way to cultivate a spirit of transfer. Involve students in brainstorming.

Step 9: (option for authorial reading) Once the text has been read the way an author constructed it to be read, then re-read it to demonstrate how you interrogate the meaning and what it asks you to know, believe, or do. Model agreement, questioning, and resistance as appropriate. Highlight to students that just like in conversation, you must first read to understand a text and the intelligence that created it as it wanted to be understood; then one should consider if one wants to agree or resist, and to what degree.

Step 10: Reinforce the process and strategies with follow-up lessons in which students use the same tip-offs and rules of notice to recognize that a strategy should be used, and then use that strategy to create meaning and effect.

Adapted from Wilhelm (2012a).

Exhibit 3.2. QtA for Authorial Reading of Texts

These are queries I've found useful with my own students that promote authorial reading. Notice the focus on interpretation (topical research into the meaning of the text as it was constructed to be read) and evaluation/application (critical inquiry into what the text should mean and lead to in the world). These are very usefully modeled and practiced with think-alouds. The queries are meant to be a menu and can be selected for use as appropriate. They can be pursued in any order that works to assist the reader's engagement with the ideas of the text.

Start-Off Queries (also known as Initiating Queries)

1. Who is the author of this piece? What do we know about this author?

2. Who is the audience for this piece? (Am I part of this audience? What would I have to know, believe, or be to become part of this audience?)
3. How does the author position me toward the topic? Am I positioned with a person or a perspective, for instance?
4. What might be her purpose and agenda in writing this text?
5. What point of view or group perspective is being expressed?
6. What is the author writing about? (What is the general subject or topic?)
7. What important information has the author presented so far? (What are the key details? How do we know to notice these details? How do they connect to other key details, both explicitly and implicitly?)
8. What is the author's point so far? (What is the main idea or central focus? What conclusion do the key details add up to? What does the author want me to know, think, believe or do?)

Follow-Up Queries (also known as Local-Level Queries)

1. What does the author want the reader to notice in this segment? And think, believe, or do as a result?
2. Why is the author telling me this information right now? In this way? In this order?
3. How is the text organized to reinforce key details and the main point the author is trying to make?
4. Did the author explain this clearly? Are we convinced of her point of view?
5. Is this consistent with what we knew before reading? With what the author communicated earlier in the reading?
6. What differences or similarities do we see between ideas from the reading, and between these ideas and those from other readings and from our experience/the world?
7. What ideas are puzzling? Distressing? Emotionally charged?
8. What would we like to know more about?
9. What strategies do we need to use to read this part of the text? How do we know (what tip-offs for strategy use have been coded into the text)?
10. Why did certain things happen? What might be the causes of certain effects?
11. How would you act or feel if you were a character or person featured in this text?
12. How might what we are learning influence the future? Our personal behavior? World consequences? What might be future effects of the situations described?
13. What could be done to change or improve the situation?
14. How do the ideas connect to what we already care about? How do they relate to our own values, attitudes, or beliefs?
15. How well does the author convince us to think or behave in a certain way? Is this case made explicitly or implicitly?

Adapted from Wilhelm (2007).

4

Using Drama to Extend the Reader

Reader response theorists have often focused on ideal reading, on the general stance and processes of proficient and engaged readers like Cora, Joanne, and Ron. Though I too worked hard to help my proficient readers outgrow themselves, I was especially concerned with those many other students who struggled with or resisted the reading act. I have always regarded reading of any kind, but especially of literature, as a unique and powerful way of knowing about self, others, and the world. Seeing students who went to great lengths to avoid reading made me ask what was different about their history, experience, and attitudes as readers from those of more engaged readers. I felt as if these reluctant readers had been sitting on the bench during the big game, completely bored, without even realizing they hadn't participated in the action. I asked myself how I could help them get into the game of reading and experience in some way its potential thrills and excitement.

I decided to use techniques of story theater (using the text as a script) to help students experience the world of a text, and techniques of story drama (using the text as a starting point) to help them explore the implications and possibilities at the edge of texts. The story I will tell in this chapter is about three reluctant readers who were helped by these dramatic interventions. Marvin, Kevin, and Libby were helped by drama to experience and take on for themselves some of the moves and strategies of more engaged readers. They also began, through the dramas, to rethink the nature and possibilities of reading.

Rosenblatt (1978) asserts that "the benefits of literature can emerge only from creative activity on the part of the reader himself" (p. 276).

She argues that the reader must evoke and exert control over the ideas, sensations, feelings, and images that are experienced while reading. The text acts both as a stimulus that activates a reader's past experience and as a guide or blueprint for selecting, rejecting, and ordering that experience. Rosenblatt even makes a specific comparison between reading and acting in a drama: "We accept the fact that the actor infuses his own voice, his own body, his own gestures—in short, his own interpretation—into the words of the text. Is he not simply carrying to its ultimate manifestation what each of us as readers of the text must do?" (1978, p. 13). In this view, literary reading requires that readers both evoke and participate in imaginary worlds whose creation is stimulated and guided by the text. Reading literature is not the reception of meaning, but the reader's participation in a "transaction" with text that produces meaning. Yet this was a conception of reading that my less engaged readers failed to understand or enact, and that left some of them scoffing.

Iser (1978) argues similarly that "apprehension of a literary work comes about through the interaction between the reader's presence in the text and his habitual experiences, which are now a past orientation. As such it is not a passive process of acceptance, but a productive response" (p. 113). For Iser, most stories cannot be fruitfully enjoyed and understood solely through explicitly articulated action because the text is filled with gaps that the reader must fill and elaborate upon to create a "virtual world."

Though Ron, Joanne, and Cora engaged in many elaborative reading activities, most of my other students did not. Eco (1978) calls such elaborative activities "taking inferential walks" and writes:

> Texts are lazy machineries that ask someone [the reader] to do part of their job. . . . Frequently . . . a text tells the reader about the event A and, after a while, about the event E, taking for granted that the reader has already anticipated the dependent events B, C, D. (pp. 214, 215)

I believe that at least for less engaged readers, the dimensions of response are order-dependent; I found that the less engaged readers I studied did not respond in connective or reflective ways to their reading unless they first overtly responded on all of the evocative dimensions. I would like to make the claim that this is the case with all readers, but the data are too murky. Engaged readers seem to respond simultaneously on many if not all of these dimensions, sometimes privileging a highly reflective dimension without really discussing their response on an evocative one.

The findings about the less engaged readers strike me as very important. The collected information reveals that we often ask less engaged readers to reflect on something that they have not experienced. This suggests that if we would help them to develop evocative, experiential response to literature, response on other dimensions would be possible for them—and the door to engaging literary worlds would finally be opened. Defining the dimensions of evocative response and thinking about questions and activities to encourage this sort of response seem to me to be important steps for teachers to take toward helping less engaged readers into the experience of reading.

My question at the point when I began to use drama, some 12 weeks into the school year, was, How could I help the rest of my student readers to think of reading as something that required the creation of meanings that were not completely printed on the page? How could I help them use words to create characters and pictures that went beyond the words? It was then that I began to think of *story theater,* or enacting *story events,* and story drama, or enacting story suggestions and possibilities, as a way to help these readers.

WHY DRAMA?

Benton (1983) describes the act of reading as the creation of "secondary worlds" (a term he borrows from Tolkien, 1964) and the involvement and enactment of dramatic activity within those worlds. Harding (1937, 1962) and Britton (1984) support this view when they describe what they call "the participant stance" of the reader as an important dimension of reading. This stance puts the reader inside the secondary world of a story, experiencing and elaborating upon it from within. The reader taking this stance, as seen with Cora and the other engaged readers, makes moves to enter the story world and to move about inside it. These theorists also describe the "spectator role" (also exemplified in great detail by Ron, Joanne, and Cora), in which a reader sees the text as an object, reflecting and commenting upon it. Rosenblatt (1978) and others have pointed out that most teaching and research have focused on the spectator stance and how a reader interprets, evaluates, and reflects on the evoked world of the text. Little emphasis has been placed on what readers actually do to go beyond simple comprehension of story action to evoke the text and elaborate upon it as a "story participant." Students are thus often asked to interpret a story by gazing and reflecting upon what they have never learned to experience.

Theory and research agree that what highly engaged readers do as they read is dramatic in nature. In just this vein, Enciso (1992) describes engagement in reading as our entry into the world of the story and the intense involvement we feel as we imagine and interpret the characters, setting, events, and thematic possibilities of literary texts. It includes a complex interplay of imaginative and intellectual processes that are typically private and elusive, yet critical to comprehension and pleasure in reading. (p. 1)

Enciso (1990) describes engaged readers taking on and enacting various roles and intensely visualizing particular settings and scenes. These same activities were apparent in the responses of Ron, Cora, and Joanne, but I had little evidence that any of my other readers engaged with texts in this way.

Other research indicates that readers must first take interest in the action and setting of the story and begin to participate in a "story world" before response can occur on other dimensions, such as connecting the story to their lives or reflecting upon the story, its construction, or its authorship (Thomson, 1987). The reader, after taking unreflective interest in the story, may then evoke and enter what Bruner (1986) describes as a "landscape of action" that is directly stimulated by the facts of the story. Such interest and participation are a prerequisite to engagement on "the landscape of consciousness," in which the reader is pulled by the possibilities and potentialities of the story facts into "what those involved in the action know, think or feel, or do not know, think or feel" (p. 14).

Many other average or less engaged readers tend to take only an unreflective interest in action, or may proceed to read in a more engaged fashion, but still only on "the landscape of action." These readers do not go beyond the text, they do not actively create meaning as they elaborate upon the story experience (Thomson, 1987; Wilhelm, 1992). Enciso (1992) points out that as Barthes (1986) suggests, these readers are often bored by reading, because without engagement on both of these landscapes the reader is unable to "produce the text, play it, release it, make it go" (p. 63).

Pulling in Reluctant Readers

But what about my many less engaged readers? In spite of these views on productive reading, a body of research on remedial reading supports the view that many less proficient readers do not naturally and spontaneously experience literature as participants. This lack of involvement suggests why they are reluctant to read and have negative attitudes toward reading. It also suggests why a highly participatory activity such as drama, or creative activities such as visual art, used in conjunction with the reading of particular stories, might help them to experience stories in the highly satisfying way of engaged readers.

Most of the research regarding remedial or less proficient reading focuses on word identification and provides little insight into the obstacles and operational difficulties experienced by these readers. The studies that have been conducted strongly suggest that these readers do not make use of a productive conception of reading or the strategies necessary to consummate the sort of reader/text relationship that allows for an "aesthetic" (Rosenblatt, 1978) literary transaction and experience. So, I found myself asking, how can classroom activity help students to take on this kind of active reading role and to rethink the nature of the reading act?

Less proficient readers have been shown to read more slowly and less accurately than better readers. They read in local, piecemeal ways and do not make use of either extratextual information such as their personal experiences, known as schematic knowledge, or larger units of intratextual information, such as a sense of textual configuration and coherence (Cromer, 1970; Daneman & Carpenter, 1980; Perfetti & Lesgold, 1979). Yet the use of extratextual information to create global meanings is a process necessary to the creation and sustaining of what Edmiston (1991) calls "a drama world," which suggests that drama would be one way of helping students to bring their background experiences, schema knowledge, interests, desires, and questions to bear on the reading act.

Johnston (1985) has posited that reading problems result from a combination of negative attitudes, conceptual difficulties, and self-defeating strategies. I thought this was true of many of my own students. Gambrell and Bales (1986) found further that lower-ability readers did not "spontaneously employ mental imagery as a strategy," therefore depriving them of full evocation and participation in a story world. And less proficient readers studied by Purcell-Gates (1991) were also at a loss for strategies for stepping into and sustaining "envisionments." They did not make use of strategies for creating meaning by building relationships with characters, taking their perspectives, and imagining and visualizing secondary worlds.

Turning Reading into an Active Process

These studies imply that less proficient readers tend to conceive of reading as a decoding process rather than as active meaning-making (Gambrell & Heathington, 1981), an attitude that is certainly reinforced by traditional questioning and discussion patterns regarding literature.

Less engaged readers' approach to reading is passive; the text itself is regarded as expressing meaning to be received, instead of constructed (Johnston & Winograd, 1983). This was certainly the case for many of my own student readers, as evidenced by their initial reading attitude inventories.

As I began to think about using new classroom techniques to support the notion of reading as the active construction of meaning, I found that the use of dramatic and artistic activity to help readers both experience and learn from text is supported by a wide variety of research in language, literacy, learning, and cognition throughout various content areas (Barnes, 1986; Knapp, Stearns, John, & Zucker, 1988; Rosenblatt, 1978; Vygotsky, 1978; Wade, 1983). Active, participatory experiences enhance motivation and concept attainment (Bransford, 1979; Reid, 1988). Active participation, such as that incorporated in the creation of drama and visual art, creates a context for more sophisticated comprehension and the creation of elaborated meanings made with text because background schemata are necessarily activated and created, a foundational aspect of proficient reading (Hansen, 1981; Langer, 1984).

Rosenblatt (1978, 1982) has repeatedly stressed that "response" to literature is not something a text may "do" to a reader, but is instead a highly complex production of meaning. Rosenblatt (1978) points out the difference between the text, made up of words on a page, and the aesthetic experience, or "lived-through evocation," of the literary work. A reader's reflection on those experiences is what is organized into an interpretation (pp. 69–70). Further, Rosenblatt (1982) emphasizes that reading is an experience and that as teachers "our initial function is to deepen the experience . . . to return to, relive, savor, the experience" (p. 275).

Less proficient and less engaged readers must learn to think differently about the reading act and learn how to participate in the experience of literature and construction of literary meaning. My own classroom experience told me that this engagement will not occur spontaneously, but that it might be taught through the modeling of expert reading strategies and the use of participatory literary activities. As I wrote in my journal:

> It's becoming clear to me that reading is one of the creative arts. The reader has to develop and use artistic tools to create people and pictures. But how can I convince my students of this; give them this experience of reading as artistic creation? Maybe by using activities such as drama and art that encourage and scaffold active response? And that

can show, right out in the open, what the reader is doing and the
meaning that has been created? (October 1992)

Semiotic theory based on Pierce (1931/1958) argues that artistic sign
systems have similar potential to linguistic ones in their power to represent knowledge, facilitate learning, and form new experiences and concepts; and that artistic representations are used by readers creating and
responding to "story worlds" involved with transactions with texts (cf.
Smagorinsky & Coppock, 1994). According to this view, readers construct a reality rather than discover it, and can construct it only through
signs and in contexts that validate the use of the signs. Pierce is particularly insistent on the vital role of the icon, or concrete image, in all
thought and communication, arguing that "The only way of directly
communicating an idea is by means of an icon; and every indirect method
of communicating an idea must depend for its establishment upon the
use of an icon" (vol. 2, p. 158). In other words, if I say the word "apple,"
it means nothing unless you picture an apple in your mind. The word is
a symbol that evokes an icon, or concrete image. If the word doesn't
evoke a picture, no meaning has been made.

If iconic response is prerequisite to other forms of response, then
reluctant readers might benefit from learning to project concrete, iconic
representations of stories such as those achieved through activities such
as drama and visual art. They then might be able to sustain or extend
these representations in their mind, and use them as objects to think
with.

So it was that 12 weeks into the school year, my students and I set off
on an exploratory journey to investigate the extent to which drama might
help less proficient readers to engage in the activities of more proficient
readers, and to reconceive of the act of reading and of themselves as
readers.

The questions driving this classroom study included:

◆ How might drama guide and scaffold student readers' development
  of the productive response of more expert readers, as defined by the
  activities of Cora, Ron, and Joanne?
◆ How might dramatic activity guide and support student efforts to
  fill textual gaps and to elaborate on and move around in textual
  worlds?
◆ How might drama engender reflection about the reading experience
  and the students' conceptions of the reading act itself?

THE STUDENTS: KEVIN, MARVIN, AND LIBBY

The drama study involved all of my students enrolled in the two reading/ language arts classes that mainstreamed the school's EEN (exceptional educational needs) population of students labeled both LD (learning disabled) and ED (emotionally disturbed). All students participated in the pre- and postdrama evaluation procedures and were observed throughout the project. Both classes included students who regarded themselves as nonreaders, who were regarded by teachers as less proficient readers, and who expressed in various ways their lack of motivation and resistance to reading.

For the purpose of collecting and analyzing a manageable set of data, I chose three case study students (from my original set of nine case study students) to help me tell a coherent story about drama as a way of entering and responding to literature. These three were students for whom drama seemed to work in powerful ways, and that is why I have chosen to tell their stories.

The first student, Kevin, was a regular education student considered to be a less proficient and unmotivated reader both by himself and by his previous teachers; the second student, Marvin, was labeled both LD and ED; and the third student, Libby, was labeled LD but differed from many of her classmates because she enjoyed reading on her own. The students were selected on the basis of how well they represented a cross-section of students having some difficulty with their reading and response, and on their availability for interviews during my one free period.

Kevin was fairly representative of approximately 40 percent of the regular education students in the two study classes who indicated on the prestudy survey that they were "nonreaders," that they read "rarely," and that they regarded reading solely as a "school activity."

A small, wiry, and very pleasant boy, Kevin could not seem to sit still. Several of his past and present teachers indicated that he could have ADHD (attention deficit/hyperactivity disorder), but a formal referral had not yet been made. He wore flannel shirts and a hunting jacket with a tag flapping on the back. He owned a game farm at home, which he ran by himself, and demonstrated complete devotion to hunting. He expressed that reading was "a boring waste of time," though his test results on the Analytical Reading Inventory (Woods & Moe, 1989) placed him on the seventh-grade level for Word Recognition and the fifth-grade level for Independent Comprehension. Kevin was described by another teacher as "fairly average, at best" and by another as "a squirrelly kid, never serious . . . a pain in the butt."

In his initial interview, Kevin indicated that he "never read stories. I mean, what for?" but that he did sometimes read "to learn things, you know. Like about hunting and fishing or raising animals." His only extra-curricular reading was *Field and Stream* magazine.

Marvin (who was introduced at the beginning of Chapter One) was fairly representative of the EEN students, most of whom indicated that they were "poor readers," that they "never" read, and that they regarded reading solely as a "school activity" that should be avoided or faked whenever possible. Marvin was a big boy for his age, both heftier and taller than his teachers, and was a very low ability reader. He liked to wear black Metallica T-shirts and unlaced black Nike high-top basket-ball shoes. His test results indicated a second-grade level for Word Recognition and a first-grade level for Independent Comprehension. His scores were approximately one to two grade levels below those of his LD classmates.

Marvin was often in trouble for hitting and pushing other students, and for constantly requesting hall passes to go the restroom. A former teacher told me: "He can't read. He'll never be a reader." Early in the year, one of Marvin's most frequently invoked expressions was: "Reading is stupid!" Marvin stated that he "never" read outside school. In fact, according to all of his teachers, he rarely read in school, usually bothering other students, acting out, or staring into space when given reading time. Marvin went so far as to state: "It's not like I'm missing something [by not reading]!"

Libby was a very small and slightly built girl with long, straight brown hair. She was very serious and shy and seemed to blend inconspicuously into the class, never drawing attention to herself. She preferred T-shirts and jeans, often wearing subdued colors such as watery yellows or greens. The Analytical Reading Inventory indicated that she could read inde-pendently and recognize words on the fifth-grade level.

Libby represented an entirely different kettle of fish, for despite her LD label, she indicated that "I like reading" and was often seen carrying and reading books. However, she felt that she was not a good reader because she had trouble answering questions about what she had read and performed poorly on quizzes and tests regarding her reading. She reported that she liked "stories about girls like me," but that she had trouble understanding stories "where the characters aren't like me." She disliked most of the reading she did for school except "when I get to choose." She particularly liked series of books such as the American Girls, Baby-sitters Club, and Nancy Drew. She told me that she disliked school because "all you do is sit, sit, sit and write, write, write . . . you never get to do anything. . . . I don't like school 'cause you can't do what you want. School blocks you from what you like to do." She told me that she could learn more staying at home and "reading what I want." She liked only the social aspect of school: "I like to see my friends." Her favorite activity was horseback riding, which she did once a week at a local farm. "I like working in a horse barn. In the barn I get to do and learn things."

BEFORE DRAMA

For the 12 weeks prior to the use of drama as an intervention, I collected information and coded student response to stories into 10 dimensions, as described previously in Chapter Three. In contrast to the rich response data revealed by these three engaged readers, Kevin, Marvin, and Libby related few codable data about what they did as readers to evoke and reflect on story worlds.

Literal Reading: But It Doesn't Say

Libby was by far the most active reader of the three, and did indicate some awareness of her reading strategies and could report on seeing story worlds and relating to characters in particular kinds of stories. In conversation and her literary letters about her free-choice reading, Libby was able to discuss characters' appearances and settings. She almost always did so by comparing characters to people she knew—usually her sister or her friend Jenna. Nearly all characters looked like and reminded her of a small group of people she knew and liked. However, when reading a story in class that was less familiar to her than the stock characters and situations of her favorite series, she often looked surprised and was unable to answer questions about character and setting. "It's really hard to tell," she'd report, "the book really doesn't say much stuff about how things are." She often told me that the stories we read in class were "kind of plain." When I pressed her on what she meant by this, she told me that "It's the characters. I don't feel like they're like me. I don't get the story. It's just kind of plain. Nothing is happening. I don't feel like I know anybody so I don't like it very much."

Though she was able to evoke characters and story worlds in particular kinds of books, Libby had great difficulty in doing so with unfamiliar material. She recognized the differences in her various reading experiences, but she seemed at a loss about how to engage with unfamiliar stories in the same way that she did with her favorite books, which she liked because "you get to know the same characters over and over again, or new ones kind of like people you really know." Reading was better for her, she told me, "when I don't work so hard on the words because I already know stuff about the people and places." (This demonstrates the importance of previous life experience and the activation of this prior knowledge, or "schema," to reading.)

Then there was Marvin. On one occasion during this first part of the year, I was reading a baseball story with Marvin. He read aloud that "Jack slid into second and kuh-nocked his kuh-nee," pronouncing both silent k's. When asked what a "kuh-nee" could possibly be, Marvin shrugged. "I just told you what it says. How should I know what it means?" Marvin often indicated that it was the reader's job to pronounce words, but not to make meaning. When asked if he could "see" what was happening in the story, Marvin replied, "No." Marvin offered that he had both played baseball and been a spectator at baseball games. So he was asked what body parts one was likely to injure when sliding into second base. Eventually, Marvin acknowledged that the "kuh-nee" was probably a "knee."

Later in the story I asked Marvin who was behind the plate calling balls and strikes. "It doesn't say," he informed me, which was true in the literal sense.

"But Marvin," I asked, "you play baseball. Who calls balls and strikes?"

"The umpire," he replied. "But it doesn't say who's doing it here!" When I pursued the issue, he pushed the story across the desk to me and said, "Okay, you find it. Go ahead. You find it then!"

Marvin was not creating or visualizing a story world in his head, nor was he bringing his life to literature to construct a meaningful experience with the text. Further, he expected everything of importance to be clearly stated in the text.

I had a similar experience with Kevin as the class began reading *The Incredible Journey*. I asked Kevin what Mrs. Oakes looked like. "It doesn't say," he answered.

"But what do we know about her?" I persisted.

Kevin became cautious. "Well, it says she's middle-aged . . . she cleans and cooks . . . sort of a maid . . . she lives down the road with her husband. . . ."

"So," I asked triumphantly, springing the trap, "what might she look like? What clothes will she wear to the house? What color hair? Do you think she likes the animals?"

Now Kevin was exasperated. "It doesn't SAY," he replied testily. Later during our conference he told me, "I know what the story says. It's not fair for you to ask me what it doesn't say."

As an experiment, I asked several less proficient readers, including Kevin and Marvin, to select a Mrs. Oakes look-alike from several photographs cut out of magazines. One photograph was of a young, stylishly dressed career woman in high heels, carrying a briefcase. Another was of an older, grandmotherly type baking bread, and so on. The students were unwilling to make a choice. "We really don't know what she looks like," one student complained. "There are no pictures of her in the book," another told me by way of explaining why he was not sure. Oddly enough, the book had included an engraved picture of Mrs. Oakes that neither student had noticed or processed.

That next Monday I asked another group of less engaged readers, including Libby, to read an Eskimo legend. The story was short, economically told, and highly suggestive. After reading it, the students were asked to describe the landscape of the story, the houses, what the people looked like, and how they dressed. Their primary response, despite the fact that they knew it was an Eskimo story: "It doesn't say." Libby told me that there was "nothing there to get. It [the story] made me feel kind of dumb."

I asked the students about the landscape near the Arctic Circle, and together they could describe it beautifully, with tundra adorned by wolves and icebergs dotted with seals and polar bears. References were made to the scenery in the movies *White Fang* and *Never Cry Wolf*.

The students knew what Eskimos looked like and about igloos and even eating whale blubber. But they used none of this information to build a story world, however, because the text did not include the information and the students did not instantiate it. "It doesn't really say anything," Libby told me. She, like her classmates, did not seem to recognize the inferential and elaborative work that the story was asking her to do.

Passive Reading: Tell Me What It Says

Like many of their classmates, neither Kevin nor Marvin played an active role in creating meaning with text. Neither brought his life to literature nor took a literary experience back to his life. Neither indicated in any way that he had "experienced" literature at all. Both conceived of reading as the decoding of words. Marvin did not expect reading to be meaningful, and if he had a goal it was to identify individual words successfully; for Kevin, if meaning existed it was "in there," inside the text waiting to be discovered. Successful reading was being able to answer factual questions about text to the teacher's satisfaction.

Though Libby had a different idea about reading that she did for herself, she too seemed trapped by the idea that good reading—for school, anyway—was answering someone else's questions. And she seemed very tied to textual details, failing to build on these details and elaborate textual suggestions or possibilities.

Marvin revealed that the whole of his reading instruction over the past several years had been exposure to DISTAR (Direct Instructional System for Teaching Reading; Engelmann & Osborn, 1976), a method in which students repetitively identify letters and words, and that he had rarely read stories or been read to. He had no memory of reading picture books or having enjoyed or completely read a book. When I once asked him what he could "see" as he read a particular passage, Marvin replied, "See? I don't see anything, man, nothin' but words!" For Marvin, reading certainly was "stupid," as meaningless as lists of nonsense words like "kuh-nocked" and "kuh-nees."

Kevin offered that he had read "lots of stories, mostly from the big book [anthology] they give you in English." For him, successful reading was "being able to answer the questions at the end . . . to know characters' names and what happened to them and stuff . . . basically you have to tell the teacher what it says."

For Kevin, stories were particularly "dumb. They're confusing and you can't really learn much stuff from them. Not like from a magazine." For Kevin, a story didn't provide information efficiently, and he had no sense that there was an experience to be created and valued through reading.

For Libby, enjoyable reading experiences were about "something you know about." The power of literature to provide new experiences and to help the reader enter new perspectives seemed inaccessible to her.

These students' past reading experiences and schooling appear to have given them a reductionist, information-transmission view of reading. For Marvin, reading had consisted of words, and he did not expect that the words would work together to express any meaningful message. Reading, for students like Kevin and Marvin, was not creating and imagining meanings (Enciso, 1990), completing the openness of the text (Eco, 1978), filling gaps (Iser, 1978), or reading along indices (Barthes, 1986) to build up meanings throughout the course of a reading. What Bruner (1986) calls the "landscape of consciousness" never entered into the reading they or Libby did. The experience of reading was, at best, the passive reception and then the retelling of what, according to Kevin, "some book is telling you, or trying to tell you."

This flies in the face of current reader-response theory, whether from schema-theoretic, psycholinguistic, or developmental orientations, which has come to view reading as a transaction between reader and text that constitutes an "experience" (Rosenblatt, 1978), as a purposeful meaning-making activity (Goodman, 1982), and as a "heightened sensory activity that imagines meanings" (Enciso, 1992). Reader-response theory argues that personal involvement and imaginative evocation of a text are necessary to the experience of a secondary world. This experience is the purpose of "aesthetic," or literary reading, and is a prerequisite to any interpretation and reflection upon that world. Without such an evocation, there is no experience, and therefore nothing to think about. Reading, in Marvin's words, must indeed be impossibly "stupid" for those readers who do not know how to evoke and enter a secondary world.

Throughout the first 12 weeks of the school year, neither Kevin nor Marvin demonstrated any sense that this meaning-making was what reading was really about. Though Libby created meaning as she read, she did not seem to create new meanings, but rather revived old ones. Neither boy showed the ability or inclination to enter or evoke a story, or any sense that they might control strategies that would allow them to do so. Libby did not seem to see or experience new kinds of stories, and I had little evidence that she reflected on stories or used them to think with. I presumed that all three possessed the cognitive ability to evoke a secondary world and to consider and reflect upon the meaning of such a world. I had observed that they were, after all, quite adept at engaging with television shows and inferring character or mood in real life. Kevin, a student in my first-hour class, liked to make announcements as I entered the room such as "He's in a bad mood today!" based on casual observation (when he made such pronouncements, he was usually right).

Through various techniques of story drama, I hoped to provide these readers with procedures that would enable them to evoke story worlds, to help them make inferences about characters and their situations, and thus find reading literature to be a rewarding experience.

DRAMATIC HAPPENINGS

At this point the drama phase of the project began; for approximately 8 weeks the students engaged in a variety of drama activities directly connected to the stories they were reading.

For my classroom purposes, I used both techniques of story theater, by which I mean the enactment of described story events, and techniques of "story drama." For the story drama activities, I used Heathcote's (1984, 1990) definition of drama. Heathcote advocates isolating moments or details from stories to create dramatic encounters that will require entry into that story moment, elaboration of it, the taking on of other perspectives, and, consequently, a challenge to the students' own current ways of thinking. Heathcote (1984) argues that "Drama is human beings confronted by situations which change them because of what they must face in dealing with those challenges" (p. 48). In drama you "put yourself into other people's shoes and by using personal experience to help you to understand their point of view you may discover more than you knew when you started" (p. 44). What is called "story drama" in this study is any activity that requires entering a character's point of view or attitude and enacting a situation or conflict that involves it. These activities were suggested by the stories we read, but were not bound by them.

All of my students first participated in several drama activities that were tied to a class reading of Sheila Burnsford's (1960) novel *The Incredible Journey* and later to class readings of various short stories and some nonfiction pieces regarding particular issues such as animal rights.

Story theater activities were used to play out the text of the story. Story drama activities were used to express, explore, and elaborate story understandings and possibilities. The story drama activities described in the following list were largely inspired by the work of Edmiston (1991). Brian Edmiston was also personally quite helpful as he discussed the use of such activities with me and helped with preliminary coding of videotaped sequences of students involved in the drama. The first, revolving role drama, was a daily activity; the others were used once or sometimes twice during these 8 weeks of intense dramatic activity.

1. *Revolving Role Drama.* The staple of our drama activity was the daily use of a revolving role drama. Each day we took on character roles and enacted particular scenes that were suggested by the story. We did the drama before reading the parallel scenes in the text so that we could bring our own experience with the characters' problems and dilemmas to our reading. In each activity the students were asked to take on another perspective, usually that of a story character, and to visualize the story world and enact movement and interaction within that world. The students acted out their scenes in pairs, subsequently switching their roles and partners once or twice

during each class. See Appendix B for a set of lesson plans using revolving role drama to explore our class reading of *The Incredible Journey.*

2. *Dramatic Play.* Students were given a prompt or situation to be used as a stimulus for imagining and filling out a story event. The prompt usually came from the story itself, as students were asked to take on the roles of story characters imagining and enacting the psychological and physical activities that would follow a particular stimulus.

3. *Guided Imagery.* Students were asked to imagine scenes, often along with the guide of my visual description or musical accompaniment, and to subsequently write about or visually depict their conceptions of these particular scenes as they mentally experienced them. Some of the visual depictions were used as "tableaux" or as "sets" for role-playing scenes.

4. *Snapshot and Tableaux Dramas.* Students were asked to physically or artistically depict the "freezing" of particular scenes as moments in time that showed physical or emotional relationships, and displayed character gestures, expressions, and activities. When a scene had been frozen I usually asked them to provide a headline or caption for the picture, and sometimes to explain how and why they had created it. Students also drew such "snapshots" or series of such snapshots in a technique called "tableaux drama," which is the visual depiction of a story sequence through the use of several pictures and accompanying captions or scripts.

5. *Analogy Dramas.* Students were asked to write and perform dramatic vignettes that in some way paralleled a story situation. I asked them to imagine a similar situation in their own lives, or in the life of someone else they knew, and to play out what would happen.

6. *To Tell the Truth Game.* Based on the old TV game show, several students at a time played the parts of characters. These characters were interrogated about their story lives by judges who decided who had most convincingly "become" that character.

7. *Correspondence.* Students wrote and responded to diaries, postcards, letters, and advertisements in the role of story characters.

8. *Missing Scene Scripts.* After identifying scenes that were suggested but left out of the text, students wrote and produced vignettes that filled these gaps, elaborated on story events, or explored alternate story possibilities.

9. *Newscast.* Students produced a videotaped news show about *The Incredible Journey* that involved interviewing characters, reporting on their activities, and editorializing on particular actions and decisions.

THE MOVES THEY MADE

In contrast to the first 12 weeks of school, once we began these drama activities, Kevin, Marvin, Libby, and many others began to make new moves to create story worlds, to connect to these worlds, and to reflect upon them. I used some of the dimensions of response gleaned from Ron, Cora, and Joanne (see Chapter Three) to code and organize the emerging new reading activities of these three less engaged readers.

Entering the Story World

Langer (1989) has argued that readers must "enter an envisionment" as a prerequisite to experiencing text. Blunt (1977) and Thomson (1987), in their respective developmental models, place "entering the text" as the first developmental stage of response. Like many of my other students, Libby, Kevin, and Marvin demonstrated difficulty in entering story worlds. During a prestudy interview, Kevin told me that he had read the first few pages of over 10 books in the past 3 weeks. "I just can't seem to get into any of them," he complained. "I try, but it's just words." After reading Chapter 1 of *The Incredible Journey*, Marvin's nightly literary letter was simple: "This story is boring. I hat [hate] animels." Libby reported that "it's kind of confusing. I don't really get it."

While the students were reading Chapter 2 of *The Incredible Journey*, I asked them to enact and role-play various excerpts from the book, such as this one:

> Twenty minutes passed and no move was made; then suddenly the young dog rose, stretched himself, and stood looking intently down the drive. He remained like this for several minutes, while the cat watched closely, one leg still pointing upwards; then slowly the Labrador walked down the driveway and stood at the curve, looking back as though inviting the others to come. The old dog rose too, now, somewhat stiffly, and followed. Together they turned the corner, out of sight. (p. 21)

When the three case study students were asked to relate what had happened in this passage and what it signified, they had no reply. The passage was reread while three student volunteers slowly acted out the animals' parts. Three LD students from Marvin's class did a wonderful reenactment. Dan (as Luath the labrador) gestured to Brad, poking him. Brad (as the comfortable Bodger, the old bull terrier) brushed him off and settled himself back into a beanbag chair as if to go to sleep. Dan continued to dance around Brad, heading toward the door, returning, and gesturing to Brad.

Suddenly the student audience came to life. "The big dog [Dan] wants to leave!" Marvin practically shouted.

At a similar point in Kevin's class, Kevin had explained that "The old dog sort of wants to go, but he's lazy. My buffalo [from his game farm] is that way, the cows will all leave for the pasture and he goofs around and bellows but when they don't come back he gets up and follows them." This analogy was the first indication that Kevin had made connections from his own life to help create the life of a story. In her class, Libby role-played this scene with two friends. "It was cool," she said. "I could kind of see and feel what was happening." I asked her to describe what she was feeling more exactly. "It was like the dog saying, 'Let's be adventurous, let's do something.'"

What Benton (1983) calls a "secondary world" had been made accessible to these readers through the dramatic reenactment, and with it meanings came alive.

The three animals were then interviewed at a postchapter news conference, with the class playing the part of reporters. Students spontaneously stood as they peppered the animals with questions: Why were they leaving? How did they feel about their departure? Did they think they were prepared? What did they expect from the trip? What would have been said in this scene if they could talk? The questions showed the students retrospecting and predicting, visualizing, and empathizing, operating on the landscapes of action and of consciousness. In addition, students elaborated on the story, filling textual gaps and imagining possibilities. As they did so, they overtly modeled different types of productive, meaning-creating response for their classmates.

That night, Marvin wrote me his longest literary letter to date: "I like the dogs and the cat becaus they are nice. I think they will like to do things together and that they will make the 250 miles to be home. I hope so."

Kevin wrote, "I think they will have to hunt to stay alive. It will be a hard trip for dogs and a cat. Maybe this will be a good book."

Throughout the study, dramatic activities regarding a story helped students to enter the story world, and this ability to enter a particular story was sustained through succeeding chapters involving the same characters without further reenactments and through rereadings not accompanied by drama.

Other information from these students (in the form of videotapes, literary letters, journals, my own observations, and running assessments of each student) also indicated that by the end of the study these students and their classmates were "entering" more stories more readily, and could more easily identify when they did not, sometimes articulating particular reasons why the entry was difficult.

Seeing the Story World

Before beginning Chapter 3 I asked the students to engage in dramatic play in order to visualize the secondary world of the story.

"We are the animals," I prompted the students. "Where are we?"

"In the woods," someone answered.

"Okay. It's morning. We had a hard day yesterday. How do we feel waking up after the first day of a hard journey? What do we see? What are we planning to do next?"

After a short episode of dramatic play, the students were asked to write the diary entry of one of the animals, and then to share those entries. Kevin wrote in his response journal: "I'm hungry. I can see the sun rising through the trees. I'm stiff from sleeping on the ground and my shoulders hurt. I'm excited to get going, and do some hunting."

When I spoke to Kevin, he indicated that he was comparing an experience he had had camping out during a hunting trip to the animals' experience in the book. He concluded our conversation by saying, "This is really getting good." To which he added, "Sometimes I do like reading, you know."

Libby wrote that "It's pretty dark under all the pine trees and so we slept pretty late we were so tired. I think we need to find the old road again." Libby told me that "It reminded me of being in the woods. . . . When I read best I guess I feel like I'm in a drama. I make up surroundings and make up scenes. I understand it better." A bit later she advised me that "Writing and reading is easier if you are a character. It's harder to write if you're not somebody. You should let us do more of that." (This points out that drama, in which you have to become somebody and take a perspective, can help students write as well as read.)

Throughout the study, my students indicated that they consciously brought their experience and knowledge of the world to the drama world.

"You have to," one boy told me, "you have to think when did I feel like that or when did I see something like that . . . otherwise you can't get started [with the drama]." This reference to their own experiences was something Kevin, Marvin, and many other students did not indicate doing while reading before we began to use drama, and that Libby had difficulty doing with new material.

Individual checksheets indicated that students who did not report visualizing a story world before the study regularly did so in both the 4 weeks after using drama and throughout the remaining semester of the school year. Anecdotal evidence indicated that this change came about at least partly because of the dramatic activities themselves, and partly because of the sharing of response that drama engendered. Late in the school year one girl revealed that she couldn't "get over the idea" that she should be in a play or a movie as she read. She also said that she referred to dramatic activities experienced several months earlier when she reflected upon the experience of the story. Some students, like Libby, made an explicit connection between the experience of reading and participation in drama.

Seeing What's Happening

As we continued our reading, I occasionally asked different students to perform "snapshot dramas," freezing their bodies into particular scenes at a moment in story time, showing the physical relationships of characters to each other, and displaying their gestures, expressions, and activities.

On one occasion I asked students to "freeze the movie in your head" and to sketch out or make notes about what they saw. Next, I asked students to create visual "tableaux"—or poster-sized pictures—illustrating a sequence of events, and to share these, in character, with a group interested in their adventures. Many students had difficulty with this task, wondering how to portray the setting. I told them the author had left it up to them to "fill in" details that had been left out of the text. As the students made their tableaux, I encouraged them to fill the pictures with weather, artifacts, and other items that would fit the story world of that particular scene.

At the end of Chapter 9, I asked students to become Tao the cat or one of the two dogs, Luath or Bodger. I then asked them, as characters, to create postcards of three scenes from the story that were most important and meaningful to them. They were to write a note to their owners on the reverse side, commenting on the scene displayed on the postcard.

Groups of three were formed of the different characters. Postcards were then shared and discussed, in character, in the groups.

On one of Marvin's postcards he had a picture of a raging river. It was almost completely water, with one tree on a far bank. The note read:

Dear Elizabeth,

I never should of swum across this raging river. But I did and my head go bashed in by a log. I didnt know what hit me. A little girl took care of me cuz I couldnt hear. She remind me of you so I hurryed to catch up with the dogs so I could get home.

Sined, Toa.

Here Marvin demonstrates empathy with the cat, her feelings of regret about crossing the river, feelings about missing her owner, and her motivation for continuing the journey—as well as composing the longest piece of writing that any of his present or previous year's teachers had seen from him.

Relating to Characters

Before reading the final chapter, I arranged for students to play a variation of the old "To Tell the Truth" game. Four students at a time played the part of one character. Their job was to do the best possible job of becoming the character, thereby convincing the "expert panel" that he or she was the most credible "real" character.

A second set of students played the part of this "expert panel," which would judge which student responded most like the character, thereby earning their votes. The rest of the students were other characters from the book who asked questions of the four students claiming to be Bodger, Tao, Luath, or one of the minor characters.

In this way students had the opportunity both to become a character and to play the part of an expert reader, testing elaborated ideas of what a character was like. This role-playing required a building of information throughout the reading of the text, a reading along what Barthes calls "indices."

When Marvin was on the expert panel, he asked those students posing as Tao: "What would you have done if you hadn't got your hearing back?" Marvin was posing an elaboration on the story, a "What If" question, because in the story Tao does recover her hearing and then leaves the isolated Nurmi family to find the dogs and continue their journey homeward. This elaboration was a clear demonstration of Marvin's engagement, that he was "playing" the text and making it "go," as Barthes would put it.

During a different round of the game, Kevin explained why he did not choose Contestant Number Three as Bodger. "He said he looked healthier than when he left. But everybody here knows Bodger got hurt by the bear and he was in the fight with the collie so he musta had scars and stuff so he couldn't of looked all that good." All this from the reader who couldn't make any guesses about Mrs. Oakes's appearance from the available details. Acting out the scenes with the bear and the collie appears to have helped Kevin to see the scene, to enter the story world, and to see the consequences of those actions in his mind.

Reports of empathy for the main characters were very high throughout the study, both during dramatic activity and in readings of the same story that followed the activity. Students who never reported experiencing relationships to characters before the use of drama later reported engaging in a variety of relationships: becoming a friend or confidant, merging with the character, and inhabiting a parallel universe to the character. The drama activities appear to have made characters come alive for them to the degree that they recognized story characters as people to understand and have relationships with.

Interestingly, each day when we would role-play some scenes that had happened or that anticipated what would be happening to the animals during that day's reading, Libby would immediately pair up with her friend Jenna. Jenna seemed to invite Libby into the drama world and to make particular moves within the world. When I talked to the girls about this, Libby told me that "Jenna helps me to become a character and to figure out how they're going to act then I can go from there." When I asked how Jenna helped her, she said that "In the drama, I try to do what she does. I don't call her by her name but by the character's name. She asks me questions and I try to answer them. . . . She listens to me. . . . I allow her to express her thoughts and feelings. I try to make her feel happy if she's sad and I react the way I should. Maybe she'll help me to solve problems, maybe say, 'What do you think we should do?' or 'Remember when you did such and such?'"

Libby told me during a different interview that during her reading of the story "I felt like I was like Tao [the cat] . . . quiet, shy, can do stuff for myself even though people think I need help. OK on my own but I like to be around my friends." She reported that at the beginning of the book, she had "trouble understanding the characters . . . but now I can see the animals are just like people." When I asked her how she came to understand the animals, she said, "By being them with my body. I got to do things and make decisions and things with my body when I was imagining I was them so I felt like them."

For Libby much more than for the other students, using her body to do things was an important part of the dramatic experience. "I can get it because I'm doing and shaping things. Drama is like writing a story with your body." She also liked drama because "other people have to listen to you when you are a character or they won't know what to do. . . . You have to do things together." This was in contrast to most of school, during which Libby told me "everyone works alone and they don't listen to each other."

Elaborating on the Story World

As we were reading Chapter 7, in which the little Finnish girl, Helvi Nurmi, cares for Tao, a student asked me what was happening to the dogs during the same time period. I seized this as a dramatic opportunity to demonstrate how readers are asked to fill textual gaps.

"Authors leave the reader many gaps," I told the students, "which they expect the reader to fill in. Sometimes these gaps are details, like what people are wearing or might be thinking, but sometimes they can be whole scenes, or years' worth of time, which we have to create in our mind in some way consistent with the cues from the story."

I then asked the students to write out the scene they felt might be transpiring with the dogs during the same time frame when Tao's experiences with Helvi are recounted. What happened to the dogs during this time? How are the dogs feeling and acting? What does the author expect us to know about what is happening to the dogs, and how do we know this?

Kevin wrote the following scene:

(Night in the forest.)
BODGER: *I sure do miss that cat.*
LUATH: *You sure do miss eating the food he gets for you.*
BODGER: *Yup. That too. But I sure do miss that cat.*

LUATH: *Shut up, Bodger. (wipes his eyes) (a wolf howls in the distance)*
BODGER: *I sure just felt better when she was around.*
LUATH: *Me too. I wanted us all to come home together. It won't be the way I wanted it now. Maybe we should just keep going. I don't feel much like sleeping or talking tonight.*
BODGER: *Maybe we should leave a clear trail, you know, so she can follow us.*

During the "To Tell the Truth" game, Libby wrote down several questions for Tao, all of which were inference questions regarding Tao's feelings and motivations during different times in the story: "Why did you fight the MacKenzies' cats and how did you feel about it?" "How did you feel about Helvi and do you miss her?" "How would you have felt if Bodger died?"

When I observed that all of her questions were about feelings that weren't reported in the actual text, she told me that "I think reading is really about feelings, about seeing and feeling things. . . . That's what I like about the drama, in a regular class you can't share your feelings."

Though there were no indications that the less proficient readers in the study elaborated on story facts before our use of drama, they were entirely capable of doing so in the context of dramatic activity. Few students spontaneously employed such elaborative activity on their own after the study, but they did seem to recognize it as an element in a reader's repertoire, naturally elaborating when coming upon a situation that required it.

Connecting Literature to Life

After the class had completed their reading of *The Incredible Journey*, I structured several activities that I called analogy dramas, designed to help the students compare their lives to the story and the story world back to their lives. The first activity was called "Two-Sided Story." Students were asked to act out a scene from their lives (real or projected) that in some way paralleled a scene from the book. A second activity, "In Through the Mirror," required the animal characters to leave the story world and enter our classroom. They used what they had learned from their journey to deal with new situations and challenges.

A third activity was called "Scrooge Looking Down." Students imagined that they were being taken back in time to view scenes from their personal histories. Applying what they had learned from the experience of reading the book, they were asked how they might have lived differently or what they understood about the situation now that they had not understood at the time. Students then met as part of an "Out of Body" seminar to share and converse about their experiences.

In Kevin's scene he was looking down on himself on his first rabbit hunt. "Kevin," he said, "don't leave those other guys behind just because they're slower and noisier. Stick together. That's one thing I learned from Luath. It's just better to do things together, and you never know when you might need someone else. . . ."

In such activities students often made statements about the significance of particular events, a story's central focus or meaning, and sometimes about the relationship of events to each other and how this sense of configuration or coherence helped make a rich experience for them. Though this reflective activity was not spontaneously occurring after the study, it was recognized and referred to by the students as a readerly activity, showing up continuously throughout the year in their work, and being then recorded on students' individual response checksheets. Further, when students were asked to reflect upon a story, they sometimes reported "imagining" themselves to be characters or to be in particular situations in a type of individual dramatic play.

READING AS PLEASURE:
"YOU HAVE TO LIVE THE STORY"

During a conference with Kevin, I was highlighting and describing the expert engagement strategies he had used while reading a "free choice" book. After I told Kevin that he was doing "lots of things that expert readers do," he excitedly turned to me and said, "Hey, maybe I can get good at this!" This expression of reader agency revealed precisely the attitude I wished to engender in all my students. I didn't have much evidence of this kind that Kevin had rethought reading or himself as a reader until later in the semester. A student doing a report on Canada asked me if I knew of any stories from Canada. "I'll take him to the library," Kevin offered. "I know where all those stories are."

"Really?"

"Yeah, I checked out some of them about the gold rush in the Yukon and one on duck hunting."

Kevin, who had earlier reported that he never read stories, had been motivated to read other stories about Canada because "I liked the book [*The Incredible Journey*]."

Libby told me after the study that "I feel more equal in a drama. People listen to me more," and that "Reading after a drama is different. . . . I can see things better and I feel like I have more choices, just like in the drama." When I asked her how reading was different from drama, she revealed that "Reading is different because it's alone—but it's the same because you have to pretend you're a character and that other people are there." Libby then went on at length about how she and Jenna were using drama together as a strategy to evoke and enjoy their free reading. "We'll talk on the phone and pretend we are the characters and are solving their problems." She reported reading a book called *Me, Addy* about the Underground Railroad and that she and Jenna "played the parts" to help them "understand and think about what's happening."

Marvin's case of thinking about the act of reading is also dramatic. After I validated strategies he was using to evoke text, and encouraging those strategies I saw used throughout our reading and response to *The Incredible Journey,* Marvin's attitude toward reading underwent a clear sea change. The ED teacher (resource teacher for the emotionally disturbed) said that Marvin came into the ED resource room for 3 days running, announced he was going to read, and proceeded to do it for the whole period. When he was finished, he proudly announced that this "is the first book I ever read by myself." (Interestingly, it was entitled *Raging River.*) He then turned to his teacher and said, "I liked it, and I don't want anybody to ask me any questions about it."

Marvin was stating that his enjoyment and experience of the book was sufficient, and should suffice for the teacher too.

A few months after the study, when he was no longer in my class, I asked Kevin what he had learned from our story dramas.

"You have to live the story, Mr. Wilhelm," he told me. "You have to be the book." Now, when I see Kevin in the hallways, he greets me with the hang-ten sign and sometimes cries out, "Be the book!" And he is almost always carrying one.

"What story are you living now?" I'll call after him as he's jostled away by the swarming students.

It is a conversation that would have been unthinkable without our involvement with drama, which helped us to share our inner experiences of reading.

EPILOGUE:
THE POTENTIAL OF DRAMA

Kevin, Marvin, and Libby had a history of reading characterized by what Michael Smith (1992) calls "submission": They expected to receive meaning, passively, from the text. They and many of their classmates seemed to learn for the first time, through the use of story-related classroom drama, to exert "control" over the strategies and processes of meaning construction with text. They began to see the text as a springboard for imagined possibilities.

To do so, these readers had to first achieve what I propose to call "entry" or "merging" with text. Drama, throughout this study, proved to be an effective technique for achieving entry into a textual world. Further, it provided a meaningful mode for moving around in that textual world, making meaning of it and in it, and of observing and reflecting on the world and its meaning. Drama enabled these readers to see that reading is an activity of constructing meaning, and that readers build and own this meaning.

All of these students seemed happy using drama as a response to literature, and they now seem happier about themselves as readers. Since the study, they have continued to talk about reading differently, and do more of it more profitably. They now exhibit the idea that reading is something "in the reader" and that it involves what Libby called "making choices" and "doing things," versus their previous attitude that reading was something "in the text" or "out there."

For them, reading literature has become something that needs to be created and constructed and enlivened. For the boys, reading literature has for the first time become an experience that holds out the promise of enjoyment. Even if they did not become passionate readers during the course of the study, this change of attitude had already made many things possible, such as Kevin's interest in reading wilderness stories in his free time, Marvin's pride in reading his first book, and Libby's use of drama with her friends to help her understand unfamiliar pieces of literature.

These readers seemed to suffer most from a passive view of reading and a concomitant lack of literary experiences that required their participation. Drama, by its nature an active, participatory experience, helped the students to experience a story world, sustain that experience as they continued to read, and eventually indicate that they had reconceived the nature of reading. Drama seemed to make story language more accessible to students such as Marvin, who had clear language difficulties, perhaps by generating interest and activating the necessary schemata. Drama also allowed for the sharing of response activities and for the "trying on" of more proficient readers' moves and strategies, such as when Libby mimicked the moves of her friend Jenna. This involvement, in turn, may eventually help them to become more engaged and powerful readers.

This classroom study suggests that though less proficient readers may have difficulties decoding words and processing figurative language and implicit meanings, the real problem may reside within the reader's view—and resultant process of reading. These readers may have been taught or may have interpreted instruction in such a way that they attended only to surface features of local text and had therefore never learned to create unified worlds and meanings by using the text more globally as a guide or "blueprint." Teachers such as myself may help such students enormously as we come to more fully understand actual processes of making meaning through reading.

In any event, the use of drama helped less proficient readers overcome their local-level decoding problems and enjoy the experience of literature. It aided them in responding on many of the sophisticated dimensions used by more expert readers of their age. Using new strategies to produce meanings helped them to also rethink the act of reading and themselves and their roles as readers.

The success of this exploration leads to other, more specific and focused questions that are worth researching. Do specific types of dramatic activity encourage activity on particular dimensions of response? Is drama useful in developing and extending the response of all readers, including those who are already highly engaged? Is drama an effective prewriting technique for reflective essays about issues the students may not have personally experienced?

Other creative artistic activities may also hold promise for changing student attitudes toward reading and their conceptions of the reading act, and for developing previously unexplored dimensions of response. I believe these questions and others are worth the attention of classroom teachers and teacher-researchers. The possibilities are dramatic.

COMMENTARY

MOTIVATION. MATERIALS, AND METHODS

Ironically, the dimensions of response were supposed to be the whole of my dissertation data. But once again, my concerns as a teacher trumped those of academia, and those of a desire (on my own part and that of my family!) to quickly finish up my degree.

Once I had learned what expert adolescent readers do, I was immediately thinking about how I could help my less engaged and less expert readers do the same things. This is a wonderful thing about all learning. It's especially true of teacher research as a way of learning how to teach by learning from your students: One question leads naturally to another. Excitement builds over time. There are always new ideas to share and try. All of your efforts help you to relate to your students as learners and model engaged learning for them. Every lesson, unit, and year is a new adventure of collaborative discovery. You model for students how learning is continual, joyful, and a heck of a lot of fun. You display how thinking and being are a constant process of revision. You demonstrate every day why teaching is one of the most exciting, dynamic, worthwhile, challenging, and endlessly interesting careers in the world. You remind yourself why you come to school each day: precisely because you embrace and are ready for new possibilities and potentialities.

Learning to Love it

My classroom project has always involved getting kids to love reading, literature, and learning, and helping them to get good at it. I've come to understand that these processes are inextricably intertwined. In our research into the literacy of boys (Smith & Wilhelm, 2002; 2006), we found that boys privileged competence above all else. As one informant told us: "I'd rather say reading is stupid than *maybe* look like I might be stupid." When the boys described why they liked doing the things that they loved to do, competence was always at the heart of their engagement and enjoyment.

We found that when boys were intensely engaged, they were either already quite competent at that activity, or were getting demonstrably better at it, with visible signs of progress. (Although our actual study focused on boys, our pre-study indicated that all our major findings were also true of girls—to somewhat different degrees.) This has profound implications for our teaching and for assessment—only if we highlight competence and growth will our instruction and assessment lead to motivation and progress.

As another informant said, when speaking about lacrosse: "I just like being good at it." The corollary is that students don't like *not* being good at it. They don't like feeling stupid, or not knowing how to proceed and improve, and they want just-in-time assistance when they are struggling. And unfortunately, school often doesn't provide the help they want and need when they want and need it. Buda was a boy I taught who claimed that "school teaches you how you are dumb, not how you are smart." Another boy charged: "Teachers give you really hard things to do and then they never help you." Still another said: "It's like the teacher throws you into the deep end of the pool, waits to see if you drown, and then marks it down in her gradebook!" His complaint was not being thrown into the deep end of the pool, but why he had not been taught to swim first, and why he wasn't given help when he began to struggle.

Competence is likewise the linchpin of the conditions of flow experience (Czikszentmihalyi, 1990; Smith & Wilhelm, 2002; 2006), which, when present, entirely explained why the boys liked to do everything that engaged them (including literate activity). When the conditions were lacking, that explained why they disliked and rejected what they did not like to do. Motivation is entirely tied up in a sense of self-efficacy and visible signs of developing competence. The findings of our pleasure reading study, *Reading Unbound* (Wilhelm & Smith, 2014), yielded similar results. When readers freely choose a reading, or freely choose to continue with a reading, there are always five pleasures in play: immersive play; social, intellectual, and functional work; and inner work pleasures. These pleasures capture all the conditions of flow, and each mirrors particular kinds of competence and ways to demonstrate that competence.

Three ways to help students develop and exercise more competence are 1) by reenergizing our methods by making them more active, hands-on, fun, social, and connected to the students' current lives, 2) by organizing learning around inquiry as cognitive apprenticeship that foregrounds an immediate functional purpose for what is learned, and 3) by rethinking and expanding the materials we use. I'll take up the first two of these here (and the third in my commentary on the next chapters).

Revitalizing Our Methods with Action Strategies and Drama

Surveys of American teaching (like those referred to in the commentary for the Introduction) match my own observations. Students sit at desks, do worksheets, engage in classroom "discussions" that are thinly veiled "fill-in-the-blank" lectures, and take quizzes and tests that require little beyond factual recall.

I contend that what our students learn and remember is a result of how we teach. We must model engagement and provide students with multiple ways of engaging, problem-solving, practicing new strategies, and making meaning. This means that we must overcome the salience of the traditional in the kinds of instructional methods we use.

Drama is now the most powerful teaching method in my repertoire. It's also the most engaging and fun. I find it to be uniformly successful with all students, from the resistant and reluctant to those who are highly accomplished students. I can't imagine teaching an elementary school class or a graduate class without using it.

I have continued to experiment, research, and write about drama and have progressed in my facility with using drama strategies. Over the years I've come to do more simultaneous drama work in pairs and small groups versus whole-class dramas. I've been doing shorter dramas and more spontaneous and scriptless drama work. I've also been using these activities more often, frequently starting class each day with a quick drama strategy.

Drama, of course, provides its own context and implies an analogous context from real life. But it still strikes me that I didn't do enough in *YGBB* with contextualizing student reading and drama work in a larger context of inquiry, nor did I use drama consciously enough to create situated cognition through meaningful contexts of use. Now I also use dramas that involve authors, or that involve characters or historical figures from across different texts.

A series of teacher research studies on drama and its various effects are reported on in *Imagining to Learn* (Wilhelm & Edmiston, 1998). A book on how to use various "families" of drama techniques for a variety of literacy and learning purposes has become a bestseller (Wilhelm, 2012a). And yet drama is the most misunderstood of all the techniques I have written about.

Ironically, when writing my drama book for Scholastic, the editors refused to allow "drama" to be in the title, eventually calling it *Action Strategies for Deepening Comprehension*. Their justification is that teachers misunderstand what "drama" is and conflate it with "theater," and that teachers just don't buy books about drama.

If I use drama in fishbowl teaching or a teacher workshop, it is invariably what most excites the other teachers, what they most immediately try to use on their own, and what they email me about and want to discuss with me. But I also get a lot of emails from people who have not yet tried it who say they don't think their kids would be able to do it.

I think this goes back to the misconception of what drama really is and what it isn't. Drama is not rehearsed, it is not staged, it does not involve people in tights dancing on a proscenium stage; in other words: *drama is not theater!* It IS active, short, scriptless, spontaneous, and often simultaneous (with pairs of students across a class all involved in their own dramatic worlds); it can be performed internally or externally; and it is always purposefully framed. Participants are always accountable for doing and creating a deliverable—something specific within the context of the drama strategy, something that they could write about, reflect on, or share.

I've found that whenever drama activities don't work, it's because the work has not been adequately "framed" (for a full discussion of framing and how to do it, see Wilhelm, 2012a). Before beginning a drama activity, students need to understand their roles, have a brief time to prepare, and know what they are being asked to do and how they will report out and be accountable to the class for the meaning they have made and are contributing to the ongoing inquiry.

Drama continues to be the hardest teaching and learning strategy to get some teachers to try—but also the strategy they and students get most excited about once they try it. In one of the schools where I work, a teacher told me that her students "wouldn't do drama." I insisted that they would, and she said that I could come in and do it with them. Since this kind of model or fishbowl teaching is something I regularly do in my PDN (Professional Development Network) schools, I readily agreed. When I asked her about the class, she smirked and said, "It's eighth-hour, twelfth-grade remedial reading."

I prepared a story drama lesson to help us navigate a previously assigned story. When I arrived at class one big boy hitched up his jeans and stood up. He was clearly the class spokesman. He cleared his throat and announced: "We DON'T DO drama!" The other kids all nodded in assent.

I replied that I was unaware of this, that it was "my bad," but asked if it be all right to read the story and "do some activities." He agreed that this was acceptable, and he sat down.

I decided to throw out any activities that would look like role-playing, but we did a "vote with your feet" activity, a radio show discussion, and a written correspondence drama and choral montage. At the end of the 90-minute block, the boy came up to me and enthusiastically told me that "this was the greatest class ever!" When I told him that all the activities had been drama, he wailed, "You tricked us!"

So maybe the Scholastic people were right—we need to call drama something else, like "action strategies." But here is my point—even if you think kids will be resistant, or if some of them demonstrate initial resistance, it will work. I start with activities that are written, or done in pairs or small groups, activities that don't look like drama, and then move from there. If some few students are resistant, I ask them to be videographers or recorders, writing down what they observe—I prompt them to record specific kinds of data and to help me as a co-researcher. As soon as they see the fun the other kids are having, they almost always want to join in. Of course I relent, but only after I tell them how much I needed them to be my secretary and note-taker!

Drama-in-education activities are powerful and work for many reasons. Foremost is that drama and enactment are an embodied and very human way of making meaning. It is a way to experiment and play with meanings and possibilities. If you have ever been around little kids, they are always doing drama, and when they role-play, they are always a "head taller than themselves"—they always role-play being more expert and older than they really are.

As such, drama moves students into their zone of proximal development. English language arts is a place to pursue personal possibilities and safely study the "shadow"—or that which is repressed and "out of bounds." It is a natural place to introduce edgy topics, ethical considerations, and limits. Drama makes all this edginess safe because it provides a "liminal" space for trying out ideas, and one is not responsible as oneself in a drama—only as the character. *Liminality* means we experiment in the space on the threshold between the real and the imaginary.

Here's another very important point for teachers: Every drama strategy correlates to a specific tool for learning, reading, or composing. For example, hotseating (where one becomes a character questioned by others, see Exhibit 4.3 for a Hotseat Planning Sheet) is a way to enter the perspective of characters and to fill in gaps, to imagine their backstory and what they are thinking and feeling. Each drama strategy is a powerful tool for learning a strategy that many adults have internalized—in an externally supported and clearly scaffolded way. We all engage in role-plays in our minds. If your principal makes you angry, don't tell me you don't rehearse a little role-play inside your head, rehearsing what you might say, or could have said! We often perform hotseats in our minds—particularly when reading—to consider what it would be like to be someone else, or to understand their perspective. Drama also works because it personally connects life to the material under consideration. Drama allows us to try things we wouldn't do in real life, and to consider ideas that are distant from us in time, place, culture, or experience. (Again, for a fuller discussion, see Wilhelm, 2012a.) Drama is transformative, and helps us to imagine what is underground, and what could be. Drama expresses a future orientation, a tomorrow mind, and a growth mindset, focused on going beyond what is to what could be (Wilhelm & Novak, 2011).

It is also hugely significant that drama can provide a set of flexible contexts that match or are analogous to historical, cultural, and disciplinary situations that can frame and co-produce the meaning that is made. An implication of this insight is that every drama/action strategy technique is useful for teaching engaged and strategic reading of informational and nonfiction texts of all kinds (Wilhelm & Smith, 2016).

Using Drama to Provide Context

Thinkers in the Vygotskian/sociocultural/teaching-as-cognitive apprenticeship tradition argue that reading and writing must be taught in contexts in which they are "necessary for something, in a way that is part of complex cultural activity, not as isolated motor skills for school" (Dixon-Krauss, 1996, p. 128). Likewise, cognitive scientists studying the situated nature of all thinking and problem-solving activity agree that situations are not ancillary to learning, but are absolutely necessary and integral to all learning (Brown, Collins, & Duguid, 1989).

Thus, drama can work as a device for framing curriculum. I have often used "mantle of the expert" dramas (Heathcote & Bolton, 1995) to contextualize learning and make it purposeful, and to foreground the need for learning to lead to application and social action/service (Wilhelm, Fry, & Douglas, 2014). For example, I have cast students as video production teams creating documentaries about civil rights issues, or web designers creating interactive relationship quizzes, or museum designers creating a museum about the settlement of America or about Egypt's contributions to modern cultures, or blue-ribbon panels proposing and implementing programs to reciprocally support and learn from our growing immigrant and refugee populations. This kind of dramatic framing casts the students as "novice experts" and helps them to learn what experts know so they can progress towards doing what experts do—and further provides the context and need to apply and use what has been learned (Wilhelm, Fry, & Douglas, 2014).

Drama can also provide more short-term contexts for imagining what it would be like to be a character or historical figure, and for imagining that one is or could be more expert—the kind of person who possesses and exerts a growth mindset: who reads, does math, creates video documentaries, writes newspaper articles, and so forth. Drama is also a context that encourages kids to play with possibilities and to collaborate and help each other.

Drama is also an excellent context for introducing inquiry themes and essential questions (Smith & Wilhelm, 2010; Wilhelm, 2007). When creating a museum about the settlement of America, students can be asked to address the question of the costs and benefits brought to North America by Western civilization. When studying civil rights and creating video documentaries about the topic, students could be asked to address the question of what best protects and promotes civil rights, or who was the greatest civil rights leader of all time and how we can emulate such leaders in our own school and community. Asking such questions helps create a context in which the learning matters in ways that are clearly connected to the students' lived experience, to the discipline, and to the world. Drama work helps to make all of these connections clear and personally felt.

Just as with authorial reading, when reading or studying an issue, inquiry theme, essential question, or any other set of material, the job is to first understand what is already thought and known (what I call "topical research"; Wilhelm, 2007). But if we stop here, as schools usually do, then we have not progressed very far beyond merely being information purveyors and consumers, instead of being producers of knowledge who have learned and practice how to create, evaluate, and use new understandings. Unless we go beyond information to see new patterns of meaning; to understand the story behind the story; to embrace, adapt, or resist, and then find ways to use and apply these meanings (what I call "critical inquiry"), we will not learn how to participate in communities of practice as developing mathematicians, historians, scientists, ethicists, linguists, and the like. Drama is an invaluable way to assist kids in using critical literacy as they engage in critical inquiry and understanding.

Exhibit 4.1. Drama Strategy Chart

BASIC DRAMA STRATEGIES

Reenactments

Reenactments can be used before, during, or after reading. Reenactments prepare and assist students in figuring out and representing the literal and implied meanings of a textual episode or episodes by reframing it into a script, or simply enacting it in some way.

Variations: Freeze the reenactment and tap individual characters awake to talk to them about what they are thinking or feeling at the moment.

Change the text by reframing, recasting, changing, or probing it in some way, for example by having a character say something different or make a different decision. This strategy will help students figure out what texts are explicitly and implicitly saying and not saying, and how a different construction would change the text as well as the effect and meaning of the text.

Role-Play

Students assume the different perspectives of characters, objects, forces, or ideas and interact with others also assuming some kind of role. Students are provided with a dramatic situation and something to discuss, achieve, and be able to deliver or report on after the role-play. Role-plays are typically quite short (60–90 seconds), although they can be extended as students get more experienced.

Variations: Carousel/Revolving Role-Play, Questioning Roles

Hotseating

Hotseating intensifies role-playing by putting students on the spot so they can be addressed, advised, interviewed, and questioned in role as a character, force, or idea by a forum of students also in role, as journalists, other characters, or interested parties. This technique helps students improve their ability to analyze characters, infer, elaborate, and think on their feet. A "lifeline" group can assist the person or people on the hot seat as needed, or the lifeline members can tap in to take the hotseated person's place.

Variations: Lifeline, Inner Voice/Alter Ego, Good Angel/Bad Angel, Pro/Con, Whispers, panel discussion or press conference

Discussion Dramas

These are techniques that support student talk and conversation about issues that matter by putting students in role and in a small or large group of other students in role. This frees students to explore issues and express opinions that they want to deal with, but without being personally responsible for these viewpoints since they are expressed in role. By using these enactments, students not only deepen their understanding through talk, but their participation increases and they are more willing to try out new points of view. Through these discussions, they also enhance their thinking skills.

Variations: In-role discussions in small groups; Forum Drama, perhaps with "teacher in role"; Radio Show, TV shows, news shows, voting with your feet, four corners, choral montage, game show formats: e.g., *To Tell the Truth*

Correspondence Dramas

These enactments are any writing the student does while in role. They provide students with a purpose, meaningful information, a situation, and an audience. Writing also helps deepen a student's awareness of how different types of text are constructed.

Variations: Character Diary, Character Facebook page and posts, Character Letter or Postcard Exchange, Choral Montage based on character correspondence

Tableaux

Tableau is derived from the French word for visual presentation. Tableaux (plural) help students visualize and explore both the text and the subtext of a narrative, including setting, scenes, situations, characters, relationships, and meanings. Using this technique, students can also represent vocabulary and create mental models of complex concepts and procedures.

Variations: tableau vivant (living pictures or statues), video clip, slide shows, captioned pictures, best/worst Scenario

Mantle of the Expert

This means to wear the cloak of a more expert person and to operate in the story world or imagined context with this more expert person's knowledge and power. This technique helps students learn the ways of thinking and knowing that experts use to understand, produce, represent, and use content knowledge.

Variations/Extensions: Create imaginary and real social actions or social action artifacts, create museum exhibits or even a complete museum, create a public service announcement, create a service learning project. All reflect and require expert knowledge from reading and inquiry.

Exhibit 4.2. Model Framing and Planning Sheet for Hotseating Activity

Title of assigned reading: _____

In groups of 3–4 students, choose a character from this story that one of you will become for the Hotseating. Or your teacher may assign groups to represent different characters. It is important that the group agree on the following information about the character so that any one of you can go to the Hotseat and answer questions from the class. If the required information is not in the story, you will have to infer or make an educated guess about it, which is something all expert readers do when creating character.

Name of character: _____

Your age and physical appearance: _____

Your house, city/area, favorite place: _____

Your passions, "soapbox" topics, deepest desires—these may or may not be mentioned in the text: _____

_____

Your main goal: _____

_____

Your biggest obstacles and problems: _____

_____

_____

Your biggest influences: _____

_____

Your greatest strengths: _____

_____

Your greatest weaknesses: _____

_____

What one or two words best describe you—give examples from the text that demonstrate these traits: _____

_____

_____

Members of your group not being Hotseated will get to ask the first two questions. What will they be? And how will your character respond? How will the questions ensure a long character response, and an interesting revelation of character? How will you know that the character responses are good ones?

Question 1: _____

Answer: _____

Question 2: _____

Answer: _____

What other questions might the audience ask? What will they want to know? How will your character respond, and why will s/he respond that way? Rehearse a few with your group.

A Few Variations on Hotseating

LIFELINE: The Hotseated student can get advice from group members if she struggles to answer a question. They quickly confer to help the Hotseated character know how to respond. Or one of the group members can "tap in" and take over the hotseat to answer the question.

ALTER EGO or INNER VOICE: Each student-in-role could have another student from the group stand behind him to play the "alter ego," or "Inner Voice" or "conscience," and, after each response, reveal the character's inner thoughts and feelings that the Hotseated character would not reveal in public, or may be in denial about, or repressing. In this way, the Hotseated student says what the character would say in a public interview, but the alter ego says what the character might be thinking and feeling behind the persona or "mask."

PRESS CONFERENCE: Do the Hotseating in the context of an interview, press conference, trial, debate, or talk show.

GOOD ANGEL/BAD ANGEL: If a character is having a dilemma, other students can visit the character in role of a good angel trying to help them, or a bad angel tempting them to make the wrong decision. Or in role as "pros" or "cons" for deciding one way or another. Students can debrief by reflecting on the strategies used, how these exemplify argument strategies (ethos, logos, pathos), and manipulative strategies of persuasion.

WHISPERS: If a character is in deep trouble and in need of help, other students can walk by and provide verbal support and advice. Afterward, students can discuss what comments were most helpful and why. This can be an imaginative rehearsal for real-life response to people suffering problems.

DEBRIEF: After the Hotseating, review with your group what went well and what answers you would change now that you have had time to think about it. One of the great things about drama is that it's like a tape recorder—you can always "rewind" and redo things, you can erase, or you can fast-forward into the future. Too bad real life isn't like that!

Adapted from Wilhelm (2012a)

Exhibits 4.3–4.6 can be found online on this book's page and the free downloads page at TCPress.com

Exhibit 4.3. The Purposes of Various Drama Strategies

Exhibit 4.4. Tips for Setting Up Work with Drama Strategies

Exhibit 4.5. Process Drama Tools for More Effective and Exciting Teaching

Exhibit 4.6. Low-Key Role-Play and Questioning Roles to Promote Discussion

5

Reading Is Seeing

used to work with a woman whose husband did the hiring for a nationally recognized investment firm. At a party, I asked him what kind of profile he used when he filled sales positions at his company. "It's easy," he told me. "I only hire teachers."

"Why?" I asked.

"Think about it," he replied. "Teachers are selling something that their clients really don't think they want, and they're doing it to groups of 30 or more five or six times a day. To be successful, they have to be very organized, very enthusiastic, and they have to make one helluva sales pitch.

"So I hire them and I ask them to sell something *everybody* wants *one* time a day to a group that usually averages about *fifteen*. They do a fantastic job." Then he winked at me. "And I pay them a lot more, so they're happy as clams in the summer sand."

I don't tell this story because I'd like to leave teaching to sell investments. I'm already selling the greatest futures investment there is: the education of our children. Besides, I'm about as happy as a teaching clam can be (especially in the summer!). I do tell the story to highlight that classrooms are very complex and intensely human places. Teachers deal with nearly 30 different individuals' needs several times throughout the day. In this context, it often seems that there are no unqualified successes; our successes are ephemeral, invisible, and intensely human. They can't be captured by bar graphs and percentages and numbers of happy customers. And it seems that every teaching story and every success is fraught with some disappointments.

STILL STRUGGLING: TOMMY, WALTER, AND KAE

Even as most of my students and I were excitedly pursuing drama and finding it a powerful way to engage with and share our reading, there were a few students who seemed reluctant participants, and who continued to struggle and be frustrated by their reading and by our classroom work. As a result, I continued to struggle to help them, and I was beginning to be frustrated too. Notable among this group were two LD-labeled students, Tommy and Walter, and an ESL student named Kae.

Not entirely to my credit, I vented my frustration in my journal in the following way:

> Tommy and Walter are conspiring to give me a headache. Not just any old headache, but the pounding, throbbing, EXCEDRIN inducing, pain piercing right through to the back of your pedagogical eyeballs sort of headache. . . . They don't want to read. I'm working hard to help them, to provide them with fun and supportive things to do as they read, and they don't *even want to try*! (October 1992)

If the truth be told, there were some other seventh-grade students who were providing them with considerable help in the headache induction department, but I mostly blamed Tommy and Walter. After all, they were both in my last class of the day—ninth period—and they could be the most unreasonable, resistant, class-sabotaging students of the day. These were basically good kids, and I liked them. I knew they had had trouble in school over the past few years, and that Walter had transferred into our school from a parochial school to get the extra help his parents thought he needed. They could be pleasant and likable as well as negative in their behavior.

Their frustration with school and with reading class was almost palpable by the end of the day. Some days it was as if they walked into class with a giant force field of rage or gloom hanging around their bodies. I wanted badly to help them, to create openings for literacy opportunities that they could enjoy and participate in and grow from. But sometimes I just found myself out and out frustrated. There were days when I gave up and let them just sit there. I wrote that "If we had prizes for 'Frontal Lobe Headache Maker of the Day,' Walter and Tommy would get my vote every single election" (October 1992).

Another student who concerned me was Kae. Kae was from the Hmong culture and had come to us from Laos, via Thailand and Chicago. She had arrived in the latter part of the previous school year with very limited English language skills. Kae seemed painfully shy and would not orally respond in class. I was impressed by her diligent struggles to pay attention and to complete her written work, which I was generally able to decipher and understand. She seemed to have little interaction with other students, ate lunch with other Hmong students, and seemed—to be honest—to be at least a little sad and out of place.

Of my 120-plus students who had participated in the dramatic activities during our study of *The Incredible Journey,* only 8 had written negative evaluations of the experience. Of these eight, only four had been consistently passive participants in the dramas. None had been actively resistant, instead choosing to not respond to others in the drama, or to drop out of the drama world and just act like themselves. All of these four had occasionally participated in some fashion, however muted. Nonetheless, these four students had certainly resisted full participation in the dramas. There was little evidence that they had been helped to grow as readers through the dramatic intervention. They had even indicated that they would prefer to not participate in future dramas. Of these four, of course two were Walter and Tommy. And they weren't just resistant to drama; it seemed they were resistant to everything in school except lunch and the bus ride home.

Kae, however, indicated that the drama activities were "OK" and told me that there were a few other students who had invited her in and helped her to take part in the dramas. Still, I had often observed her during the dramas to be at a loss for something to do or say; whether it was because she didn't understand what was going on or could not think what to do next, I just didn't know.

Kae was labeled an ESL student and participated in our ESL program. This was the first time that she had been mainstreamed into language arts classes. She told me that her family had fled from Laos to Thailand, where she lived in a camp, and that she had spent most of her time there "drawing in the sand." More than a year earlier her family had arrived in Chicago, where, she confided, she didn't like school. Kae was very small and very quiet.

When I addressed her in class she would hang her head, turning from me as if trying to hide. When I spoke to her personally, before or after class, she would always give me a very big smile of gleaming white teeth, though she would say little. When I talked to her she usually answered with pat replies. "How is it going?" She would answer, "Good." "Do you understand what we're doing?" "Pretty much. I trying." I did not give Kae an Analytical Reading Inventory, but her word recognition and comprehension seemed on a par with some of the LD students. Because the typical homework assignment each night throughout the year was for students to free-read for 20 minutes, choosing material of interest to them, Kae took the opportunity to read almost exclusively from her brother's extensive comic book collection. She did not seem to discriminate between different kinds of comics and told me simply that they were "easy to understand." She read mostly about superheroes. She told me that she liked "the pictures" and that they helped her "to understand story." Later in the year she read other comic books such as *Classics Illustrated,* which I provided, and then stories with illustrations, such as *Little House in the Big Woods.* She also pursued other reading in English, reading some of the American Girls series and short romances, which she seemed to especially enjoy. She revealed that she sometimes read in Hmong at home.

With some struggles and difficulties, she seemed to achieve some literal understanding of her reading, as evidenced by literary letters and reading logs. But she seemed to be working hard and had difficulty achieving and expressing other forms of response. Most clearly, she seemed estranged from the classroom community and had trouble taking an active part in many of our language activities. She was obviously bright and diligent. I hoped that I could find a way for her to enter into the life of the classroom and to help her improve as a speaker and listener, as well as a reader and writer.

I had also noticed that Kae liked to draw pictures; she seemed highly artistic. A few early literary letters were spontaneously accompanied by illustrations that she smilingly shared with her reading partner. On one occasion, she pointed to an illustrated letter and told me, "She understand it!"

Both Tommy and Walter were labeled LD (learning disabled) students. Both were small for their age, fragile looking. Tommy was olive-skinned, with stringy black hair swept across his forehead, and liked to wear camouflage clothing. His friends called him "The Camo Man," and his dream was to buy a car and cover it with camouflage paint. Walter had wispy blondish hair hanging in bangs in front of his eyes. Every single day, no matter what the heat, he wore a gray hooded sweatshirt, jeans, and beat-up Reebok sneakers. His moniker was "The Ninja." He made ninja stars out of paper and threatened to impale people with them.

"These are two kids we're probably just not going to get. They just don't like to read. They just refuse to," the LD teacher told me. Her description, to my mind, was fairly accurate. On the ARI (Analytical

Reading Inventory; Woods & Moe, 1989), Tommy and Walter both scored on the second-grade level for Independent Reading. Their scores for vocabulary and comprehension were similar—second grade—and their Instructional Reading level was only about a grade level higher—slightly above third grade. But in class, no matter how carefully I chose the material to match their abilities and interests, they refused to read. Tommy would often just sit in his desk staring straight ahead. He would become extremely angry and agitated if disturbed from his trance. No amount of coaxing or cajoling would convince him to read. "I can't do it," he'd say. "You can," I would reply. "CAN'T. Never Could. Never Will," he'd say with finality. Even when he had chosen his own book for free reading, he wouldn't crack it, or would crack it to draw pictures inside. Tommy, in fact, spent most of his active classtime drawing pictures, sequences of them such as cartoon stories, pictures of faces and animals, and ornate etchings of exotic settings and monsters and amazing machines.

Walter's reluctance to read was also interesting. He would carefully set aside the assignment and, usually, begin to "read" a book of his own. His chosen book was always filled with photographs, pictures, or drawings. He especially favored *Calvin and Hobbes* or *The Far Side* and could often be seen quietly chuckling, head down in the book. Walter did quite well on the free-reading component of the course, which made up about 40 percent of class time—for free reading itself, response to it, and sharing. But on shared readings and projects he refused to take part. "I can't read that stuff," he snarled at me on one occasion. "Why not?" I asked. "I don't know. I just CAN'T!" Walter, normally quiet and almost mousy, typically friendly and polite, would explode when pressed on this issue, the ninja side of his personality rising to the surface. On two occasions when the LD teacher gently tried to cajole him to read the assigned text for the day, or offered to help him to read along with his classmates, he threw books, once yelled an obscenity, and stormed out of the classroom.

I was agitated myself. How could I encourage these boys to read more widely, or at all? How could I convince them that reading literature was an experience worth pursuing and enjoying?

SEEING THE VISUAL POSSIBILITY

Much of what these students revealed to me made me begin to believe that these students did not "see" anything when they read, and that therefore they could not experience and think about what they had read. They had no ownership over the process, and no sense that it could work for them in personally meaningful ways. Tommy and Walter seemed to have very low expectations of print and no sense of what to do as readers to make their print experiences meaningful. And Kae seemed to struggle with her language difficulties and not get beyond the meanings of words to see the world of a story.

I knew that visualization was considered to be an important part of reading and that it has been shown in various ways that the use of mental imagery has various powerful positive effects for readers. It has been demonstrated that visual imaging encourages students to access and apply their prior knowledge as they read, increases comprehension, and improves the ability to predict, infer, and remember what has been read (Gambrell, 1981; Gambrell & Bales, 1986; Pressley, 1977; Sadoski, 1985). Gambrell and Jawitz (1993) have also shown that the use of visual imagery while reading helps students to monitor their comprehension. Jacob (1976), in a review of imagery, has emphasized that the ability to use imagery is a central difference between good and poor readers. Yet Belcher (1981) has reported that teacher's guides designed for use with basals and anthologies rarely mention the use of mental imagery, and never as a strategy for experiencing text and improving reading ability.

So despite compelling evidence of its importance, neither teachers nor materials seem to emphasize visualization in reading as an important element of active reading, comprehension, comprehension monitoring, and response. And the need for such instruction has been demonstrated: Gambrell and Bales (1986) found that lower ability readers did not "spontaneously employ mental imagery as a strategy," therefore depriving them of full evocation and participation in a story world. Less proficient readers studied by Purcell-Gates (1991) were also at a loss for strategies for stepping into and sustaining envisionments by building relationships with characters, taking their perspectives, and imagining and visualizing secondary worlds.

I wrote in my journal:

> I'm beginning to believe that students who do not "see" what they read won't be able to do so just because I ask or tell them to! Telling them to "see what you read" just doesn't work—they don't know how to do it. I wonder whether letting them create visual art as a response to their reading would help them to start seeing how to build visual meanings

from text, reinforce the importance of this, and interest them in participating more actively in class. (November 1992)

The confluence of three events helped me decide to use visual art as
a classroom intervention and to pursue a study about how art might
influence and help develop student response and discourse about what
they had read.

First, I was interviewing Ron, whom I had decided to use for a case
study early in the year. Ron had enlisted his friend Chris to read some
Tom Clancy books together with him, for the purpose of "talking about
it" and "doing a project together." "It's a funny thing," Ron told me.
"Sometimes we'll be silently reading the same part of the book, and I'll
be laughing and snorting and practically rolling on the ground, and Chris
won't be giving any reaction at all." When I asked Ron why he thought
that was, he replied, "I guess . . . he must not see the story the same way
I do. He can't be, because for me a part might be hilarious and it doesn't
affect him. He can't be seeing what I'm seeing." Later in the interview,
Ron told me, "It's like he can tell me what's happened, so he knows that,
but it's like he hasn't, like lived it like I have. It's not like . . . there for
him or something." I found this idea of "seeing" the work in order to
experience it fully a compelling idea that was corroborated by a lot of
other student data that I had collected.

Later that same day I was interviewing Tommy about a one-page story
called "The Dinner Party" that involves a cobra that is found underneath
the table during dinner. Tommy insisted that he had experienced nothing
by reading the story. When I began to poke around, asking different
questions about the reading and what he thought about it, even disliked
about it, he exploded: "I can't think about it, talk about it, do anything
about it, if I can't see it!"

This made me pause and think. A few minutes later I was doing a
cued protocol story response with Walter and the story "Larceny and Old
Lace" (Arthur, 1960). At every cue he gave either no or very thin indications of what he was doing. "Nope, nothing here." When I asked what
the two protagonists looked like, he indicated that "They're women, you
know. . . ." When pressed he indicated that they had blonde hair, red
dresses, looked pretty much, he guessed, like "Mrs. Kirst," Walter's
young and very athletic science teacher. I then elicited from him that he
knew that the characters were former schoolteachers and were retired,
and that he knew at what age people typically retired. But he had not
translated this knowledge into a picture of what they might look and act

like. He had not seen the world and characters of the text. At the end of the story, Walter indicated that he "didn't get it." And that the story had "done nothin' for me. Sorta boring."

The interview completed, Walter hurried back to his seat, opened *Calvin and Hobbes,* and immediately began chuckling. It was then that I experienced a teacher's epiphany, Walter enjoyed the humor of *Calvin and Hobbes,* which was often quite sophisticated, at least partly because he was helped to see and therefore experience the imagined world of the story through the cartoon pictures!

I then remembered two separate occasions when I had experienced and discussed the enthusiastic and powerful reading of two deaf children. Apparently, profoundly deaf children typically do not learn to read beyond the second- or third-grade level (Allen, 1986). There was a constant factor in both cases, however: both children, one a boy and one a girl, had been inveterate readers of comic books. The girl's mother told me that her daughter had "consumed" the series of comics called *Classics Illustrated* and *Classics Junior.* The boy was more typically interested in *Superman* and *Spiderman* adventure comics. My hypothesis began to develop: the pictures, paired with words, helped less engaged readers to visualize the action of a story and to understand how words suggest various characters, settings, and activities.

One of the powerful lessons my case study students taught me was later recorded in my journal:

> Listen to your students! If you want to know how to teach your students, get to know them! If you want to know how to help them, look at what they can do and build from it! If you want to know what they are thinking, ask them! . . . It's almost as if Libby and Kae, Tommy and Walter and so many others have been demonstrating to me how I could help and encourage them, but it just didn't register. . . . Libby's dramatic play with Jenna in the hallway and Tommy and Walter's constant doodling . . . why not pick up on it and use it? So many kids just seem to love using the arts for any purpose, it's personal and meaningful and fun for them . . . and now it seems that visual art is helping them to understand their reading and to participate in class. (January 1993)

Eisner (1992) asserts, "We cannot know through language what we cannot imagine. The image—visual, tactile, auditory—plays a crucial role in the construction of meaning through text. Those who cannot imagine cannot read" (p. 125). And, according to my classroom experience, don't want to.

THE VISUALIZATION PROJECT:
ART IN THE CLASSROOM

So I began a second study project that ran as a sort of mini-theme through the last two and a half quarters of the school year. Though the project included all of my classes, I emphasized it most heavily in my two LD mainstreamed classes. The project was designed to convince reluctant readers that reading involved seeing, and to find ways that would scaffold and support that sort of "readerly" visualizing and image-making for the students.

The "aesthetic experience" of a textual world was first described by Rosenblatt in *Literature as Exploration* (1983) and in *The Reader, the Text, the Poem* (1978). She has stressed the difference between the "text," made up of words on a page, and the "aesthetic experience," the reader's lived-through evocation of the text as it is imagined and visualized and experienced in the mind's eye. Rosenblatt insists that reading must be seen as an experience and that teachers must help students to actualize the potential experiences of texts by helping develop their repertoire of reading strategies.

By looking back at the literacy histories I had collected from my most reluctant readers, including Tommy and Walter, I noticed that none had recalled being read to much, nor did they have any memory of ever reading picture books. I wondered if they had ever learned to "experience" literature, to evoke and "see" textual worlds in their minds. In any case, it was my job to help them do so in more vital and meaningful ways, and I set out to use their penchant for creating visual art to help them do so.

Talking to Tommy and Walter, I asked them if they had ever been able to use their artistic skills in the classroom. "Usually we get in trouble for it," Walter offered. They did remember a poster contest in science, drawing maps in social studies, and making a life-sized drawing of the body's internal organs in health. Neither had yet had the opportunity to enroll in an art class. "We pretty much had to draw what we were told to," Tommy commented on these projects, "when we do what we're thinking about we pretty much get in trouble." They then proceeded to recount some of these misadventures, which often involved both of them. This was the first time that I realized that Tommy and Walter were friendly, and that they exchanged and talked about their drawings in exactly the way I was trying to encourage students to share their responses to reading.

When I talked to Kae, she said that creating art was "easier" for her than writing or talking, and that she liked to "do it when I can." She felt that people "understand my drawing" better than they understood her when she spoke and wrote. She said that reading and writing took a lot of her time and energy and that she wished there were other ways, such as art, for her to do schoolwork.

Eisner (1992) cites three critically significant aims of arts education: (1) to increase the variety and depth of meaning people can secure in their lives, (2) to develop cognitive potential, which is achieved only through the exercise of various opportunities, and (3) to achieve educational equity. These aims had certainly not been met for Tommy and Walter, nor for Kae. School had limited the variety and depth of meaning they could secure through their drawing. They were not encouraged to use their artistic strengths to develop cognitive potential in related areas, such as reading. They had been educated against the very grain of the way they liked to think about and know things. This can hardly be considered educationally equitable.

Representing ways of knowing is discovering or inventing a private world and then making it public. Tommy and Walter did not know how to invent and enter the "secondary world" (Benton, 1983; Tolkien, 1964) good readers experience when they transact with text. Kae had difficulty doing so in English and difficulty communicating about her reading with others. Visualization activities regarding literature, I was sure, could help them to do so. Representation stabilizes thought, serving what Eisner (1992) calls "a place holding function." This conception can then be shared with others, and tested, negotiated, and revised communally. The drawings of these students, I hoped, could help their responses to literature be part of our classroom community. It could then lead to the refinement of their own individual responses and reading processes, and those of the classroom community.

I had been tracking the response of all students, including these three, throughout the first quarter of the school year and then through the drama study. I continued to track their response on different dimensions as they participated in the following activities making use of visual art.

Symbolic Story Representations

The SRI, described earlier, involves creating cutouts for characters, the reader, the author, and any props, settings, ideas, or forces that played a part in the student's reading. The students then used the cutouts, explaining them and moving them around to describe the action of the story and how the story had been read and experienced by the reader. The SRI seemed to provide a natural bridge between the drama and visualization projects. Students were necessarily representing essential story elements visually as they dramatized a story for their classmates. Their reading, made visible, could be talked about, critiqued, manipulated, and revised. New moves and elements could be added and experimented with.

Visual Protocols

During the classroom use of visualization techniques, students were asked to read a story and to stop whenever they had formed a strong visual impression and draw a picture of that impression. Some students began to stop and draw when they felt the need to get a visual impression clear in their minds, and they were encouraged to do so. Though some students participated in cued protocols, during which they were asked to either describe or draw their visual impressions at particular points in a story, Kae, Walter, and Tommy participated only in uncued protocols, so they drew pictures only when they indicated that they wanted to.

Reading Illustrated Books

During the first part of the project, in mid-December, I brought a book cart of picture books into the classroom. Each day, I would share one of these books as a companion piece to another nonillustrated reading. We discussed how the picture books worked: how the pictures worked with the words to contribute to our experience of story. We then discussed the type of pictures the nonillustrated story might have, the sort of pictures we could imagine in our minds that would fit the story, how using different types of pictures (different color schemes, techniques, photos versus drawings, foldout, pop-up, highlighting different scenes or moods) would affect the reader's experience.

After Christmas I brought in sets of the complete series of *Asterix* and *Tintin* comic books, some copies of *Classics Illustrated,* and two copies of the illustrated Holocaust tale *Maus*. There was a stampede for these books, and it continued for months, on the part of the less proficient readers. Many of these students read nothing else but comic books for their free reading for the rest of the year. On the other hand, these illustrated books were pretty much ignored, with one or two exceptions, by the more proficient readers. (An exception was Art Spiegelman's Holocaust stories *Maus* and *Maus II*, which were read and traded by several very proficient readers and discussed at length among themselves and with both myself and the social studies teacher.)

Kae had been reading comic books since the beginning of the year and was now reading other sorts of books as well. Tommy, over the course of the next two quarters, read every single *Tintin* book and most of the *Asterix* series and did some library research to see if there were other such series of books. This activity was from a boy who had refused to read on his own for 10 weeks. Walter read most of the *Tintin* books while continuing to read his own comic books involving various super-heroes. Walter also began to branch out to books with a few illustrations, such as *Scary Stories,* which had an illustration at the beginning of each story, and one or two embedded in the text. Though Tommy remained fairly reticent, Walter would often excitedly discuss the illustrations in comics and books with me, coming into class with his finger holding his page and exclaiming, "Look at this, Mr. W!"

One of their classmates and friends, a boy named Jeremy, after reading *Maus* and running to the bookstore to buy and read *Maus II,* exclaimed, "Why don't they write more books like this?" These students, I observed, enjoyed reading such books, finding something engaging, supportive, and helpful about them. Once students were introduced to picture books and encouraged to read them, they did so vigorously. I wrote in my journal that "I just have to wonder if school conveys a very limited view of literature that does not include picture books and comics, and if this limited view of literature contributes to how bummed out and distanced many of my student readers become from literature and the literary experience. School denigrates what experience is accessible to them, and denigrates how they read. Could it be?" At the same time, I wrote that "It's amazing to me how much I enjoy reading the comics. I've spent several free-reading periods that I had intended to conference with students reading *Tintin*. So there's something in it for me too!" (January 1993).

Interestingly, the German teacher and I spoke about this phenomenon and she gave me several comic books in German, which I read with gusto. I wrote in my journal that "Reading comic books in a foreign language gives me a little insight into why it is so supportive for kids who have trouble reading. It's much easier to figure out words from context and to follow the story line. It's a lot of fun too!" (January 1993).

Illustrating Books

In the next stage of the project, taken up just before Christmas and continuing into the next calendar year, students were asked to illustrate nonillustrated stories that we read as a class, and then to write and illustrate their own picture books with original stories, or adaptations of stories they knew or had read. During an integrated unit with social studies, each student (as part of a learning group) performed a tableau drama of at least four poster-sized drawings. The tableaux helped to share an important myth or fable from the studied culture, and were accompanied by narrative as they were presented to the class.

Picture Mapping

Picture mapping is a way of note-making with pictures. Students were asked to visually depict the key details of particular texts, usually nonfiction, in the most efficient way possible. Students were encouraged to draw reminders of the key details any way that they liked, and to combine several details into one drawing if they chose. It was emphasized that there was no right or wrong way to depict ideas, it simply had "to work" for the student. Students were also encouraged to graphically show how the key ideas related to each other. The picture map took the place of summarizing and note-taking, and students were allowed to use their maps to complete other assignments that required them to use information from the text.

Collages

In this project, students were asked to create poetry and story collages that would represent their response to a particular piece of literature, usually a song or poem of their choice. The completed collage was then used as part of a presentation about their response to the literary selection, guiding the sharing of their literary response with classmates.

THE ART OF READING

The art these students created and discussed as a response to literature typically encompassed two or three dimensions at a time, centering primarily on the dimensions of entering and seeing the story world. But once they had achieved these reading milestones, I was excited to see that they began to make moves on other response dimensions, such as considering the significance of details and how various details work together to create meaning.

Entering and Seeing the Story World

The first thing that struck me about student response using the SRI was how naturally students of various abilities made use of it.

> After my brief presentation modeling the SRI it was like everyone knew exactly what I was talking about . . . showing what the story was about was easy for them to grasp, symbolically representing characters, settings, even ideas or forces—which I had worried would be difficult for them— did not cause the anticipated confusion. Even creating cut-outs of themselves as readers caused no consternation; everyone did it though not everyone made use of this cut-out in their presentations. Overall, I was astounded by how richly the students recounted their scenes, and especially by how they discussed how they actually read the scenes and what they [the scenes] meant to them. I hadn't expected this level of discussion on the first try—if ever. Another thing that really psyched me was how students were trying out new ideas and moves as they made their cut-outs and presented their scenes, and how they responded to each others' presentations. All in all it resulted in tremendously rich small group discussions, group after group after group, such as I have rarely seen in my career. . . . Conversations leading to new moves, deeper understanding, sharing and discussion—it was truly a great success. Can't wait to try it again, maybe with a new wrinkle. . . . (December 1992)

When creating his first SRI, Tommy asked if he could use the story as a reference. Of course, I told him. He constantly referred to the story as he created his cutouts, studying it in an intense and interested way that I had never witnessed in him before. Though many students made highly symbolic cutouts, or used icons that related to characters (e.g., a gun or helmet for a soldier, a crutch for a crippled person), Tommy created very detailed and literal pictures. Typically they consisted of pencil or ink drawings on typing paper, cut out and mounted on construction paper. He also liked for the cutouts to stand up, and in later SRIs he sometimes created 3-D scenes such as a basketball court with upright standards in which the cutouts, like chessmen, could move around.

He had gone over this story carefully, he told me, so he could be sure he'd "got it right." Tommy had never much cared before about getting answers to quiz or test questions right, so I asked him what the difference was here. He stopped short of scoffing at me. "I'm *making* this," he told me, "and other people are gonna see it." I asked Walter about the care he took with his cutouts and he simply replied, "It's fun to do."

Walter's cutouts were also quite literal, though usually less ornate and more colorful. Walter also created scenes for his cutouts to move around in, though his were usually flat.

This creation of scenes during an SRI proved to be an exception throughout the use of this technique by the class. Some students used cutouts of props to indicate a scene (e.g., a tree meant the scene was in the forest, a bed indicated a hospital room), but only a very few students continually created elaborate "stages" for their SRI presentations as Tommy and Walter did.

I asked Walter about his use of the elaborate scenes and he told me:

> It's like when I see the people then all of a sudden I'm seeing where they are too. . . . It's kinda weird . . . it's like I don't see much but I start to make the thing [cutout] for a person and before I'm done doing it I can see exactly where they're at and that's just got to be part of it [the SRI] then.

Tommy simply asserted that "You're not telling the story [through the SRI] unless you have where it happened. . . . I don't care about these other ones [from other students], we [Walter and I] got it right and theirs aren't as good." This feeling of doing superior work was an important step for Tommy and one that I encouraged him to make as I told him, "Let it all hang out. Show the other kids what they could do too if they wanted their SRIs to be better." Tommy nodded and said, "Okay." I wrote in my journal that this was "an incredibly positive step. I suggested that he had something to teach other students and he agreed!" (January 1993).

During their initial SRIs of scenes from "Pandora's Box," both Walter and Tommy dramatized complete summaries of the action that their respective groups found totally complete and understandable. Tommy did little in the way of explicitly discussing what he had noticed and done as a reader, but his emphasis on the turmoil of Dorie in deciding how to classify Max during triage ("She was thinking will he hate me when he doesn't have a leg and I could have let him die?") and Max's subsequently amputated leg indicated his involvement all the same.

Walter discussed his involvement as a reader with more awareness. "Here I was feeling like I was him and would I want to die and be a cripple? But then I wasn't him anymore."

Kae's initial SRI recounted the story action and little else. Her cutouts were highly stylized and artistic, and she spoke confidently to her group when giving her presentation. She was very excited by her work with the SRI, telling me, "This is so good!" and that the other students "could see what I see!" Kae drew very elaborate characters, props, and sets onto cutout shapes of paper. She told me that "When I draw I just draw, I don't really think. . . . I kind of discover and think what person look like when I draw." She explained that she usually had a very sketchy idea of what people and places in a story looked like until she drew them. "I kind of just do it and draw dresses and faces which I did not really know but then I know what they look like and be like and feel like." She felt strongly that she saw and understood a story better. "I see the hospital and people now."

I wrote in my journal:

> Kae really seemed to enjoy class and participate fully for the first
> time. . . . I think that making the cutouts required her to go beyond the
> words of the story to think about what they mean and to start creating
> a highly visual model of the story in her head. From what she said it was
> almost as if making the artwork was what made her discover the
> story. . . . The SRIs helped Tommy and Walter to enter and merge
> themselves into the story—not immediately as we expect students to do,
> but over time as they created the SRI—and the creation and perfor-
> mance of the scenes made them want to do that. . . . I have never seen
> them so motivated or involved in response to a story. I've never seen
> them be so much a part of the class. (December 1992)

Relating to Characters

Kae, who often expressed romantic sentiments while reading, indicated that she had come to know and understand some of the characters in "Pandora's Box" when she said, "I think they kind of love each other" when referring to Dorie and Max. "I think she really love him all years. That's why she so sad," she explained, inferring relationships and emotions not explicitly stated in the text. This move excited me, and I wrote that "Kae is finally moving beyond her struggle with word meanings to create a textual world that is personally meaningful to her!"

Walter, too, demonstrated that he had come to know and understand the characters in this first SRI. In response to a question, Walter said that Max "didn't know what he was talking about" when he said he'd rather die than be crippled. "That's stupid!" he almost ranted, then pointed to his head and said, "Think about it, man!" He was evaluating Max and his beliefs, but he backed off a little, saying, "I guess it would be hard to know." Walter then commented that his own leg "hurt" when Max had to have his leg amputated. He clutched his right thigh as he made the comment. "You just can't imagine it," he repeated. When I asked him to explain, he just said, "You can never know." Though it is unclear exactly what Walter was thinking, he was certainly putting himself in Max's situation, trying to know and understand him. And he certainly felt for Max and his situation. He ended the interview by saying, "I'd be really P.O.'ed if she [Dorie] hadn't of saved him! Really P.O.'ed!" It struck me that "the story was something *real* to him—this is something I haven't seen before! Big step!" (December 1992).

While watching another student perform an SRI for the nonfiction piece "Swish" (Robinson, 1991), about a boy who can make half-court baskets with his back to the basket, Walter twice started to interrupt the presentation. When the student was finished, Walter took issue with the student's interpretation of the story.

"You said he wanted to be good at basketball," Walter pointed out, "but he didn't—he already got cut from the team. He wanted to be good at anything!"

When other members of his group wanted an explanation, the normally taciturn Walter went full steam ahead. He explained that the boy's sister was a basketball star and that he wanted to be, too. He explained how this probably really "killed him" that his sister was a star at something he wanted to be good at but wasn't. Finally, he concluded that:

> *He just wanted to be good at something. Shooting baskets that way ain't being good at basketball—it's just being good at something! If he could have been good at something else and got attention he would of done that.*

This was a subtle point Walter had made, and he had made it by trying to know and understand the position of the character. It was also the most thorough response Walter had ever given to another student's response. His comment stimulated some discussion in his group.

Tommy demonstrated activity on these dimensions of knowing and understanding characters less often, but the visualizing activities seemed to scaffold his own preliminary efforts on these dimensions. After Max's amputation, for example, he commented, "That would really suck."

When the story was over, he indicated that "it [the story] kind of makes you feel sorry for everybody."

Kae's artwork continued to help her operate on this dimension of response, and to think about characters long after she had read a story. A few days after her SRI of "Pandora's Box" she said, "Now I know nurses and how they sad."

During our reading of *The Incredible Journey* she became very excited by our postcard exchange. She drew a scene of Tao being washed down the river with the other animals helplessly watching. "Now I know how everybody feel," she said. "They so scared and so sad." She then went on a slight tangent as she talked about how sad her owner Elizabeth was that Tao was washed down the river. When I told her Elizabeth was still in England and didn't know Tao was missing, she said, "Oh, then she will be sad if she knows."

When I asked her how drawing the postcard worked for her, she said, "If I draw a person I know them. I know their feelings." She also said that drawing the postcard had helped her "see things in my head."

Kae's tour de force was a symbolic story representation of a Hmong cultural tale, orally told in her family, called "The Seven Daughters," which she presented to part of the class during an integrated unit on cultures that we pursued with the social studies classes. Kae's elaborate performance lasted nearly 25 minutes and held her listeners enthralled. It was a love story about a prince from a valley town and his beloved, a princess who lived high on a mountaintop.

The story begins with the prince befriending a man by killing a dragon who lives on his lake. The man gives the prince three magic arrows. The story was very nuanced and involved, with several subplots about the theme of love, but the basic plot is this: The prince and princess fall in love. Before they can get the proper parental approvals to be married, he must go off to war. His parents are then turned against the match by an evil crow. In interesting subplots the princess uses two of the magic arrows to save other girls in the town who eventually find love and happiness. But the princess then begins to die slowly of a curse from the crow and is saved through magic by her father, who takes her back to his mountain kingdom.

The prince returns to find the princess gone. He rebukes his parents for not taking care of his love and goes off on a journey to find her. He finds a magic horse and is able to overcome several supernatural obstacles, such as stone elephants trying to keep him from the Mountain Kingdom. The crow makes a last-ditch effort to stop him with snakes and fire, but the prince overcomes them. He reaches the palace and uses a hand-maid to communicate with and then meet with his love, but the king won't consent to the marriage because of the problems his daughter has suffered. The prince must prove his worthiness, which he does by shooting the final magic arrow through the princess's crown. Kae ended her presentation with a flourish. "So the king think, 'Maybe he strong enough to marry her,' and so they get married. Then they try to get the evil bird and shoot it with same arrow. Then they very happy."

Kae used a white cutout of herself as the reader, because "I feel like a ghost, go everywhere, see everything, but no one see me." She often positioned this reader cutout to show how she was relating to the characters. She placed this cutout near the Mountain King and said, "I really see the king and queens. They very sad about their daughter and wonder what to do."

During the princess's great troubles under the curse, she placed the princess cutout over the cutout of herself as reader and said, "I cared about princess the most. She did nothing wrong. Why do they want to burn her up and stuff? I feel like I her and I feel very sad. She not understand why everyone so mean to her." She then placed the reader cutout over that of the crow and said, "I hate him. He evil. I want to cover him up." At the end of the story she again overlaid the princess cutout on her own, and said, "I am like princess the most. I love her the most. I want to be strong like her."

At the end of the story she placed her reader cutout right next to the prince and princess and said, "I like prince and princess. They have really strong relationship."

As we talked after her performance, she said, "It [the SRI] helped me to see the story and show it to other people. . . . It helped me know the people and they feeling." She told me that she had drawn some of the cutouts several times, until she thought the cutouts really "look and feel like people in story."

Considering Significance

At the end of her SRI performance of "The Seven Daughters," Kae told her group that the story was meant for Hmong parents, and was a warning to them not to stand in the way of their children's romantic desires. "Parents shouldn't try to always be boss. They should listen to story and see what happens when they don't listen to child." She explained that if the prince's parents had respected their son's love for the princess, all of the trials and tribulations could have been avoided.

She then told a story of her cousin and his girlfriend and how his parents would not approve of the girl, thereby destroying their hopes to be married. She ended by saying, "My parents doesn't do that," and commented:

> I want to be Hmong but I don't want stuff to happen to me like what happens to other Hmong girls. I want to finish high school or college before I get married. I want to find good man and have his parents approve me. I will take care of them but I want them to take care of me too.

Here Kae explicitly reflects on the meaning of the story and connects it to her own life.

Throughout the visualization project, Tommy, Kae, and Walter were interviewed about their reading, and were asked to complete periodic "visual protocols." Sometimes we read the stories aloud together, but usually they read the stories silently on their own. During the protocols, the students were asked to stop and draw a picture or to verbally describe what they were seeing whenever they had formed a strong image, or felt the need to get a sense of one. Many students involved in the studies chose to verbally describe what they were seeing. Notably, Tommy, Kae, and Walter always chose to draw. If they discussed what they had seen as they read, it was by discussing the drawing.

The first protocol selection used with Tommy and Walter was Liam O'Flaherty's "The Sniper" (1923), a story set during the Easter uprising in Dublin, Ireland. The second protocol was completed with Donald Westlake's "The Winner" (1970), the futuristic story of the poet Revell, who is imprisoned for the expression of personal and individualistic views considered inappropriate by the state. He is in a model prison without walls or fences, imprisoned by a "black box" implanted in his body that will make him reel in pain when he wanders more than 100 yards from the prison compound. Despite the intense pain, Revell continues to try to escape, because if he stops doing so, "They would have made me stop being me." A third protocol was completed with "The Little Boy Whose Friend Died on Him" by Ana Maria Matute (1968). This story involves a little boy whose best friend dies in the night. The boy can't believe it because all the toys they played with are still in the yard. He will not eat or sleep. The next morning he proclaims the toys worthless, throws them away, and goes home. His mother exclaims, "How this child has grown. My God, how this child has grown!"

In the first two protocols, Tommy and Walter chose to stop twice to draw pictures. On their own initiative, they independently stopped to draw a third picture after the story was over. On each occasion, the first picture was drawn after reading the first few paragraphs. In these protocols, Tommy and Walter separately stopped to draw within two sentences of each other, Walter stopping first on each occasion. The boys were eager to make the drawings, Walter calling out "I've gotta stop here," and Tommy murmuring, "Wait, I need to draw now. . . ."

The first drawing was used in both cases to situate the story world. From it, the boys could recount who the characters were, the conflict, how the conflict involved these characters, and a somewhat elaborated view of the setting the characters found themselves in. Tommy explained drawing at this point as "figuring out what's going on," and Walter as "getting it like, set in your head." The actual act of drawing itself seemed to help them to enter into the "secondary world" and to imagine and get this story world set in their minds.

The second pictures involved the climaxes of the stories. Tommy twice drew a climax earlier than Walter. In "The Sniper," Tommy drew it at the point when the sniper dropped his rifle over the building's edge to trick the other sniper into thinking he was dead.

Walter, on the other hand, waited until the sniper actually shot his enemy. Both readers seemed eager to stop at those points and then to finish the drawing once they had decided to do so. When asked why they drew at this point, Tommy said, "because it's important"; Walter said, "now he's won . . . he's safe now." Both indicated that they felt the drawn event was climactic and important to pay attention to.

Both readers also chose to draw a picture after the story was read. The purpose seemed to be to reflect on the ending of the story. In contrast to the previous two drawings, which were quick sketches, both students took their time with these drawings, sometimes staring into space for periods of time before continuing to sketch. In "The Sniper," Walter drew the sniper springing to the side of the dead enemy to turn him over. "That's the last thing he did." Since this action was not stated in the text, the drawing seems to have helped Walter to fill in textual gaps, imagining how they should be filled.

Tommy's final picture moved back into the story to the point at which the sniper shot his enemy. "That's the big thing in this story," he said. "If he had missed—KER-BLAM—he's dead, man, and the other guy's turnin' *him* over." Tommy did not reflect on the ending as much as rethink the climax of the story and how it affected the ending.

Their visual responses to "The Winner" were similar to those created for "The Sniper." Both figured out that Revell was a prisoner and identified with him, but had trouble figuring out what he was imprisoned for. Tommy dismissed this problem; Walter thought about it until he decided that "Somebody doesn't like him." Tommy's climax was when Revell crawled into the woods, "escaping" from the warden's sight and defying his prediction that Revell couldn't make it that far; Walter drew later, when Revell and the doctor were arrested at the doctor's office. Tommy's final drawing was of the doctor being arrested. He observed that "They [Revell and the doctor] can't get away with it. Ever." Walter's final drawing was of the doctor and Revell in prison together. "Now there's two of them going to try and escape."

In "The Little Boy . . ." both Tommy and Walter drew one picture, to set the story world at the beginning. They did not draw further pictures, commenting instead on what they perceived to be the stupidity of the story. "Nothin' happened!" Walter complained. Tommy, in his protocol, sneered, "What a stupid story!"

In the first two protocols, these two boys used their drawings to set the story world, set and reflect on the climax, and set and reflect on what they considered to be the resolution—in the form of a resolving action. Bruner's (1986) conception of the "landscape of action" and the "landscape of consciousness" is useful here, I think. Tommy seems to operate almost solely on the landscape of action; Walter makes moves into the landscape of consciousness somewhat only at the very end, after absorbing all of the story's action. In this final story, which has little action, operating instead almost exclusively in the consciousness of the boy and his mother, these readers did not experience nor visualize a complete story world. It was not a story to them at all.

Kae completed three visual protocols with different stories. She always drew three pictures. One typical visual protocol was for a science fiction story called "Human Frailty." In this story, the captain of a space ship overrides the computer and has a rescue ship save his young female apprentice instead of himself. At the end of the story, this decision is explained by the computer as being due to "human frailty." Kae drew a first picture five paragraphs into the story "to tell me what I seeing and where I am." The second picture was drawn toward the middle of the story, "because I want to know for sure what happening." At the end she drew a third picture, "to help me think about story." Her final picture was of the captain drifting off through space as the spaceship disappeared in the other direction. "I guess he really love her. That's all," Kae said of the ending.

Kae seemed to draw her pictures less to record what she was seeing and more to actually work out her visualization of the story. Like the boys, Kae also seemed to use her first drawings to set herself inside the story. She used the second to understand story action, and the third to operate on the landscape of consciousness to understand the story's meaning. "After I draw," she said, "I can think about what story mean. That's hard when I just read." On another occasion she had told me that "Art and computer [hypermedia] help me to understand what I learn and how to work with other people. It help me know what to do and I get to know things. . . . Without pictures it hard to know what things mean."

Remembering

In addition to helping these students enter the story world, see people and places, and get the "story" set in their minds, the visualization activities seemed to enhance their memories of the stories they had read. Earlier in the school year, for example, while reading *The Incredible Journey,* Tommy and Walter could often not comprehend story sequences, nor remember what they had read the day before. In contrast, they could discuss in detail the scenes they had responded to through the SRI or through drawings, sometimes weeks after the reading and response.

A particularly striking example of this phenomenon was with the picture map these students completed with David Quammen's "Republic of Cockroaches," a nonfiction tale of the cockroach, framed by why it will probably inherit the earth.

With the Quammen piece, all three students picked out and drew key details of the tale. Kae's and Tommy's pictures corresponded to key details on a one-to-one basis; Walter had one picture that expressed two key details and another that expressed three. The picture maps were completed before Christmas; I produced them again in May. All three students could tell me exactly and correctly what each picture expressed about the cockroach, including Walter identifying the multiple meanings of his two pictures! Drawing the pictures was a powerful memory prod for these students that was not fulfilled by note-taking or other conventional study techniques.

The boys indicated during this session that drawing helped them to read, understand, and, as Walter put it, "to talk about, you know, what you read." They were amazed at how the pictures helped them to remember and think about stories. Kae indicated that she already drew pictures as part of the notes she made in school. Walter indicated that he would now take notes for other classes, "in pictures, as much as I can . . . it works better for me." This indicates a tremendous amount of metacognitive awareness about how he best learns and responds, and a new willingness to use it to his advantage.

Five weeks after her initial SRI of "The Seven Daughters," I asked Kae to do it again for me. I had kept her cutouts and gave them to her from my filing cabinet. Without any review, she launched into a full 23-minute rendition of the story, complete with comments about how she read and felt about the story. When I told her how amazed I was at her memory, she told me, "When I make it, I remember it."

The SRIs and drawings also seemed to help these students build up an awareness of intertextual connections, and the ability to remember and draw upon these connections. After reading "The Sniper," Walter commented that his reading of this story was similar to that of "Pandora's Box," "because they're both war stories and the people wonder if they did the right things." Kae compared "The Seven Daughters" to the Greek myth of Perseus that another student performed through symbolic story representation. "He [Perseus] love this girl and magic help him to get her."

Kae, as mentioned earlier, quite often used her artwork created around a story to talk about incidents that occurred or that she thought about from her own life. After her second SRI of "The Seven Daughters" she said, "Sometimes I look at the stars and wonder what going to happen to me. I want to get marry and be happy too, but without all the troubles."

MOVING TOWARD A REFLECTIVE RESPONSE: "THE BOOK SAID ALL THAT"

As if unleashed by the "go-ahead" to respond artistically to their reading, these students, especially Tommy and Walter, submitted a continual stream of artwork to their classmates and teachers (myself, their LD teacher, and occasionally the social studies teacher). In Tommy's case, much of the artwork did not reflect what I would consider to be full or rich readings in that they sometimes missed, subverted, or violated important textual details. But at least he was doing some sort of reading, often doing it enthusiastically, and creating and sharing his responses to that literature. He had become a member of the classroom community.

When given a choice among various activities introduced in the class that would incorporate artistic response, Kae almost always stuck with small drawings that corresponded on a one-to-one basis with story scenes and ideas. Throughout the year, after making a drawing she often made the move of explaining how the pictured scene or idea was important to the story, and why the author had put it there. Tommy and Walter usually stuck with simple one-page drawings, usually drawing one scene or event from a book. They almost always chose to spurn more complex uses of visual art that required more interpretive or reflective artwork. Throughout, Tommy's drawings got bigger and on occasion more colorful, taking on a mural-like quality. At the end of a class reading of *Roll of Thunder, Hear My Cry,* Tommy made an action-packed drawing of the fight between the Wallaces and Mr. Morrison on the Vicksburg road, complete with Papa's broken leg and head wound, gushing blood, gunshots, Kaleb's broken back, a muddy road, the red pickup and its shining headlamps, and the dark rain of the night. Walter made a series of pencil drawings of major scenes: the sabotage of the bus, the fight with the Wallaces, and the fire at the end of the book. In their discussions of the pictures, these two boys pointed out what had happened in the scene, how they had seen it—sometimes referring to textual clues that helped them to see it that way, and on one or two occasions, to what the scene meant to the story. For example, when explaining one drawing to his learning group, Walter had this to say: "So they dug the hole to wreck the bus because they were always getting crapped on and they wanted to get back. . . . I put them in the woods all covered with mud and laughing because the book said all that."

Particularly effective for helping these students organize and share their personal experiences and responses to literature was the collage project. The process of making the collage both motivated and scaffolded their attempts to understand the meaning of the poem or song in question, and the presentation of it scaffolded their move from nonverbal to verbal expression. Both Tommy and Walter found it much easier to talk about their collages and what they did to make them than to struggle with the often abstract and suggestive nature of the literary works to which they were responding.

Tommy's collage was of John Ciardi's poem "The Shark," which we had read in class. In the poem, the shark is described as having only one thought, which he thinks constantly, "of something, anywhere, somehow to eat." At the end of the poem, the speaker says, "Be careful where you swim, my sweet."

In Tommy's collage, there was an interesting pattern of three separate levels of drawings mixed with photographs cut from magazines.

On the middle level were drawings and photographs of sharks, whipping and swirling through the water with snarling faces. The drawn sharks had gaping jaws and huge teeth trailing thin streams of blood. Above the sharks was a top level that included mostly photographs of food: hams, turkeys, gourmet meals, a McDonald's hamburger, and much more. Tommy drew a thought bubble containing a single chicken drumstick from the head of one shark. This, he explained, corresponded to the line in the poem that the shark "has only one thought, but he thinks it a lot."

On the lowest level was a fatherly figure wagging an index finger in the face of a young woman. This was a father "warning his kid not to go swimmin'." Tommy further explained that the whole poem "was this guy talking to his kid about how dangerous it is to swim where there's sharks." He indicated that the scenes of the sharks and foods that were placed above these two characters' heads were "what they were thinkin' about in their minds as they were talking. Mostly the dad, but then the girl too as she thinks about what he's sayin' . . . except she thinks about herself getting chomped—like the girl in *Jaws*."

Tommy has done some very sophisticated literary reading here. He knows that on one level the poem is about the dangers of the food-obsessed shark and was able to visually depict this and explain it to his discussion group. He has recognized a speaker and an implied audience within the poem, and has spectated as a reader upon the scene that transpired between them. He has participated in the drama of the shark's appetite and has expected that the two characters also participated in this imaginary experience. He articulates that the collage is a created evocation of the text that he imagined as he read, and that he expects characters implied by the poem to imagine things when they speak and listen to that same text. This, in my estimation, was the high point of Tommy's response during this school year. He did not create it spontaneously, however. The final line of the poem, "Be careful where you swim, my sweet!" gave him fits. "I don't get it!" he told his reading partner and then me. "It don't fit!" I was quick to point out that he was right—it didn't fit, and that I was pleased he had recognized that. "It introduces something new," I told him, "and you have to figure out what that is." Tommy cared enough about his collage that he undertook to canvass other readers about the final line until he was satisfied that he had a coherent and complete understanding of the poem.

Significantly, after his presentation his group proceeded to discuss how the poem could be about the many dangers and consequences of single-mindedness, and the danger of encountering people who, as one student put it, "only want to use you." Tommy did not make this thematic generalization himself. But the group's discussion of this point was stimulated and scaffolded by his artistic rendering of the poem. The group was helped by his picture of a father and daughter and by the notion of advice-giving and warning as they came to a general understanding of the poem's thematic implications. "It can't be about sharks," one boy remarked. "What dad goes around making a big deal of sharks?" This began a discussion about what parents did make a big deal of. As the group discussed these possibilities, Tommy could be seen shaking his head in agreement, and once said, "Yeah, that's it!"

EPILOGUE:
OPENING DOORS WITH ART

The artwork considered in this study helped me as the teacher, and helped the students themselves, to see the various ways in which one text could be evoked and the various possibilities that it held to be read in different and potentially richer ways.

Tommy and Walter, for example, practiced reading much in the way described by the phenomenologist Georges Poulet (1969). For Poulet, reading is a passive submission to the world of the text, which assumes a life of its own. Textual details are submitted to in order to "concretize" a world defined by the text. Readers, in Michael Smith's (1992) terms, "surrender" to the text, creating as closely as possible the world it suggests. In Poulet's terms, preconceptions and assumptions are "bracketed out" so that the reader can engage with the text's ways of perceiving. Tommy and Walter were attempting to understand exactly what it was the text was saying. At least when their reading would serve as the basis for an artistic project, they wanted to "discover" the textual world, and "get it set." This was very difficult for them, and artistic activities helped them to do so.

As such, their readings were what Vipond and Hunt (1984) call "information-driven": The questions they asked themselves and the subsequent evocations of the secondary world that they created had to do with information "Right There" (Raphael, 1982) in the text. They seemed preoccupied with what Peter Rabinowitz (1987) calls rules of notice and signification, asking themselves, What details should we pay attention to, and what do they mean? This was true of Kae as well, though as her language and reading proficiency grew, she moved beyond this.

Perhaps this is a necessary starting point for unengaged readers. It is a starting point from which other, more creative forms of reading may be launched.

The use and discussion of artwork with other students began to move Walter beyond this rather passive way of reading into more productive and participatory dimensions, anticipating the more active roles of filling gaps and adding meaning to text that were exhibited by other readers in the class. Tommy's artwork involved him in discussions and interchanges where other readers were doing this sort of elaborating and connecting with literary works. During these discussions they were able to involve him as a member of the literary club, and perhaps, in time, these exchanges could help him to become a more active reader as well. Kae quickly used stories as a way of telling other stories, stories about her family, her life in Laos, and herself. She introduced herself to others through her art and built up relationships with them.

The greatest recommendation for including artistic response in the language arts classroom is that it encourages very different readers to respond in natural ways, to share that response with each other, and to extend and develop it in unforeseen, socially supported, and personally validating and exciting ways.

The idea of "art for art's sake" can be replaced by that of "art for the reader's sake." That is an idea that my readers and I found quite compelling.

Individual and Democratic Response

The experiences we had together suggest that artistic response activities may help less proficient and less engaged readers to respond on various dimensions to enter, evoke, comprehend, and sometimes elaborate and reflect upon the experience of reading. Further, art may provide a means for experiencing what it means for a reader to enter, create, and participate in a story world, especially for readers who may not naturally see and experience what they read, whether because of operative reading difficulties or because of limited language proficiency.

It is a central tenet of reader response theories that a reading is an experience created by the reader. The use of art as response stresses the individual's control in creating, organizing, and constructing experience and knowledge. Using art is also a way to get children both to move beyond simple comprehension and to do the work of responding, instead of having it done for them. Since art requires drawing on personal experience of the world, it reinforces how prior experience is the raw material we bring to a transaction of text to create a literary experience with it, and it encourages students to connect what they read back to their own life.

Visual response is a very democratic form of response not only because it is useful in different ways to different students, but because it validates a form of knowing and exploring not normally made use of in core academic classes; it offers perspectives not usually considered in the classroom. And art, unlike traditional forms of response, is not perceived by students to be "correct" or "incorrect." It may therefore open doors for readers who have become resistant to contributing in class because they have been so often told they are wrong, or because their response has been in some way devalued. Artistic response encourages risk-taking because it is traditionally freer from judgment than the answering of authority-generated questions about a reading.

Art encourages and celebrates spirited thinking. It therefore has possibilities for building self-esteem and the belief that the reader "can do it" and can "contribute" to the grand conversation about literature. The use of art in my own classes, I believe, helped to express the attitude that every student can respond to literature in unique ways, and that each response adds to everyone else's experience. Because it encouraged risk-taking, it was a way for students to attempt and perhaps fail at something difficult but interesting, such as when Walter believed that his depiction of important scenes from Roll of Thunder did not quite "get" or capture his experience of the book. He then began to consider how more of the experience "could be got."

This sort of controlled floundering is what education should be about. Walter knew he was doing something difficult, he was critical about the process and product of doing it, yet he felt entirely capable of taking on the challenge and considering what to do next.

The use of artistic response as a springboard for literary discussions decentered the teacher as the authority, and foregrounded the students as conversants and generators of discourse. That the students often explored and developed their private visions as they created their artistic renderings, and that these visions continued to be negotiated and developed during small group sharing, allowed the readers to experience themselves as productive theorizers of an evolving literary landscape and meaning. The use of small group sharing encouraged every student to become part of a meaning-making community; the sharing of artistic response enhanced both individual and group understanding. In the case of Kae, the use of art brought her into classroom conversation for the first time and provided her with a way of communicating and sharing with other students in a way that she valued and they appreciated.

Artistic response reinforces the reader's role in the reading transaction precisely because students immediately see that they are dealing with their own private visions and experiences. It is interesting to them to share the visions of others, and they know it is unlikely that such a vision could be considered "wrong."

As Tommy told me, "I don't usually like to talk in class, but I didn't mind talking about my pictures because people seemed interested and nobody was telling me that what I did was wrong." Tommy also used art to include himself as a valuable member of collaborative groups. "I used to not want to work with other guys, but now they know they can give me the drawings and stuff like that to do." During the making of a mural of the civil rights movement, in fact, Tommy was drafted by a group of students who normally operated as an exclusive clique because they valued his artistic ability. He responded with two highly elaborate and complicated panoramas reminiscent of the confusion and texture of Bosch's *Garden of Earthly Delights* or the social vitality of a Brueghel scene, with layers of people involved in different individual activities. One was of the March on Washington, and the other of the Watts riots in Los Angeles.

In an art class, such risk-taking is rewarded. Divergent views are "interesting" rather than incorrect. Students are prodded to explore and express their visions and understanding, not simply to justify them. By bringing art into the reading classroom we open the doors to these same possibilities with literary response.

Engaging Multiple Intelligences

The artistic activities were not universally embraced by all of my students. Though no student refused to attempt them, many students selected other options when given a choice. Some students indicated that they did not really feel that they possessed "artistic talent" and chose to respond in different modes when given an option, and by cutting and pasting photographs rather than drawing when required to create something visual. Still, the use of such activities may convince some students who feel less compelled by visual activities that artistic response may work for them in some way, and it may enhance or become a part of their response repertoire. And using such activities as a choice among several options opens wide doors for many previously disenfranchised students, such as Tommy and Walter, or students trying to find a way into the classroom such as Kae.

The artistic activities did include new members in the conversation about literature, and seemed to encourage students such as Tommy and Walter to think of themselves as readers with private visions worth sharing. Other students, such as Kae, were able to extend and develop their thought about literary works, and to converse more fully and fruitfully about their response through the use of art. A few very proficient readers seemed enabled to explore tangential worlds and visions through their art, and were able to share these visions with others in ways not normally encouraged.

Howard Gardner's work (1983) with multiple intelligences has helped to debunk the notion that there is one way of learning, or that there is such a thing as a fixed IQ. Gardner suggests that instead of asking "How smart are you?" we should ask "How are you smart?" School should be a place where students are encouraged to use their natural talents and aptitudes. So language arts classes become a place where student strengths and interests are called on. If they are not, students will be unrecognized, bored, and unhappy. Gardner suggests that every child is gifted. By providing various opportunities and choices, we help students to develop their own unique combinations of talents.

Researchers working on the problem of how the brain works and learns have corroborated Gardner's ideas. Hart (1984), Ornstein (1990), and others have shown that all learning is auditory, visual, or kinesthetic in nature. None of these researchers' work has been disputed by any other. So we have fairly good information that certain types of brains and learning styles privilege certain ways of learning. Yet almost all classroom experience is auditory. This excludes many students from using their preference to learn in kinesthetic (like Libby, who wanted to learn by "doing things with my body") or visual ways (like Tommy, Kae, and Walter). And it precludes auditory learners from expanding their own repertoires.

When we use a wider variety of techniques and emphases in our teaching of reading and response to literature, we create richer possibilities for exploring, experiencing, and knowing through literature. We provide more opportunity for engagement, and higher expectations from print.

It is, I think, the job of the teacher to encourage students to use their natural talents and aptitudes as they construct meaning. It is the teacher's job to call on children's individual strengths and to build upon these. The use of various meaning-making activities such as drama and art helps us to reach the various strengths and multiple intelligences of our various individual students.

Art as a Metacognitive Tool

The creation of artwork provides students with concrete tools and experiences to think with, talk about, and share.

My team teaching colleague Paul, upon hearing one group share and discuss their artwork with each other, told me: "This artwork is as sweet a piece of metacognition as you can imagine. The kids are seeing how they think and seeing how other kids' minds work. They can actually be let into their heads and see what others see when they read!" (March 1993).

Students have a concrete reference as they ask themselves and each other: Why did you do that? What else can you do? Possibilities can be considered, widened, and narrowed as students ask themselves such questions.

The artwork can then lead to more reflective response on more abstract levels, once these students have a concrete reference and anchor point from which to engage in more risky explorations.

COMMENTARY

SEEING THE SUBSTANTIVE POSSIBILITIES

In the Commentary after Chapter 4, I noted that teachers are often reluctant to use drama and action strategies for fear that they will lose control, or because they don't really understand how drama strategies work and how to purposefully frame and focus them for powerful instructional goals and ends. (In fact, I feel more in control while using drama than at most other times, because I have not only framed the work and required concrete deliverables, but also because I can see what students are thinking and doing, and I can help to shape and further that).

My concern with teachers' use of visualization techniques is much different. I have found that teachers readily embrace the use of visual strategies, but in ways that fail to actualize the possibilities for teaching students *how* to read, learn, organize, analyze, and synthesize more powerfully and with deeper understanding. The activities become "throwaways" that do not scaffold students' practice of new strategies and attainment of new stances and understandings. What is produced are not knowledge artifacts that are extensible, revisable, and usable by others, but something to display briefly (if at all), and then throw away. This is why I use the drama/visualization strategy teaching guide shown in

Exhibit 5.1 whenever I teach preservice or inservice teachers how to use both drama and visualization techniques.

In addition, it strikes me now how much I privileged the reading of fictional literary texts in *YGBB*, especially narratives in the form of stories and novels. Now I'm much more apt to use narrative and creative nonfiction of all kinds, nonnarrative texts, electronic texts, visual compositions, video, and graphic novels in my teaching (see Wilhelm & Smith, 2016).

This has become a throughline of my recent teaching and research: to take a wider view of textuality and literacy, to use more and different kinds of texts (paintings, photographs, videos, children's picture books, etc.) to introduce and deliberately practice and consolidate threshold processes, and through this, to promote a wider notion and understanding of literacy (Wilhelm & Smith, 2016).

Now I model and have students do SRI with arguments, websites, and video clips as well as with fables and stories. I conceive of multimedia texts as important in their own right, as well as a way to help students visualize, and to bridge the developing strategies of visualization and mental modeling to less visually supported texts. I know now that I was not sufficiently respectful of my students' out-of-school literacies and the new literacies that have come with the rise of electronic technologies (see Smith & Wilhelm, 2002; 2006).

I still love and privilege literature, and I know that there are benefits that accrue only from spending extended time with characters and their experience, but now I cast a wider net, use many more visual and shorter texts on the way to reading longer ones, and define more widely the notion of literature and the kinds of texts I think are worthy to consider and reflect upon in our work together.

Seeing What We Read

It's a simple but profound insight that "reading IS seeing," and that students who struggle do not see what they read, or even know that they are supposed to see what they read.

This insight has served me well as a teacher of struggling readers over the years. I've seen countless lightbulbs go on, and numerous struggling readers climb over the hump of their reading challenges by using visual strategies in ways that assist them in learning to "see" what they read.

But there is more at stake. I also think visualization explains the difference between recall and true "understanding," defined by current cognitive science (e.g., Wiggins & McTighe, 2006) as the capacity to explain, differentiate from other possible perspectives, interpret, use, and transfer what has been learned to new situations. I have found in my current work with science teachers, and with my longtime work with content-area teachers, that students must possess a working and highly visible mental model of a concept, process, or phenomenon to truly exhibit the facets of understanding listed above.

I've continued to experiment with various instructional techniques that use visuals and that promote visualization as a strategy, but also as a way to represent, share, and use understandings. I've reported on these ventures in my book *Reading IS Seeing* (Wilhelm, 2012b). This keeps visualization techniques from becoming throwaways done only for a class, and turns the techniques into scaffolds and prosthetics that develop threshold concepts and strategies that can be further developed, or that are part of a knowledge artifact that represents deep, shareable, and usable understandings.

This work has reinforced to me how essential visualization is to engaging, comprehending, and experiencing texts of all kinds; how assistive visual texts can be in developing threshold knowledge; and how necessary visual strategies are to understanding, as well as representing and sharing understanding. My current work with visualization and non-fiction texts has also led me to consider ways in which visualization strategies can take students back into a text in ways that will help them reflect on, more deeply understand, and learn from text.

Using Visual Techniques with Data

Over the past several years, my work with reading and comprehension has taken place almost exclusively in inquiry contexts. Because of this, I have experimented widely with visual techniques for placeholding, "seeing," organizing, and analyzing data from a wide variety of nonfiction texts (video documentaries, charts, statistics, tables, etc.). I have found that my students are all familiar with a variety of graphic organizers, but that they don't really understand how to use these as tools to do what they were invented to do: represent, organize, and analyze data. Instead, they seem to use them as a glorified worksheet for repeating what they have read or learned, not for analysis, nor for "figuring forth,": as a tool for seeing new patterns in the data and constructing new kinds of knowledge and representing this knowledge (see Exhibit 5.2).

In my inquiry projects, I require students to create visual data displays using semantic feature analyses, family trees (webs), flow charts, and much more. When students use these techniques to operate on data, analyze, and interpret, and to represent new understandings, then they are not only making new knowledge, but making this knowledge conceptual and visible, and they make themselves and their insights account-able through the data.

Students using visual techniques in these conscious and wide-awake ways are learning to see data and to think like inquirers. They are learn-ing to think with data, to use evidentiary reasoning, to come to under-stand and to make meaning, to contribute as researchers and public intellectuals to ongoing disciplinary and community conversations.

Learning how to read across a variety of nonfiction texts and data sets, mine these texts and data sets, see connections, organize patterns of data, and extrapolate patterns is a literacy skill that is necessary for expertise in all disciplines.

We have certainly found this to be so in our work with scientific lit-eracy. What good is it, for instance, to know facts about the troposphere, unless they help one to understand the difference between the tropo-sphere and the stratosphere? And what good is that if one does not understand the differences these layers of atmosphere make to Mother Earth and all forms of life, and if one cannot extrapolate patterns about the damage being done to the troposphere and imagine where this might lead, particularly in terms of how life will be affected?

Symbolic Story Representation/Reading Manipulatives

SRIs are another technique that I have used continually and at all grade levels over the years (Wilhelm, in preparation). I have worked with kin-dergarten and 1st-grade teachers using SRIs to model engaged reading and the use of various strategies, and to help students begin to take over these strategies as they use the cutouts and objects to position themselves in the story and to practice and rehearse using the strategies and meta-cognitive language of a real reader. I have used the technique in middle and high school classrooms and in undergraduate and graduate classes to help students learn how to navigate various genres like fables, ironic monologues, satires, and arguments, as well as various informational text structures (Wilhelm, Smith, & Fredricksen, 2013), and to learn how to recognize and make meaning with conventions like irony and symbolism.

Recently, I asked 9th-graders to do SRIs to different inaugural addresses and share these in jigsaw groups so that they could compare these texts, see similarities, develop a sense of the genre, and identify what all inaugural addresses expect of a listener/reader.

I've also continued to use SRIs as a teacher research tool, and have advised several teachers who used them in their own research. Of course, they always work as a method for helping teachers to model their use of reading strategies and of noticing textual cues and interpreting them (Wilhelm & Smith, 2016). They are also useful for helping students engaged in inquiry and self-study of their own reading processes, which is so necessary to metacognition, self-regulation, the growth mindset, and future continued growth. Finally, they address both the spirit and the letter of next-generation standards and their call for metacognitive awareness as readers and writers.

I have found SRI to be a powerful teaching and teacher research tool. It not only reveals what a student reader is doing, it also demonstrates what is possible by identifying what is in that student's zone of proximal development, and helps to actualize these possibilities. The technique demonstrates in its classroom use that it is toolish instead of schoolish, that it creates extensible and generative tools for the readers who use it. This is true in content-area classes, with nonfiction texts and data sets, and with videos and multimedia texts. This past year I used it to great success with middle school science students reading a Bill Bryson text on the atmosphere along with various charts and data sets about different aspects of the atmosphere.

Like drama, it seems that many teachers are intrigued by SRI but may have difficulty getting started with it. But I receive a couple of emails a month from teachers who have tried it with great success, and from many students who have tried it, enjoyed it, and learned a great deal from it. (See Exhibit 5.4 for an introductory guide sheet to creating a model or helping students to create one.)

The following emails are typical examples:

Dear Jeff,

Have to admit I found it hard to make myself do it with my kids [symbolic story representation], but once I did, the results were amazing. The kids worked harder at it than any assignment all year, and I saw things about them as readers and people that I hadn't ever seen before. The technique seemed to provide a powerful scaffold for getting them to see what they did do and could do as readers, and encourage them to try new things.

I'm sending you a packet of photos and of letters from the students about their experience. Thanks for your help and advice. . . .

Dear Jeff,

Here is an article from *The Times* that lends hard scientific law to your often-seen-as-metaphorical "You gotta BE the book." To heck with this as merely a metaphor, in a very real sense, way down in the synapses, you ARE the ART you choose to view:

http://www.nytimes.com/2006/01/10/science/10mirr.html

The passage that sealed it for me: "Art exploits mirror neurons, said Dr. Vittorio Gallese, a neuroscientist at Parma University. When you see the Baroque sculptor Gian Lorenzo Bernini's hand of divinity grasping marble, you see the hand as if it were grasping flesh, he said. Experiments show that when you read a novel, you memorize positions of objects from the narrator's point of view." (Moreover, from the passage above, it seems that metaphorical transfigurations—in this case, stone to flesh—are "hardwired" in our brains.)

Wow, so reading IS seeing, and you do have to BE the book!

Exhibit 5.1. Visualization Response/Drama Response Activities Criteria Guide

When using drama and visualization strategies to teach reading, you'll want to demonstrate your understanding of how adolescent readers read and respond to literature, as described in *YGBB*, and how expert readers "bring meaning forward," learning text by text and activity by activity, as we know the best instruction helps students to do.

When designing drama and visualization activities, you might give students a handout to guide them through the process of engaging in and completing that activity, and/or you might choose to create a model of the completed activity (with video if you are doing drama work) with an attached description. In my experience, the most successful assignments of these kinds meet the following criteria:

____1. Each activity should require students to **evoke** the world of the text.

____2. The activities should encourage students to **elaborate** on the story world, to fill in gaps, to make inferences, and to extend their reading beyond the text.

____3. The activities should encourage students to **reflect**—to revisit **textual facts**, details, and experiences, and to reorganize, bring forward, and represent their experience and what they learned.

____4. The activities should encourage students to achieve a **richer and more "valid"** reading of the text.

____5. The activities should ask students to hone other skills and develop knowledge outside the domain of the text, e.g., learn about interviewing skills, news show formats, review writing, etc. (cf. use of visuals [Wilhelm, 2012b] and drama [Wilhelm, 2012a]).

____6. The activities should be **fun** for the kids, and should ask them to learn something they didn't already know (instead of just revisiting what they already know) and to achieve or practice some new learning processes they have not already mastered.

____7. The activities should **do some real-world work,** that is, pursuing and completing them should help to teach kids in the class about one another, about the book or unit topic, or about ways of reading, and may perhaps be part of a community service or partner school project. In any case, the work should have some real-world audiences.

____8. The activities should demonstrate how art and drama work **as assisted performance in the creation of new responses and knowledge creation.**

Exhibit 5.2. Picture Mapping

Before you start, work on your own, then with a partner, to consider the following (as you read, mark or list each key idea about the topic):

» Pay attention to the Key Detail clues/Readers' rules of notice we have studied:
  - Paragraphs often signal a new key idea
  - First and last sentences of the text and of paragraphs
  - Highlights, italics, bullets, bold print
  - Surprises, shifts, changes in focus or emphasis

» Now identify the topic of your reading—this will be what every key detail has as a point of connection. There might be multiple topics—choose the one that you think is most important to our current inquiry and purpose.

How can you symbolize the topic with a visual (no words allowed)?

Now, consider how you can symbolize the key details and how they were organized and arranged in the text.

  - Symbolize each key idea with a picture or a symbol; do this as simply as you can!
  - Show the relationships and the patterns of the key details, e.g., how they are organized and expressed, perhaps through text structure.

Finally, what comment, or theme, is expressed by this arrangement and organization of the key details about this topic? How do you know? Be sure you can explain!

» Now, what visual or symbol would be best to express this topic, comment, or theme? How do you know that this will express the theme to your audience?
  - Share your picture map and tell someone else what each picture/symbol means and how the pattern of details works toward communicating a main idea. See what they think.

Or, if you really get good at this:

» Demonstrate several key ideas with one symbol or picture.

> Show connections between ideas or progression of ideas if the organization or structure of the text is important to the points it makes (e.g., through a timeline, a family tree, a Venn diagram, etc.).
> Create a picture map of all the readings in a unit, reporting on all the key details, the common topic, and the main idea expressed across several readings.

Exhibit 5.3. Tableaux Directions for Narrative

In groups

1. Choose the text or text segment that you wish to depict and to visually share with your audience.
2. Consider why the audience will be interested in the text you have read and what they will need to know about it.
3. Review the important scenes and details your audience will need to know from each scene. Please consider the journalist's 5 W's and H (Who, What, Where, When, Why, and How). Remember that the author signals us to notice particular scenes: the first and last ones, ones that are surprising, that signal a climax or change in direction, that offer new and important information, that are different in some way, that are described in great detail, etc.

    Challenge: Use as few details or scenes as possible to communicate the whole story or meaning of a text.
4. Brainstorm how to present these scenes visually in a way that will communicate all of the important details of the scene to the audience.
5. Create the visual depictions of the scenes on newsprint sheets. Make notes on the back about what you need to point out to the audience about each scene. For example, you might include a topic word, a one-sentence summary of the scene, explain how this scene connects to prior or following tableaux, point out key details and explain how these details are important, cite the theme or deep meaning of the scene, relate this theme to the topic of the excerpt, etc.
6. When you are done with individual tableau, you should be sure that your audience will have completely understood and "seen" that whole section of the text.
7. When all tableaux are done, make sure that they work together to show the shape of a story, the stages of the process, or the whole shape of the ideas presented.
8. Rehearse your presentation as a group, making sure everyone is involved.
9. Present it!
10. Get feedback about how well you did and what you could do to improve your presentation.

Tableaux Variations

Idea Tableaux. I've found that tableaux lend themselves particularly well to remembering and recreating scenes from a narrative. **Picture mapping** (see Chapter 5) is a technique that is excellent for representing key details and main ideas from expository and other texts designed to convey information.

However, tableaux can be adapted to add depictions of main ideas, motifs, or themes that occur in any kind of text. Students can be assigned an excerpt and asked to depict a major point (or points) that the reader must carry away from that scene or text excerpt. (This is a prerequisite stage to creating symbolic story representation.) Students can make concepts into people, and invent contexts or settings in order to personalize and communicate the meanings of informational texts.

Slide Shows. Students can use **PowerPoint** (or more sophisticated kinds of software applications) to make simple slide shows of tableaux. These can be very spare and symbolic, or highly detailed and realistic. Just like a traveler from abroad will want to show the central places and events of a past trip to her friends, here the creators depict the central scenes or ideas from a text, and can even animate or blend the scenes together so that the audience will get a sense of their journey through a text and the important sights, seminal experiences, and meanings that capture the essence of their reading experience.

Interestingly, these techniques scaffold readers' consideration of key details, and sharing them with one another offers another scaffold as they debate why certain details are key, what needs to be included in a slide show, what is lost if a particular idea is deleted, etc. In this way, the kids learn a lot from one another about identifying key details and creating summaries.

Exhibit 5.4. Quick Guide for Composing a Symbolic Story Representation/Reading Manipulative

Step 1: **Select a Short Text or a Short Excerpt of Text.** Choose a short excerpt or scene that you enjoyed and/or that seemed really rich, interesting, and important to the overall text.

Step 2: **Consider How You Read This Excerpt.** Create a representation (e.g., a symbolic cutout from construction paper) of yourself as the reader that will help your audience to understand your stance, perspective, and how you read and interacted with your chosen scene.

Step 3: **Write Down the Moves.** List five moves you made as a reader while reading this excerpt/scene and list them. How will you "perform" and demonstrate these moves to your audience?

Step 4: **Consider the Author's Moves.** Create an author cutout or a symbolic representation of the author. Think about how the author constructed the scene and made particular moves to create meaning and effect. List significant moves made by the author.

Step 5: **Show the Details.** Create cutouts or symbolic representations, or use found objects for the important characters, elements of setting, ideas, and forces in your excerpt/scene.

Step 6: **Illustrate the Central Focus.** What takeaway did you get from reading this excerpt—a theme, generalization about life, application? How can you represent this with a symbolic cutout?

Step 7: **Include Extras.** Music? Backgrounds?

Step 8: **Rehearse.** Practice performing the story of your reading in a way that will also highlight the important elements from the text excerpt.

Step 9: **Anticipate Questions.** Try to predict the kinds of questions your audience will ask you after you have presented your SRI and consider how you will answer them.

Extensions of Exhibit 5.4 appear online.

Exhibits 5.5–5.15 can be found online on this book's page and the free downloads page at TCPress.com

Exhibit 5.5. Using Visual Response

Exhibit 5.6. Using Graphic Organizers Purposefully

Exhibit 5.7. SRI/Reading Manipulative Planning Sheet

Exhibit 5.8. Symbolic Story Representation/Reading Manipulative Evaluation Sheet

Exhibit 5.9. High School Teacher Samantha Archibald Mora's Symbolic Story Representation Model for Assisting with Student Reading Throughout *The Grapes of Wrath*

Exhibit 5.10. Symbolic Story Representation/Reading Manipulative Checksheet for Teacher Modeling

Exhibit 5.11. Symbolic Story Representation/Reading Manipulative in Mathematics

Exhibit 5.12. Kae's Symbolic Story Representation Cutouts of *The Seven Daughters*

Exhibit 5.13. Censorship Unit Summary Picture Map

Exhibit 5.14. Republic of Cockroaches Argument Structure Picture Map

Exhibit 5.15. Sleep Picture Map

6

✿

Expanding Concepts of Reading, Response, and Literature

Through this school year of studying literary response with my students, the focus of class became reoriented. We came to focus on the *how* and the *why* of using various reading responses and strategies instead of just the *what* of that response. With this as the focus, students were given time to create and share responses to literature. "What was most exciting," I wrote, "is that they then began to learn from each other, evaluating and trying on each other's response moves" (June 1993). I also came to believe in the importance of providing time for both individual and group readings so that students could compare their response to the same story, and bring their own unique contributions and responses to the class. Our class became a study of self and world and response, instead of an exercise devoted to curricularly defined content, and this proved to be motivating and interesting for the students. Making the *process* of reading a major subject of the class and emphasizing the sharing of moves and strategies helped the students to rethink reading as a personally meaningful, productive, and creative activity.

Studying response with my students allowed me to get to know my students as people and as readers. It allowed me to validate who the students were and what they did as readers, and gave me the possibility to develop, build on, and extend these abilities.

I came to see that research techniques such as the protocol and the symbolic representation interview could be adapted for the instructional purpose of helping students to see what they did as readers, to extend and develop their use of these moves, to share and learn from each other, and to set their own goals. The research methods, when used by the students, helped them to gain more awareness and ownership over their own reading strategies.

For teachers interested in practicing reader response theory and natural language learning in their classrooms, the stories I've told here may have some informing power. My work with student readers has impressed the following points upon me with particular force.

READING AS ENGAGEMENT

First, I found that thinking about literary reading as engagement was a powerful move for me as a teacher, and for my students as readers. Engagement means that the reader uses a variety of moves and strategies to enter and involve herself intensely in worlds of meaning. In these "story worlds," the reader interprets characters, setting, events, and thematic possibilities through her interaction with and movement through that world. Adopting this perspective helped me to implement reader response theory into my classroom, to get to know my students as readers, and to provide opportunities and activities that helped develop them as readers in both their abilities and attitudes. This development was especially notable in the cases of many learning disabled students and reluctant readers.

The notion of reading as engagement, in turn, expanded my view of what constituted reading and response. I found that truly engaged readers responded to texts in a variety of creative and productive ways that were not encouraged or privileged by my own typical classroom activities. As I came to know my student readers through the research procedures that we used together in class, I was very surprised at what individual readers could and could not do. The variety, intensity, and often stunning sophistication of the most engaged readers' responses was an amazing contrast to the virtual nonexistence of available moves and expressed response on the part of the less engaged readers. Even among the most engaged readers, response was highly individual and idiosyncratic, their response on each of the 10 different dimensions drawing on the personal experience, interests, and even mood of the reader.

I realized that the response of engaged readers is intensely visual, empathic, and emotional. By focusing in class on the importance of these evocative responses, that is, entering the story world, visualizing people and places, and taking up relationships to characters, less engaged readers were given strategies for experiencing texts and were helped to rethink reading.

As a result, many were helped to become more enthusiastic readers. These less engaged readers' use of insufficient or impoverished strategies was then used as a springboard to richer and more reflective response.

I think it was an important finding that none of the less engaged readers ever responded on the connective or reflective response dimensions unless they had first fully evoked and experienced the world of the story. This indicates that teachers might well begin to privilege the development of evocative response before asking students to reflect on their experience of a text. This creation of a textual world or a "mental model" (such as we did through drama and art) is an activity that is almost completely neglected by classroom instruction and curriculum guides in reading, and yet every other kind of response and thought about reading depends on this.

ALTERNATE TEXTS AS LITERATURE

In the context of expanding my notion of response, I also began to adopt a wider and more inclusive view of what constitutes literature. I began to encourage readers to read young adult novels, picture books, comic books, illustrated books, organic nonfiction pieces, and student writing—and to respond to and share all of these works as literature. This invited more students to become readers, composers of literary response, and conversants about literary experience.

As the word suggests, *canon* is a holy word, and there are many teachers and parents who think that there is a particular set of texts so culturally important that every student needs to know them. This becomes the job of schools. I think, though, that we need to ask what our purposes are as teachers: to teach texts, or to develop readers who can and will want to engage with and know texts in personally powerful ways throughout their lives?

A colleague of mine once told me that "we have to teach Shakespeare or the kids will never have read him." He later told me that his own students didn't enjoy his Shakespeare unit, but "it was for their own good." As a teacher who loves Shakespeare (and who thinks his work can be taught in a way that connects to students' current lives), I thought this was pretty cynical. In my experience, when someone says something is for your own good, it's not; it furthers his own agenda. My response to him was, "Do we want to stuff Shakespeare down their throats like castor oil so they'll hate it and never want to read him, or do we want to develop readers who love story and language and who will want to read and go to Shakespearean plays in the future?"

A transactional view of literature makes the case that any intense and personally fulfilling experience with text is an aesthetic literary experience. Readers who know the power of the literary experience will return to it throughout their lives. These are the kinds of readers we should be working to develop in our classrooms.

USING STUDENT EXPERIENCES:
ART AND DRAMA ACTIVITIES

Developing a richer vision of the reader's response repertoire also led to expanding my teaching repertoire. Now I try to encourage student growth along what I came to see as various dimensions of response. For example, a relatively new move for me as a teacher is working hard to help students enter story worlds, to see these worlds and move around in them, and to take on various relationships with characters. Two major techniques that were shown in the studies to develop these student response strategies *and* more positive reading attitudes were the use of story drama and visual art activities. When used in conjunction with particular reading selections, these activities worked particularly well for many reluctant and learning disabled readers.

I found that these reluctant readers possessed a passive, text-bound view of reading, in which they submitted themselves to texts. Drama activities were motivating and helped them to enter and merge with texts, and to begin to exert control over their reading and to see reading as a constructive, meaning-making activity. The use of drama with reading also helped these students decode words and process implicit meanings.

The use of visual art was also powerful for many students, including some few who were not engaged by the dramas. Art, as in the case of drama, helped reluctant readers to enter texts and respond on new, untried dimensions, opening up their notions of reading as well as their repertoires. Art and drama both reinforced the necessity of drawing on the reader's prior experience to create meaning. Art also helped the students both to explore and create new meanings, and to "set" and place-hold what they had come to know. As such, art became a powerful metacognitive tool for many students.

Taken together, the studies reported here show the possibilities of considering and encouraging the use of multiple intelligences in the reading classroom. New ways of thinking can be engendered and developed. Spirited thinking, response, and risk-taking can be encouraged. Different ways of knowing can be validated, and more students can be included in conversations about literature.

THE ROLE OF THE TEACHER

For me, pursuing and completing these studies wrought a personal change that provided a larger context in which to understand my own role as a teacher and as a researcher. This political realization of a new role and position has become another result of my year of teacher research. As I wrote in my journal:

> I've come to realize that I have a political agenda as a teacher. I have to work towards valuing my different students' abilities and perspectives. I have to work towards changing school so that many students, who really are downtrodden in some sense, can feel they have a place in the school, that they have a say and choice in what happens to them here and out there in the world. I think it all has to do with conversation. Conversation means I engage other viewpoints and value them. I have to do that with other teachers to work towards change. I have to do it with students to grant them some authority and respect. If they can't pursue their own reading and learning and creating, then can they ever be said to really be learning? (June 1993)

I have therefore chosen to conclude this book with a discussion of the teacher's role as a highly professional educator who creates learning environments and researches learning *with* students.

I believe that what I discovered about readers and reading will have implications for other teachers in the field and that these findings would be generally true in other instances. However, what I found was certainly particular in many ways to my own community, classroom, and students. So, more importantly, I want to argue that teachers should take a look at their own classrooms with students, and create new learning environments along with them.

Testing Situations

At a faculty meeting earlier this year, we were doing a "postmortem" on the recent two-week period of standardized testing for the seventh grade.

It was at this point that I asked the question: "Why is it that we give a week of standardized tests anyway?" I was told, rather frostily, that the testing committee had chosen this test as the one that best fit our curriculum.

I had been on that committee. The first question I had asked was whether giving up standardized tests was an option for our district, if we could find an alternative assessment procedure. The answer was the unceasing monosyllable: NO. In effect, I said, we had been free to choose the "best-tasting poison."

The frosty atmosphere became positively polar at this point.

"Do you want to be a scientific educator, or are you satisfied with practicing voodoo?" I was asked.

"What do you mean?"

"If you are a professional educator, then you had better want to evaluate whether students have learned what you have taught them!"

"Oh, I agree, wholeheartedly," I replied, "that we should evaluate student learning. I just don't think that a standardized test is the best way to do that. I think teachers and students should work together to demonstrate what has been learned. I think we should be turning to teachers for assessment, not to the faceless tyranny of testing companies! Then the teachers and the students might have some control over their own learning, and they might get some benefit and learn something from the assessment."

I really hadn't intended to be a gadfly, much less a full-fledged nuisance, but the atmosphere was getting pretty thick with tension.

"Do you really think that a teacher's evaluation of student learning would have any objective validity?" an administrator asked.

I was less astonished by this barb than by the total lack of response from the rest of the faculty. There was complete silence. No one took issue with their supposed incompetence to assess student learning.

It was hard to know what to say—the room didn't feel cool to me anymore—instead, I was feeling the room heat up like a hot air balloon ready to explode.

"Do you mean to tell me," I questioned, measuring my words out carefully before giving way, like a weakened levee, to a flood of emotions and words, "that one kid fills in circle B because he's guessing and it turns out to be right, and the next student fills in circle C because she has several reasons to believe it and she turns out to be wrong, and you mean to tell me that you believe we have learned something about what students know, how they think and how they learn? Are you going to tell me that these tests are not curriculum-altering and mind-altering devices?

That the kids don't know they're being labeled as one of these or one of those? Are you suggesting these tests actually measure the many sorts of complex learning we try to engender in our classrooms? Do you mean to tell me that taking these tests is good for the kids, or good for educating them?"

My voice echoed in the silent room. I was breathing hard and sweating by now. I heard a brief spasm of dry, humorless laughter—like the sound of a rattlesnake.

Then the edict was made clear, with careful pronunciation of each word: "The issue of whether we will give standardized tests is not under discussion. The board has decided that we will give standardized tests to evaluate student learning and progress. We will do so to compare our success to other schools."

Punto. Period. End of meeting.

And there I sat, feeling some warmth in my face and shakiness in my knees, wondering why educators agree to this situation.

What Counts?

There are some pretty big issues at stake here:

◆ What are the purposes of education? How do curriculum and evaluation contribute to these purposes?
◆ What is the role of the teacher? Are teachers simply people who deliver prepackaged curricula, who teach to premade tests? Or are they individuals who create learning environments based on individual students' present needs, desires, interests, and abilities? Are we simply technicians painting by numbers, or are we educational adventurers guiding our students on their personal paths of learning?
◆ What measures, in what situations, best capture the sorts of learning we hope for in a school? How do these measurements help our students to be better, more empowered and more "wide-awake" learners, and to feel better about themselves?
◆ What is the role of the teacher in shaping curriculum and assessing learning?
◆ Most of all, what sort of research and evaluation "count" in school settings?

All of these issues are tied to the issue of teacher professionalism, and as a corollary, to that of the teacher as researcher.

They have much to do with what I see as the personal and professional implications of pursuing and reporting the research projects I have described in this book.

Knoblauch and Brannon (1993), in their work *Critical Teaching and the Idea of Literacy,* make the same point as my faculty meeting story: that power resides with those who name and define what education should do and how to do it, and that these people are not teachers.

These commentators' view of critical teaching is that it values difference and attentively fights subordination. Its purpose is to consider how education will help students to "address inequities and renegotiate the terms of their lives" (p. 97). Critical teaching is visionary; it is about offering possibilities and ways of pursuing these possibilities. This work must be pursued "in the pragmatic terms of stubborn advocacy, continuing conversation, and small gains" (p. 23).

Teachers can help to develop their own critical literacy and that of their students when they engage in teacher research. They can observe what is, pose problems and solutions, converse with students and other members of the community, implement change, and observe whether students are actually enlivened and empowered by the changes. By assuming responsibility for constructing our professional lives, we help students assume responsibility for constructing their own, and we give them ways of doing so.

In my own case, I attempted to observe and analyze what my most proficient readers did to engage deeply with literature. I then asked what my other, less engaged readers were doing, what they might be able to do next, and how I might help guide and support that new, creative readerly activity. I asked: "What might my students be and do as readers? What possibilities can be made accessible, or be realized for them through the reading of literature? How can I help these possibilities to become real?"

My role as a teacher depended upon what I found out about my students: the readers, therefore the teacher.

As a teacher, I left behind the role of curriculum delivery boy and became a dealer in what might be possible for my students. My new role was that of co-researcher, collaborator, mentor, information broker, attention payer, success celebrator, encourager of experiments, and believer that every single student could read in more satisfying ways, and share that reading for the benefit of the classroom community. Instead of taking on the job of teaching solely for myself, I became one who enlisted students to help each other, and who used the community and the computer, paints and music, video camera and microphone, and the possibilities of drama and art to aid students in their development as readers.

THE TEACHER AS RESEARCHER

Teacher research is really about evaluation: an evaluation of what kids have learned; how they learned it; and what stances, methods, and situations are most empowering for the learning.

Teachers are necessarily researchers. They are continually evaluating, interpreting, and making decisions—or they wouldn't survive 2 minutes in a classroom. Teachers must deal with numerous kids' individual needs for some five or six different hours a day. Is Joanie too upset to do her work? Does Max understand the lesson? What can I do differently to help Shana? Why didn't Joe do his homework? Does Tommy really have to go to the bathroom? Why won't Tanya read?

Little questions and big questions, moment-to-moment survival, and a constant conversation of theory with classroom practice—these are the sorts of research and evaluation teachers engage in each day.

In my own classroom, I began to notice the gaping difference between my attitudes toward reading and those of many of my students. I began to compare the experience of many "expert" and highly engaged readers (myself, my wife, my friends, my daughter, and many of my students) with that of the reluctant and resistant readers whom I taught. This became a driving question behind my teaching. How could I uncover what readers "do" when they are engaged? And what could be done in the classroom to encourage the activity and attitudes of those who love to read? Because I was interested in transforming my classroom in order to better teach my students and develop them as readers, teacher research was the most potent instrument at my disposal.

Just as I had a relatively unformed view of what readers do until I studied it in my own classroom, my view of teacher research was similarly vague until I found myself undertaking it. Teacher research has helped me to reimagine my role as that of a democratic worker: reading and learning with my students in collaborative fashion; helping to establish a community where we listen to, value, and learn from each other; and establishing democratic values and processes as we read and learn and work toward better ways of being, understanding, and acting both as individuals and as a community.

My experience has brought me to the position that the educational research and evaluation conducted by or with teachers needs to be highly valued. It tells real stories and is highly informative for classroom practice and student learning. Conducting teacher research in conversation with the field's theorists and professional researchers can have powerful consequences in awakening teachers and students to as yet unrealized possibilities.

TOWARD A CRITICAL LITERACY

Perhaps it is necessary to step back and ask a set of more fundamental questions that we do not often attempt to answer: Why do we teach the language arts? What do we hope to achieve for our students and for ourselves through this enterprise? How will it make their lives better and their living more powerful?

Such questions as these require a look at the framing issue of literacy itself, what it is and what it can achieve. And what it can achieve, I believe, is the ability, first, to look inward to define the self; second, to imagine and enter the selfhood and perspectives of others; and third, to look outward to critically read and converse with the world. Such a conversation allows the reader a sense of agency, and the ability to "rewrite" and help transform the world. Being literate, that pursuit of reading and conversing with the world's many "texts," continually develops those three abilities that I would call "self-definition," "social imagination," and "critical literacy."

Knoblauch and Brannon (1993) also frame critical literacy in these terms when they argue that it is a commitment to understanding language use and its relationship to power in order to use "language for self-realization, social critique and cultural transformation" (p. 152).

Literacy is both the willingness and the ability to evoke, conceive of, express, receive, reflect on, share, evaluate, and negotiate meanings, in the various forms that meanings may take. In this view, literacy is not limited to proficiency with written and oral language, but extends to the making of meaning with other sign systems: music, art, drama, physical movement. In my own work, I found that if students' work with one sign system was valued and encouraged, they could use this work as a springboard to operating in other systems.

Literacy is both a private and a public phenomenon. As a private act, it helps the reader in the process of self-discovery and definition, in that continual odyssey of "self-realizedness" (such as when Kevin realizes that "maybe I could get good at this," or when Kae dreams about her future and how she wants to define it differently than it has been planned for her).

But such a process, though it has private moments, is really only enacted communally. Johnston (1993) calls the capacity to value and explore multiple perspectives a "social imagination"; this includes the ability to imagine the worlds and possible worlds of others different from ourselves. Literacy is a window into the social world, where it empowers and emancipates the reader, helping us to become social by understanding other perspectives and to develop a personal sense of agency in the world (versus just in the classroom). Literacy, in this sense, is both social and political; it allows one to secure satisfactions in the world and impinge upon that world in an effort to make it more satisfactory for the self and for others.

For those students who have been outside the conversation, ways must be provided to include and value their voices, to make them a part of the meaning—making community. Drama was a way in which Kevin, Libby, and Marvin came to value their voices and contribute to class; visual art was a bridge for Kae, Tommy, and Walter.

Literacy is the ability to traffic in meanings, which allows the reader to participate in democratic meaning-making with others. Without such participation, literacy loses its ethical and democratic edge. Literacy should be helping students, much as Giroux (1987) and Boomer (1987) argue, to become aware and attentive to realities, penetrating and interpreting what is happening to them; and to possibilities, to the means in which the world can be transformed. This "critical literacy" includes a sense of "wide-awakeness," as Maxine Greene (1978) describes it, that is necessary to a sense of agency. Giroux argues that this kind of literacy is a "project of possibility."

Essential to this teaching for the possible is what Simon highlights as a "moment of transformation," during which students think critically, make choices, and "believe they can make a difference in the world" (cited by Giroux, 1987, p. 179). Both writers stress the need for students to be supported in becoming "agents." Giroux proposes that the purpose of education is not to foster "functional literacy," that is, to train workers, operating as an adjunct of corporations, but to operate "as vital sites for the development of democracy," developing critical citizens who have "civic courage," who see possibilities and act as agents.

> Democracy requires citizens who can think, challenge, and exhibit long-term thought. This means that public schools need to become places that provide the opportunity for literate occasions, that is, opportunities for students to share their experiences, work in social relations that emphasize care and concern for others, and be introduced to forms of knowledge that provide them with the opportunity to take risks and fight for a quality of life in which all human beings benefit. (Giroux, 1987, p. 181)

Being literate in this sense means that the student can make conscious choices, see possibilities, and judge and evaluate the truth and usefulness and limits of what is read, heard, and experienced. Critical literacy includes knowing the worlds of a particular writer, and being able to explore and judge why he wrote in a particular way.

When Tommy suggests that the class respond to a story by making a collaborative mural, he has seen a possibility. When the class agrees, we have made him a member of the community who can help to set its agenda. When he judges the completed mural to see if it "works," he is evaluating its possibilities for entering the world of another's experience. When the mural helps him to enter a conversation about the way the world is and might be, he is entering the grandest of literary conversations: about the ways that he and his classmates might envision and find of being human in the world.

Literacy, for myself and for the profession at large, used to mean the mastering of basic sets of skills to "correctly" extract other people's meanings from text. This set of meanings is the body of knowledge that curriculum lays out for us. This is the set of facts standardized tests can measure. This may be part of being educated, but it is not all of what we most want for our students, or what education should really be about.

As a result of my learning with students, I have come to know something new about literacy: that it requires readers who bring personal meaning to bear on a dynamic and critical interaction with texts, *and* with the world, in order to "outgrow our current selves" (Hanssen, Harste, & Short, 1990), to augment our knowledge base, and to revise our theory of the world.

Susan Hynds (1990) argues that literate behaviors are only engendered in situations that move beyond skill-building to provide opportunities to make and judge meanings. This is what promotes the actual experience of being literate and thus the desire to become literate. So it was that Kevin began to read on his own, visiting the library to find stories from the far north of Canada, and creating "movies in my mind" after the drama project empowered him to make meanings with texts that were rooted in his own experience. Thus it was that Tommy and Walter began to create and share cartoon versions of stories they had read when their way of knowing and exploring meaning through their drawing became valued.

How we teach literacy is of great importance if students are to understand the acts of reading and writing as productive and evaluative pursuits, and if they are to become empowered as lifelong readers and writers. As Anne Dyson (1984) has pointed out, and as many of my own students quite articulately confirmed, children and young adults see the difference between reading for school and reading for the self. In classrooms, they learn to "do school," developing a "pragmatic sense" of how to demonstrate competence according to the idiosyncratic demands of the school situation. School reading revolves around what is discrete and testable; personal reading revolves around a powerful experience that is organic, personally meaningful, and satisfying. Teachers must move beyond teaching skills and testing for comprehension if students are to embrace a new way of being literate. If we do not, students like Libby, Marvin, Tommy, and Walter will trudge through school days filled with frustration and failure, without the possibility of discovering how reading can be a unique, personal, and powerful way to both experience and know themselves and the world. And students like Ron, Cora, and Joanne will complete their schoolwork in perfunctory fashion, never bringing what they know to be the vital private experience of reading into the classroom, where it can be shared and extended with others.

This sort of program to embrace a new classroom agenda of literacy can only be undertaken by teachers with their particular students; their year of sharing and growing and keeping track together is research at its best.

This is not to argue that traditional research cannot be useful to the teacher. It is only to insist that it must be complemented by a body of teacher research that builds upon what is known; that explores what the data might mean, how they might inform instruction, and how they will be played out in classrooms full of learners so that they can improve real lives.

When I became interested in "what readers do," as I referred to it in my journal, I searched the professional literature for theories of reading and literature that focused on the reader's role; for studies about the engagement, moves, strategies, and activities of individual readers; and for stories of classroom practices that would help develop these activities.

This professional reading was then, and continues to be, invaluable to me as I think about reading, and pursue researching the reading act with my students. Still, I found that there were great gaps in the literature. Literary theory looked at model readers instead of real ones; theories of expertise focused on adults. The very few studies that looked at the moves of individual student readers focused on both younger and older students than I taught. And no study looked at how a theory of reading as "engagement"—as the deployment of various strategies to construct and imagine meanings, to live and move around inside the world of a book—could be played out in a real classroom. Such a study, or series of studies, that would address the concerns of myself and my students was left to me to undertake.

When these stories are shared, as I have tried to do here and by participating in round-table discussions at schools and conferences, they will provide a unique angle on the thinking of teachers about reading education, an angle that can only be provided by a practicing classroom teacher-researcher working with his or her particular students.

I don't believe that the abilities of self-definition, social imagination, and critical literacy can be developed or measured through set, fact-based curricula or standardized tests. I do believe that these abilities can be developed through knowledge of students, celebration of what they can do, and the use of creative activities such as reading and writing, drama and art, sharing and discussion that build upon, extend, and develop what students already know.

Such a project requires a teacher who embodies a wide-awake agency through a clearly articulated theory of the purposes and processes of learning and, as I have stressed, of reading.

Such a project requires a community of teachers who listen to children, and who make critical readings of their own theories and practices of teaching. We need to share teacher views and stories about children and learn to listen to them, "so that we can come to imagine those perspectives ourselves—developing social imagination. Imagining two different interpretations gives us both depth of vision and the grounds for self-correction" (Johnston, 1993, p. 428).

If we can work together with our colleagues and our students, sharing stories and meanings and building upon these, we can help our students to become the caring, involved, empowered citizens necessary to a democracy made up of diverse people and voices.

Education is experience in how to learn; it is an exploration and an expansion of what it means to be human in the world. It is practice in the construction of meanings with others.

As I make my way with my students, I try to equip them and guide them through the first few stages of an educational journey that I hope will be neverending. I am a teacher-researcher because if I improve instruction, the lives of those I teach can be enhanced. The meaning of our work, as Eisner (1993) reminds us, is in the lives it enables others to lead.

COMMENTARY

A MORE HUMANE AND DEMOCRATIC CLASSROOM— FOR A MORE HUMANE AND DEMOCRATIC WORLD!

Since the original writing of *YGBB*, there have been many macrolevel policy changes that have had their inevitable effects on the classroom. But over these many years, I have become even more positive than ever about the individual teacher's capacity to shape her own classroom in such a way that it will benefit all students, no matter the policy environment. I see it happen daily in the classrooms of my National Writing Project fellows. I experience it in my own classrooms and those in which I coteach. Throughout my own teaching at middle school, high school, and university at the pre- and inservice levels, I am constantly reminded that although my thinking and teaching have expanded since the writing of *YGBB*, they have always remained connected to the book's central questions.

I have come to the awesome conclusion that it is the teacher, through relationships with students and responsive teaching of the human threshold knowledge that really matters, who makes all the difference to learning and to student lives.

I have lived and taught through many ill-conceived policy environments. And yet I have taught with great energy and joy and, I maintain, with effectiveness. I have done so through support and collaborative work with many other thinking partners. *Together, we have made a new path by clearing and walking that path together.*

Even when policies are misguided, I have told myself and the teachers with whom I've worked that it is up to us to leverage whatever policies exist for the good of our students and the profession.

That said, and as I argued in depth in the commentary to Chapter 1, the Common Core and next-generation standards worldwide exemplify a paradigm shift toward the learning of threshold knowledge, particularly of strategies and stances, ways of thinking and being in the world. These new standards are consistent with what we know about effective teaching and learning and with cognitive science and literacy research, and the context and elements that are missing can easily be added by any expert teacher teaching students *how* to read and compose in a context of inquiry as apprenticeship. I have never taught at a time when I have been more hopeful about how the policy situation abets the capacity of teachers to teach for engaged and reflective reading, composing, thinking, and problem solving. In this environment, I have high hopes for the continuing professionalization of teaching. We must grab this opportunity, and grab it with two hands and the utmost urgency. We must find like-minded colleagues to do the work and walk the walk together to *be* the change we want to see both in our classrooms and schools, and in our world.

I agree with John Milton that truth was never bested by a bad argument unless all the arguments were not made. We now have a welcome opportunity to make a counterargument to the traditional curriculum-centered, information-driven, decontextualized kinds of teaching that have dominated American education. We must make our argument through our classroom practice, and by sharing the value and success of this practice. This is how professional knowledge is made, and how the path of professional progress is mapped into future directions. We make the path by walking and talking, and doing it together.

We need not only to explore alternatives to the salience of the traditional, but also be willing to share our stories. Educators have many stakeholders, and like any stakeholders they rightfully want to know that their needs are being addressed. As teachers, we must be able to verify that we are teaching well, and to show with proof positive that students are engaged and learning what has been identified as important to our culture.

If we do not, then systems to make us do so will be imposed. Such systems will almost always be inferior to those we can responsively design on our own. To get out from under repressive systems, we must transform our situation from within, devising and testing alternatives in our own schools and classrooms, showing how they work and explaining why they work better than standardized curricula and standardized tests. The Common Core explicitly and implicitly encourages this kind of innovation. Yet I have seen many schools that are implementing the Core in the most closed-minded and reactionary ways, thereby risking the loss of what I am experiencing as a once-in-a-lifetime—or at least once-in-a-career—opportunity. In one neighboring school district, dominated by information-transmission teaching, the district spent 3 days asking teachers to justify how what they already did met the Anchor standards. The teachers I know from this district recognized the process as a charade and façade—"a fake-ade" in the words of one teacher. Two of my NWP fellows left the district in protest.

The district engaged in this facile process instead of taking on the significant challenge of retheorizing teaching and thinking how to implement new curricula that actually assist students in deliberate practice of the anchor standard strategies. The district missed an opportunity for innovation in favor of defending past practices. By clinging to a fixed instead of a growth mindset, they failed to model for the students and community how knowledge and progress are actually made. They remained mired in the past and present instead of using the past as a resource and as a springboard to move toward a different future.

I often tell experienced teachers that they must provide leadership in their school; they must articulate resistance to ill-conceived projects. But more than that, they need to provide positive alternatives: They need to have the courage to innovate; they must protect and apprentice young teachers into the profession; they must give voice to the concerns of the voiceless—and primary among the silenced are our students, particularly those who might be marginalized or possess damaged learner identities. We cannot give our students a voice unless we know them and their concerns, and unless we work to teach them to become independent, confident, and more expert in ways that really count in the world beyond school. *As professional teachers, we must model pathfinding and pathmaking.*

I like to compare teaching to baseball. It is a complicated game with numerous options. In baseball, you don't expect get a hit every time at bat, or to win every game. In fact, if you win three of every five you will go to the World Series and may be world champions. Likewise, you won't hit a home run as a teacher every day, but win three of five, just three of five, and your students will thrive. What I wrote about in this chapter are salutary reminders to me even today: Don't expect to win them all; work for small gains; be stubborn and consistent in advocacy; make sure your teaching helps students renegotiate the terms of their lives.

One challenge this chapter throws down to me is the critical literacy piece—have I emphasized this enough in terms of my own work inside the profession? Have I promoted it specifically and explicitly in my own teaching with students?

Do I get distracted by the day-to-day and forget the bigger picture I am working for? How can I remind myself to keep my eyes on the prize? *To make sure that I am working, as Robert Frost puts it, for heaven's and the future's sake?*

Have I created enough ways for students to be different and to learn and contribute differently in my classroom? John Dewey (1916) reminds us that democracy is not everyone doing the same things in the same ways—democracy is "complementarity," that is, different people using their different interests, strengths, and capacities to contribute uniquely to a common project. Reframing my curricular topics in terms of inquiry has helped me more than anything to implement a democratic classroom (Wilhelm, 2007), but what more might I do? How can I catch the kids who still fall through the cracks? How can I relate to them and teach them so they know they are valued and have something to contribute, and that they can and will learn? This continues to be a challenge. It is a challenge we can strive to meet in part by thinking more expansively about choice, texts, instruction (as inquiry and apprenticeship instead of telling), and literacy itself.

As we strive in this direction, new challenges inevitably arise. As I write this, the schools in my hometown are flooded with immigrant and refugee children. In the last decade Boise has accepted 12,000 immigrants, and we now have nearly 200 different languages in our schools. All of these immigrant children have experienced tremendous challenges, some of them almost unimaginable. How can I integrate these children into the classroom community, into the wonders and the power of speaking and reading English, into the world of our larger community?

When we invite and allow these students to become a necessary and integral part of the classroom, this enriches the learning of everyone. Here's a favorite story about this. A few years ago I was coteaching *Romeo and Juliet* around the question, "What makes or breaks relationships?"

There were two girls in the class from a refugee camp in Somalia. They wore burqas and spoke some limited English. We began the unit by playing favorite love songs to the class and identifying what these songs expressed about love that we accepted or believed. We did this as a backdrop to autobiographical writing and justifying our response to survey statements like "Love means never having to say you're sorry" and "Teenagers cannot experience true love." The two girls immediately waved their hands in the air and asked if they could sing their "promise songs"! Before I could respond, another girl from the class asked what a promise song was. "The song you sing to your future husband when you are promised to him." The class eagerly asked if the Somali girls were "promised" and were shocked to learn that the girls were both promised to men whom they'd never met. But you sang them your promise songs! "Oh, you do it beneath his window or outside his tent. You cannot see each other until wedding day." But how did you meet him, then decide to marry him? "We not decide; our parents decide." The class erupted. I was able, due to recent reading, to put some statistics on the board about satisfaction and longevity in arranged marriages and told the students: "Maybe all your parents should be picking your partners?" What ensued was one of the most enjoyable, far-ranging discussions of successful relationships I've ever seen, with the Somali girls at the center. They continued to be a go-to resource for the class through the rest of the unit and beyond.

Following are a few of the teaching moves I think are most important in regard to differentiating instruction for all students and integrating all students meaningfully into the classroom projects.

Expanding Choice

When I teach in an inquiry context, there are natural ways to differentiate—students can read different texts, be taught with different methods, pursue different angles, work in different groupings, and complete different projects, and still be contributing to a single common project of pursuing the inquiry question. In our *Romeo and Juliet* unit, all students chose which one of the three graphic novel versions to read—one in simple English, one in modern English, one in the original—then some read the play and others *Shakespeare Made Easy*. Students can likewise compose various kinds of texts to share with the class; several Bosnian boys composed their own tableaux and graphic novel translations of Bosnian newspaper accounts and folktales of situations reminiscent of *Romeo and Juliet*, while other groups composed video glossary entries defining literary terms using examples from the play, and so forth. All of these were shared with the whole class.

In other words, we made our own paths together by walking the inquiry journey together.

Inquiry provides a measure of choice for students inside the required curriculum. Choice is motivating; choice helps us stake our identity; choice *can be* accommodated within the constraints any of us work under.

When students read outside school through free reading programs or summer reading, let's really give them a choice. Many reading programs, such as Accelerated Reader, limit choice—as any reading from approved lists limits choices. Such programs generally also limit how one reads and responds (to answer literal-level quiz questions) and why one reads (to get points, instead of for joy, enjoyment, or learning about personally compelling and social topics through inquiry).

As students in our study on the power of pleasure reading often indicated, summer reading lists proclaim to students: "Hey, here's a good idea! We wrecked reading for the whole school year, so now we are going to ruin it for the summer, too—by limiting why, what, and how you can read!"

Widening Our Notion of Texts

In this last chapter I argued for expanding our notion of text.

I see it every single day and throughout every day. My middle school students are carrying back-bending backpacks full of texts they are uninterested in reading and find boring and insipid if they do, and that in many cases they are not capable of reading. One of the more salient findings in our boys' study was how virtually all of the boys—including accomplished students—detested textbooks. They wanted deeper and more storied explorations and "uncoverage" of important issues versus the superficial and universal kinds of "coverage" they experienced through textbooks, worksheets, and classroom lectures.

When my daughters—both of whom are engaged and inveterate readers—came home from school they invariably complained about how boring school was for them, and they often complained about the canonical texts they are asked to read in English. This was true of their university experience as well as of their primary and secondary school years.

The NEA study *Reading at Risk* (2004) shows that people are the least likely to read for the first several years following their formal schooling. The Pew Foundation (Zickuhr & Rainie, 2014) found that one-quarter of Americans reported that they did not read a single book of any kind during the 2013 calendar year. When you consider that self-reported data are notoriously biased in favor of positive behaviors, this is even more worrisome. If we are trying to create lifelong readers and enthusiastic learners, we are certainly failing. I am more dedicated than ever to using children's and young adult literature in the classroom instead of or in addition to canonical texts. Children's and YA lit is written for students in their current state of being and for their current capacities as readers, learners, and developing human beings. One of the many great things about inquiry-oriented teaching is that students can read any text that helps inform them and allows them to weigh in on the essential question. Free reading around the inquiry theme can be the daily homework, or become an adjunct to the required curriculum. *We show what we value by what we give time to*. It's time to show that we value reading by giving students time to do it, both in school and outside. *It's time to walk the same walk with students that engaged readers walk in their out-of-school reading lives.*

Of course, in the time since writing the First Edition of *YGBB* in 1995, the kinds of texts students are drawn to read have widened more and expanded further from traditional school texts. Today, my 7th-graders are all free reading around our inquiry topic and essential question: What are the costs and benefits of technology? Joanie is reading anime; Ahmet and Roz are reading video game–based graphic novels; Iqra is reading a graphic novel version of *Frankenstein*; Sasha is deeply immersed in the YA dystopian novel *House of the Scorpion*, which she is reading in her native Bulgarian; Orly and Tamil are on the Internet reading and writing Facebook entries in which they have assumed the roles of literary characters from *Frankenstein*; and Tommy is on bbckids.ca checking up on climate change research and how climate change is related to technology. Several students are on video game forums that relate to the costs and benefits of technology. As we found in our pleasure reading study, the video games themselves are experienced by students as narrative texts, and massive amounts of associated reading must also be considered texts (Wilhelm & Smith, 2014).

Expanding Our Notions of Literature—and of What Counts

Here's a central argument of this book: Any text that provides a reader with an aesthetic experience can be considered literature. What constitutes literature or literariness resides in the transaction of the reader and the text. Likewise, any text that operates as a "transitional object," helping one to outgrow and transform thinking, perspective, and being, can be considered literature. Again, literature is a function of the individual reader's transaction and resulting experience. It is not a function of the text itself.

As I've mentioned in the commentaries to the Introduction and Chapter 4, in our recent studies on the power of pleasure reading, reported in *Reading Unbound* (Wilhelm & Smith, 2014), we found that students tended to gravitate to texts that helped them navigate current challenges, which led us to this mantra: "They read what they need." When students did so, they experienced five kinds of pleasure (play, intellect, social, functional work, inner work), each providing ancillary benefits that are valued in life and school. This has foregrounded for me the absolute need for free choice reading and free reading programs.

Add this to the mix: free reading in youth is more explanatory of future educational attainment and social mobility than any other factor, including parents' educational attainment and socioeconomic status (see, e.g., Clark & Rumbold, 2006; Sullivan & Brown, 2013). This makes free reading a civil rights issue.

Expanding Notions of Literacy

If we do not widen our notions of text—and of what counts—we will fail to make use of powerful new forms of textuality, we will lose the opportunity to connect what students already are interested in and know to what they could become interested in and know, and we will disenfranchise students by not valuing their literacies and by practicing literacies distant from what they see practiced in life. We will also fail to meet next-generation standards for multimodality and multimedia composing/reading, and fail to prepare students not only for the future, but for critical engagement with the present moment.

In the technological age and a flattening world (Friedman, 2005), we need to expand our notion of literacy to include the use of electronic media in all its forms. As Jay David Bolter (1991) argues, literacy has always meant the ability to use the most powerful tools to communicate and receive meanings. Those tools are now electronic. If students are not critically and carefully using the Internet and designing knowledge artifacts with the latest technologies, then we are not promoting literacy—in fact, we are failing to address the demands of modern literacy.

Expanding Our Goals: Thinking Big

I've spent the last 33 years on the front lines of teaching. Even as a professor, I spend most of my time in schools, "where the action is," teaching and coteaching and co-researching with my NWP teachers and often with student teachers. As such, I tend to think on a micro level: about units and lessons, daily challenges, individual students, and the interventions that might help a student or group of students right now!

In contrast, my colleague and co-author of *Teaching Literacy for Love and Wisdom* (2011), Bruce Novak, is a philosopher and a big thinker. Bruce is always urging me to talk and write about the "big stuff."

I've already mentioned some of my own big goals and what I think are big implications throughout this book: teaching for deep engagement and joy, expertise, deep understanding and use, service and social action, civic engagement and democracy. I've explored these ideas in depth in both *Teaching Literacy for Love and Wisdom* (2011) and *The Activist Learner* (Wilhelm, Fry, & Douglas, 2014).

But I think Bruce is right. We should not undersell the profound knowledge that teaching expertise requires, nor the profound personal, social, disciplinary, and cultural purposes that we work for. So, in closing, I'll make a few comments about expanding our articulation of purpose—because I think such articulation will remind us why we teach, help us get through the inevitable rainy days, focus our work, and help to justify teaching as the significant and central profession that it is—and that in any democratic culture that it absolutely needs to be.

John Dewey and Arthur Bentley (1949) wrote that our lives and our planet are at risk if we don't develop what Dewey called "transactional consciousness"—a consciousness marked by a continual stance of inquiry, an attitude toward all knowledge as tentative, and an embracing of the essential relationality and reciprocity of all human beings, cultures, objects, and the environment. But Dewey was far from the classroom at that point, and he didn't give any specific advice to teachers about how to accomplish transactional consciousness. Drawing on Dewey, Louise Rosenblatt (1978) then made a convincing case for the transactional nature of literary reading. But she, again, provided no concrete discernible method for teaching transactionally.

Bruce maintains that what *YGGB* did, centrally, was to establish a transactional method of both teaching and reading any text as literature—intuitively drawing on the three-dimensional path to wisdom in any wisdom tradition, and on the narrative structure of human time proposed by Paul Ricoeur (1984, 1985, 1988). And what our book *Teaching Literacy for Love and Wisdom* did, centrally, was to develop this method of teaching transactional reading, not just of literature but of life.

The Path to Wisdom and Wholeness

Bruce argues (see Wilhelm & Novak, 2011) that the path to wisdom begins with deep and full immersion in experience, then connecting that experience to other experiences, and then deep reflection, questioning and moving forward more consciously from this experience. These three stages are mirrored by the three major categories of interactive response to literature reported on here.

That is: To read transactionally we must 1) bring our prior experience to the text and use that prior knowledge to enliven and deeply evoke, live through and feel a new experience with the text, 2) we must connect that experience to other experiences both personal, textual, and out in the world, real and imagined, and then 3) we must reflect on the experience of our reading to take away insights and knowledge for transformed reading and living in our yet-to-be-experienced future.

Paul Ricoeur's (1984, 1985, 1988) notion of narrative and human time works the same way. First, we *evoke experience* freshly and fully. This is what Ricoeur calls "the present made fully present," and what Ellen Dissanayake (1992) calls art as "making special." Next, we *connect*, what Ricoeur calls the "past made present" and the "present made past"—connecting the self to text, text to text, self to other, text to the world and environment. This reminds me of David Perkins's (1986) injunction that knowledge is not a line but a network. Finally, we *reflect*, what Ricoeur calls "the present made future"—what Santayana designated as "imaginative rehearsal for living" (cited in Booth, 1983, p. 212), critiquing what we read and learn, applying, transforming, acting, serving, *becoming and being something different, outgrowing our current selves through this experience.* This is what we mean when we argue (Wilhelm & Novak, 2011) that the text (material or data) acts as a "transitional object" propelling us into newly possible understandings, selves, communities, and futures.

This trajectory also mirrors Carl Jung's journey to human wholeness (Johnson, 1986): We move from simple immersive consciousness of current experience; through complex consciousness of connection, particularly to what we repress; and if we persist and do our inner work, eventually to enlightened consciousness and wholeness. Reading response, in these terms, is like a dream world that we inhabit to do inner work and to explore more fully our true selves and potential (see Wilhelm & Smith, 2014).

In my experience, when we assist young people through inquiry in their desire to become something more, and to become a part of something larger than themselves, to engage in significant learning about themselves and about important issues and the world, then they tend to learn with what can well be called deep engagement and joy and to become far more accomplished and active in the world.

This process works toward a *transactional* consciousness of how all beings are meaningfully and existentially entwined with one another, and of how human beings become most fully human only when they are actively and meaningfully enwrapped in a world they have come to care about.

Like all art, literature, widely construed as any crafted text, fictional or nonfictional, that provides an aesthetic experience, is a special kind of gift, a "third space" of experience in which we live for a time enwrapped in the consciousness of another as well as our own to create the third space of possibility that is neither the book nor ourselves, but something that happens uniquely between the reader and the text. The central purpose of art is to prepare us to imaginatively *live through* this third space and then to make what is now merely possible and imagined into something real.

Here's the takeaway: Be the book—to be the change. I want my students to be changed and more competent readers, for sure, but also more transactional and transformed human beings living in community, asking "what if it were otherwise?," engaged in critical democratic conversations about who we want to be and how we want to relate to one another and to the environment—both as individuals and as a community.

It seems to me that these ideas are so easy to get behind—the justification for doing so is so clear, and doing so has so many benefits to our students and to our world. So what's stopping us? Is it the salience of the traditional?

Whatever it is, a future that is radically unique is here. It is a future that breaks in significant ways with the past. If we do not teach the students for the world they do live in, and the one they will live in, then we will fail to engage them, and we will fail in our calling as teachers. *We must walk a new walk with one another and with our students, and we must make a new path with our communal walking.*

The challenge is great. The importance of literacy has never been greater. I know that as a profession we can rise to the challenge and that the benefits will also be great in terms of enriched lives and the capacity of our students to meet the challenge of their own futures.

APPENDIX A

∝

Questions and Activities for the
Ten Dimensions of Reader Response

1. ENTERING THE STORY WORLD

What the Readers Do

Express "excitement": "want" to read, "think about" what reading
   will be like
Anticipate pleasure; generate enthusiasm
Show willingness to read and to help create an aesthetic experience
   under the guidance of the text
Activate linguistic capacities and strategies needed to comprehend the
   text's guidance
Bring personal experience to help enter and build up a story world
Activate necessary schema for genre, topic, and theme

Questions to Ask (Tell me . . .)

When you first saw the book, what kind of book did you think it was
   going to be? What made you think this? What were your feelings?
   How might your feelings influence your reading?
Tell me anything that caught your attention about the book: the cover,
   the book itself, layout, pictures, anything else.
What will the book be about? What do you know about this topic/
   text/author/type of story? How will this influence how you read?
   What would you like to know about the topic or about X, Y, Z?
   How will this influence how you read?

Many questions that appear in Appendix A come from Chambers (1985) and Iser (1978).

How will the story be told or organized? Have you ever read other stories/books/poems like this? What sticks in your memory most vividly about these types of books? What will you want to know right away?

Possible Activities

Book talks or previews to get students interested

Simulations or drama activities that connect to or foreshadow events and scenarios that will occur in the reading

Look over the book, make predictions

Brainstorm what is known about the topic of the reading

K-W-L: students list what they *know* about the topic, what they *want* to know, and (as they read) what they are *learning*

Prereading activities that focus attention on topics or themes to be explored in reading: surveys, opinionaires, anticipation guides, rankings, case studies, autobiographical writing

Activities to build necessary background knowledge for reading: expert speaker, demonstrations of activities or ideas from reading, constructing a timeline or museum exhibit, sequence texts so that students build background knowledge text by text, review texts previously read that were of a similar genre, style, or topic

As part of literature circle or reading group activity, have students describe when and how they entered the story

2. SHOWING INTEREST IN THE STORY

What the Readers Do

Begin to "get into" or "enter" the story world

Comprehend literal meanings: "I understand"

Make an undifferentiated response: "It's good because I like it"; decide to go on with reading

May summarize, giving a brief description of the event or a condensed version of a whole section

Predict and anticipate what might happen next, in the short term: "I think," "I predict"

Form expectations: "This will be good/interest me"

Begin construction of a story world

Create rudimentary mental images, usually stereotypes from film and television

Recognize some "rules of notice" to make contact with the text; accept the "game" devised by the author, though reader may not show understanding of all basic conventions of this game

May be confused or tentative; may express lack of background knowledge, too narrow a response, indifference; could give up on story at this point

Questions to Ask (Tell me . . .)

Did the first pages meet your expectations? What has caught your attention?

What is happening in your head as you read the first paragraphs?

What do you think the author wants you to notice? How is your attention drawn to these items? What is the text signaling you to notice?

What do you know that is helping you to understand the story? What might you need to know more about to understand more of the story?

What type of story will this be? What characteristics will it have?

Are you asking yourself or the text any questions?

What are you imagining might happen next?

How do you think the story might develop?

How did these present circumstances arise?

What do you think will happen next, or what will happen when or if X occurs?

How do you think it will all end? How would you like it to end?

Possible Activities

Students write telegrams summarizing the beginning of a story

Prediction games

Ask students to make a personal statement about what they are noticing, what is catching their attention, what kind of book they think this will be

3. RELATING TO CHARACTERS

What the Readers Do

Create character and expectations about characters: "I think/hope she will"

Feel emotions in relation to character activities and situations: "I'm scared/excited/worried/happy for X"

Become a presence in the story world, as "character," "friend," close observer, distant observer, "in the midst"; may use "spy" tool to see, hear, and move around in story world (e.g., peephole)

Make judgments about character and character actions

Project self and personal knowledge of people into the story world; life brought to literature

Identify, empathize, or merge with ("become") character, jumping into character's head

Role-play—how would I feel if/what would I do if I were in character's situation?

Enact: physically become or represent character

Achieve parallel focus (Enciso, 1990): refer to friends as characters, or imagine scenarios that seem parallel to story

Become agent: may desire to act on character's behalf

Define frame: designate a relationship between self and character

Questions to Ask (Tell me . . .)

What clues do we have to the character's personality?

Do you like the character? For what reasons?

What do you think the character will do? What problems will she have?

What are the character's problems? How are they solved? Are any not solved? What would you do differently?

What feelings are you experiencing as you read? How did you feel when X happened to the character? Are you feeling pleased or irritated with the character? How would it feel to be one or more of the characters?

What personal experience have you had that helps you to better understand these characters? (Note: This is different from connecting because there is no reverse analogy from character to understanding one's own life.)

What do you feel about this character? setting? incident?

What character interests you most? Is that character the most important character? Or is the story really about someone else?

Which characters didn't you like? Which bored you? Did any character remind you of someone you know? Has anything like this ever happened to you? Did you feel the same as the people in the story?

Did we ever get to know what the characters were thinking about? Did you agree with what character X thought about Y?

When you were reading the story did you feel it was happening now?
Or did you feel it was happening in the past and was being
remembered?

What in the writing made you feel that way? Did you feel that things
were happening to you? As if you were the character? Or were you
an observer? If so, where were you watching from? From different
places? Can you tell me where in the book you felt a particular way?

Possible Activities

All drama activities (see Chapter Four)

Retell episodes from different perspectives

Write character diaries

Discuss characters in terms of whether you would like to know, meet,
or be that person

Write a letter to a character; a classmate could answer the letter as the
character

Write a story about the character as if she were in your town today

4. SEEING THE STORY WORLD

What the Readers Do

Notice cues for visualizing a "secondary world"

Create and sustain a "secondary world" in the mind

Create visual pictures of characters, physical features, physical gestures,
placements, settings, situations, and mental images of affect

Questions to Ask (Tell me . . .)

What impressions are you forming in your mind of people and places
in the story? What pictures do you have in your mind's eye?

Are you able to see in your mind the characters and the places where
the events take place? Do you see pictures in the text? All of the
text? Or only in some parts? What in the text helps you see a
picture? How and when does the clarity of your visualization
change? Where are you seeing the story from? What sort of vantage
point or perspective do you seem to have?

As you read this story, do you see it happening in your imagination?
Are you unaware of images, but seem to have a sense that you are
"seeing" in another way? Can you describe that way?

What kind of details in the story help you see it most clearly? Can you
tell me some of those details? What do they suggest to you? How do
they connect to your experience?

Where did the story happen? What was it like there?

Did it matter where it happened, or could it have happened anywhere?
What did you think about the setting as you were reading?

Where are characters placed in relationship to each other? To
important objects?

What is the setting like? Can you describe it? If you were going to
take a picture or make a movie of this scene, where would you do
it? What would you include? What sort of music would be
playing?

Possible Activities

All visual art activities (see Chapter Five)

Describe an important setting or scene from the book

Draw a floor plan or map of an important setting

Write about how the story would be different if it happened in your
town

Make a character book or yearbook including drawings and
descriptions of characters; cutouts from magazines could be used

Create a hypermedia version of the story, or a hypermedia scrapbook
of important elements

5. ELABORATING ON THE STORY WORLD

What the Readers Do

Build meaning through accumulated clues: "I added X and Y," "X
made me remember Y"

Recognize openness of the text

Draw on repertoire of personal experiences both as a reader and as a
person to extend and develop the story

Begin to play "detective"; actively fill out textual cues and gaps in
creating a secondary world

"Imagine" new situations, characters, settings, and episodes

Imagine alternate or parallel endings or consequences

Ask "What if?"

Elaborate: imagine details, situation, character qualities, conversations, and actions not apparent in text alone, but still consistent with experience of the story world

Generate expectations about alternatives and possible long-term outcomes; extend and hypothesize, taking character and events beyond time and frame of the story

Questions to Ask (Tell me . . .)

What episodes or information did the author leave out? How did you fill them in?

What if X had not happened? What if Y happened? What if character Z were different, or the setting or situation or timing were different?

What other adventures might these characters have? What would be an alternate ending for this story? A sequel to this story? What was left out of the story that you wish had been included? How would you include it? How would the story be different/better/worse if the author had included these changes?

What other books have you read that the story you are reading reminds you of? Have you ever read other books, stories, or poems like this one? Tell me about them: What sticks in your mind most vividly about them? How are these two works alike? different? How could this book be made more similar to or different from that one? What characters from this book might fit in a previous book? How would they behave differently from the characters in this book?

What will you tell your friends about this book? What won't you tell them because it might spoil the story or be misleading?

Possible Activities

Keep a detective's log of clues regarding important questions you have or patterns you notice

Write a new ending

Compose a flow chart of cause-and-effect relationships; change the resolution of one major conflict and trace how it changes the rest of the story; or create a Choose Your Own Adventure flow chart of the book, showing what other alternatives could have eventuated and what would have happened next

6. CONNECTING LITERATURE TO LIFE

What the Readers Do

Make explicit connections between personal experiences and the character's experiences; between story experience and own life; use intertextual references: "I connected/compared/related"

Take a perspective: may consider what someone else might be seeing, thinking, or feeling; consideration of most likely experiences and interpretations others would have in a situation; may switch or coordinate various perspectives, e.g., mutual perspective-taking (Selman & Byrne, 1974); take third-party view to reconcile two other perspectives (*Note:* Perspective-taking differs from empathy in that it requires contemplation of other's feeling, and this depends upon projecting own experiences, attitudes, and feelings.)

Questions to Ask (Tell me . . .)

Tell me what things have happened in your life that are similar to some of the things that are happening to characters in the story.

Do any of the characters remind you of people you know? Does knowing the characters help you to understand the people you know who have similar qualities or situations? Tell how so.

How does what is happening in the book make you more aware of your own life? How does it inform how you think about your own life and identity?

Have you learned anything important about other people? Has your understanding of others increased? Have you learned anything new about the world? others? yourself?

Has the book influenced what you believe in, what you think is right or true? Has it helped you think how you might behave in some future situation? Or helped you to think how you could have done things differently in a past one?

Possible Activities

Many drama activities (see Chapter Four)

Create a Life's Little Instruction Calendar of Ideas or Suggestions for Better Living that were found in the book

Two-column notes comparing situations and problems in book to situations and problems in your life

Cast your friends in various roles for the movie version of the story

7. CONSIDERING SIGNIFICANCE

What the Readers Do

Establish significance

"Know": state with conviction that they have knowledge about
something in the story, historical period, character's thoughts, author

Ask "how did the text work?"; ask how experience fits together

"Remember"/retrospect: refer to earlier parts of story to make sense of
the present

Perceive changes: shifts in reading experience; changes in character or
plot, diction or setting, style or tone

May express wonder or surprise, implying reader expectations about
what would occur, and wondering why it did not

Formulate puzzles, enigmas; accept (or reject) "hermeneutic challenges"
(Iser, 1978), "I wondered why," "I tried to figure out"

Apply rules of signification, and elaborate upon possible meanings

Begin to consider matters of coherence, and how separate elements fit
together to indicate meanings

Compare (character's view to own), classify, critique (communicating
what is of value, enjoyable, interesting)

Questions to Ask (Tell me . . .)

Tell me about the parts of the story you liked the most/the least. What parts
excited you? Bored you? If you stopped reading, what stopped you?

What is the connection between events that are seemingly unrelated?
What is the point of a particular event or description? What did the
author leave for you to explain or fill in? Why was a certain
character or passage included in the story?

What patterns of meaning are being created by you and the author?

Was there anything that puzzled you? Things you thought were
strange? That took you by surprise? Did the author try to do these
things to you purposefully? For what reason? What was the author
expecting of you in these situations?

What idea was the author exploring through this story? What
comments or generalization would the author make about that idea?

If you were filming the story, when would lighting and music change?
Why? When would characters change? How would you capture this
in costumes, gestures, looks? What changes in feeling or tone would
be captured by these changes?

Possible Activities

Radio or news show in which you discuss or debate what you think the book reveals about people and their lives

Share one new idea about people and their lives that you realized after reading this piece

Dramatic interview or debate with author in which you disagree with at least one of his ideas

Create a main idea book or a picture book version of the story that captures all major scenes and ideas

Write a script for and videotape a part of the story to capture its mood and meaning

8. RECOGNIZING LITERARY CONVENTIONS

What the Readers Do

"I noticed" a change, shift, literal meaning that author "couldn't have really meant" or that "didn't make sense"

Recognize literary event as a highly conventionalized and socially constructed experience

Recognize highly sophisticated rules of signification involving the subversion or undercutting of literal or usual expression, e.g., story inversions, prolepsis, analepsis, symbolism, irony, unreliable narrators

Draw on literary and cultural repertoires to construct implied meaning: "I thought about Dad/Mom/movie/previously read story when X didn't make sense"

Questions to Ask (Tell me . . .)

How long did it take for the story to happen? Was the story told in the order that it happened? Why or why not? What effect did the changes have on you as the reader?

What information did the author know that she withheld? Have you ever withheld information while telling a story? For what purpose?

Who was telling the story? Do we know? How does this make a difference?

Are there parts of the story that took a long time to happen but are told quickly? Are there parts of the story that took a short time but take a long time to tell? Are there events that happened once, but are repeated in the telling? Events that reoccurred but are told only once? Why did the author change the actual time and order of events when she told it? Have you ever done such things when you have told stories? For what purposes?

How do you recognize when X device is being used? What subtle clues are you given to be alert? How do you feel about the use of this particular device for telling this story? In what ways does it change or add to the story? Were you surprised when it became clear that the surface story could not be taken literally? Do you think you were meant to be surprised? For what purpose?

Possible Activities

Assignment sequences (see Michael Smith, 1986, 1991) to develop student problem-solving strategies for recognizing and using conventions

Have students write their own Ripley's Believe It or Not that displays irony

Have students rewrite stories from other perspectives, with new time sequences, or with new elements and discuss how the story is different

9. RECOGNIZING READING AS A TRANSACTION

What the Readers Do

Question significance: step back from ongoing experience to see how that experience fits together

Refer to how story is told; may critique authorial choices

Recognize implied author

Generalize; concerned with understanding the world through the literary work

Interrogate text and the author as a presence shining through the text in order to evaluate author's construction of meaning and to match the author's representation of the world with one's own

Apply rules of configuration and coherence in an attempt to understand author's expressed vision

Accept, reject, or resist (parts of) the author's vision

Questions to Ask (Tell me . . .)

What kind of person is the author?

Did you find her to be someone you could like or not? For what reasons?

What values or attitudes does the author want you to affirm or question? What ideas of the author's did you respond to with a "Yes, she's right!" or "No, that couldn't happen/could never be," etc.?

Do you agree with how the author sees the world? In what ways?

Did you notice things in the story that made a pattern? (Could play "I Spy" game with students, asking them to cite striking elements. List and see if patterns are formed.) Why did the author create the patterns that she did in the story? Why did she write the story in the way she did?

How do you feel about the way the story is told? Is there anything you enjoyed or were irritated with about the way the book is written?

What do you feel is the most significant word/passage/event from the story?

If the author asked you what could be improved in the story, what would you say?

Possible Activities

Dramatic interview or debate with the author

Create the author's yearbook page or a scrapbook page

Write a letter to the author explaining your reactions and asking questions

Brainstorm what authors you would most want to invite to a dinner party, to be with you on a deserted island, etc.; discuss why

10. EVALUATING AN AUTHOR, AND THE SELF AS READER

What the Readers Do

Recognize implied reader, and relationship between implied author and implied reader

Acceptance/resistance/rejection of assigned role as implied reader or as member of reading community

Apply rules of coherence and exercise awareness of process of meaning-making undergone in concert with author and text; awareness of how process worked or did not work for them in this case

Recognize text as socially constructed and role of reader as part of literary community

Exercise reflexiveness, leading to an understanding of textual ideology, personal identity, and one's own reading and learning processes

Questions to Ask (Tell me . . .)

What kind of reader was the book written for? What kind of person do you think the author imagined in his mind's eye? Are you that reader? Could you become that reader? To what degree?

Did you sympathize with the author's worldview? Did any of her attitudes or opinions make the book difficult, enjoyable, reassuring, or annoying?

Would you like to get to know this author?

How did your experience as a person and as a reader guide your reading?

Where were you as you were reading? When you read, did you hear the words being said in your head? Whose voice was it you heard?

What was your reading rate? Did it vary? When and for what reasons?

How did "meaning" happen? Were you conscious of the text's language? Did you note unusual words, images, style? Did you reread certain sections? For what purposes? With what results?

Would you read the story again? If so, would you read it differently?

Has your reading helped you understand yourself any better?

If you read the story before, was it different this time? What did you notice that you didn't notice the first time? Did you enjoy it more or less? Because of your experience, would you recommend that others read it again as well?

We've listened to each other's thoughts about the story, and heard all sorts of things about what we've noticed. Are you surprised by anything someone else said? Has anything been said that changed your mind? Helped you enjoy the story more? Understand it better? What struck you most about what others said?

Now, after all we've said, what is the most important thing about the story for you? Should you give the book to others? Who? How? Should it be read aloud, or should it be read silently? What would be best for the story? For the reader?

How do you feel now that the reading experience is over? What would help you to reflect further? What might distract you?

What will you do differently the next time you read? What are your goals for the next time you read?

Possible Activities

Nominate the book for an award based on what it did for you as a reader

Write a letter to your librarian explaining why the book should or should not be purchased based on what the book expects of a reader

APPENDIX B

∝

Revolving Role Drama Lesson Plans
for *The Incredible Journey*

DAY ONE
(Before Beginning Reading)

The revolving role drama project will be explained to the students in the context of our purpose of learning how to enter and experience "story worlds." It will be explained that each day we will enter an imaginary "drama world" that will anticipate and parallel the "story world" of the book we are reading.

The class will engage in a few warm-up exercises: imagining we are in class on a hot day, at the North Pole, Christmas morning, the day of a test. We will discuss how we imagine and express our entry and experience in these imagined worlds. Concerns will be discussed.

We will then, as a class, enter a drama world, via guided imagery. The teacher will explain that at the end of school one day we were escorted to a bus without windows. We were taken on a long trip. No one explained where we were going. After about 14 hours we finally stopped and were allowed off the bus. We were then put on a plane and flown over the wilderness, finally landing on a remote lake, and left at what appears to be an old hunting lodge.

Within the drama world, students will be asked to share their feelings and concerns about our current situation.

For several weeks we are well cared for, but also carefully guarded by several friendly guards, none of whom seem to be able to communicate with us or tell us why we are here or how long we must stay. We are in the middle of a wilderness area, and all we can see from the top of the house we stay in are lakes and trees—for as far as the eye can see.

One day, we awake and find we have been left alone. We call a town meeting to address the following questions: Why are we here? Should we try to find our way home, now that we have the chance? What preparations must we make if we are to journey across the wilderness? As a group, what problems do we foresee and what rules do we wish to make for our group?

The students will conduct the town meeting.

DAY THREE
(Parallels Reading of Chapters 2 and 3)

It is the second day of the animals' journey. Today students will be assigned to play the roles of an A or a B. They will find a person playing the other role to enact the story drama in pairs. After 2 to 3 minutes of role-playing, students will be asked to switch partners.

Role-Play #1

We are still in the wilderness. We have no idea where we are and have seen no people or travelled roads. We have been out for a whole week. Role A has some food but is still quite hungry. Role A has had some limited success hunting and fishing.

The students in Role B, however, are weak and starving—having not eaten since the first day of the journey. The person in Role B finds the person in Role A and asks for some food. Role-play the drama.

Role-Play #2

Role A finds a new Role B partner. Role B2 is a friend of the person who role-played B1. You are worried about B1. You think that your friend will die if some situation is not worked out to find and share food. Try to work out a situation. Role-play the drama.

Role-Play #3

Role A finds a new Role B partner. Role B3 is a friend of B1. You tried to wake up B1 this morning and you cannot do so. B1 is totally unconscious, but is still breathing. B1's lips are cracked and bleeding, cheeks sunken, skin a greyish color. Talk to Role A about what to do. Role-play the drama.

Reflection

Write short diary entries that explore your reaction to today's role drama. Tell how you felt as each character in each situation, etc.

DAY FOUR
(Parallels Reading of Chapter 5)

We are now 10 days out on our journey. Tonight we can see lights up in the sky ahead. We decide that we are perhaps only 2 days' walk from some sort of town. Unfortunately, we are camped on the bank of a wide and torrential river filled with rocks and white water. There is no easy place to cross as far as we can see.

Role-Play #1

Role A does not want to cross the river, at least not at this particular place. Role B does want to cross the river, right here and right now. The two roles must give their reasons, explore possible options, and come to some sort of conclusion.

Role-Play #2

Find a new partner. Role A2 is a hermit who is slightly unbalanced and lives in a fantasy world. A2 has lived in the wilderness for many years. Role B2 has become separated from the group during the group's river crossing. What are your concerns? What can you do for each other? Role-play the scene.

Role-Play #3

Find a new partner. Roles A3 and B3 are both group members who have just realized that one of the group members was lost during the river crossing about an hour ago. What should we do? Role-play the drama.

Role-Play #4

Find a new partner. Role A4 is a park ranger who has just found the one person who was separated from the group, played by B4. What are your needs and concerns in each role? What must be done immediately, and what plans must be made? Role-play the drama.

DAY FIVE
(Parallels Reading of Chapter 6)

Option A

In pairs, students will write a scene about the two dogs that occurred when they were separated from Tao the cat. The scene should include some sort of adventure and a conversation about the cat. The dramas will then be rehearsed and performed for the class.

Option B

In pairs, create a tableau drama of "snapshots" of key episodes from the last three chapters (4–6). These tableaux will be presented to the class. Class members will guess which episode is depicted by each tableau.

DAY SEVEN
(Parallels Reading of Chapter 8)

Students are members of the intact group. We are walking along a set of telephone poles and wires. We believe that we are very close to civilization and that we will reach a town in just a few miles. We have been under way now for over 2 weeks. We are tired, dirty, scarred, and sore. What other feelings do we have?

Role-Play #1

Role A is a guard from the camp where all of us were originally held. Role B is a lost group member. You run into a cave and the guard refuses to come in. Role-play your conversation.

Role-Play #2

Role A2 is a member of the intact group and a special friend of group member B2, who is the lost group member. B2 is approaching the group and is reunited first with his friend A2. What will you say to each other? How will you greet each other? What are the first stories you will need to tell? Role-play the reunion.

Role-Play #3

Role A3 is limping along with Role B3, behind the rest of the group and out of yelling distance. Role B3 falls into a hole and suffers a broken leg (parallels porcupine quills in Luath's mouth). What are you going to do? Role-play the scene.

DAY NINE
(Parallels Reading of Chapter 10)

The group believes that they are close to civilization and that everyone should just try to make it there as quickly as they can, so that the slower and weaker members will not hold up the others any longer.

Role-Play #1

Role A is a best friend of one of the group of missing people, and has spent the past few weeks very worried about her missing friend. You have just been informed that two of the missing group members have reached civilization, but there is no news of your friend. Role B is your mother or father. What are your feelings? What attitude should you take toward this news? What do you want to do?

Role-Play #2

Role A2 is the local police chief in the town that the two group members have finally reached. Role B2 is a parent of one of the still-missing group members. How can you find the rest of them? What plans do you need to make?

DAY TEN
(Parallels Reading of Chapter 11)

Role-Play #1

Role A is a friend who thinks that all of the group members have survived. Role B is a friend who is sure that they did not. Role-play a discussion between you.

Role-Play #2

Role A2 will write a letter from Bodger, Tao, or Luath, still away from home but pining for it, to your masters. Tell them the most important things they need to know about your trip and about your current feelings.

Role B2 is Elizabeth, Peter, or Mr. Hunter. You are worried and pining for your lost pet. Tell them what you would want them to know as they struggle through the wilderness—if they are still alive.

DAY ELEVEN
(After Reading Chapter 11)

Throw your letters into a pile at the center of the classroom. Choose a letter from a Role A if you are a B, and vice versa. Choose a powerful word or phrase from the letter and circle it or write it down.

We will now create a choral montage for Group A. Before we start, we will decide who has a phrase that will serve as an appropriate opening and who has one for the ending. Then we will spontaneously read out our phrases to form a choral montage letter for the owners.

Then we will do the same for Group B to form a choral montage for the animals.

REFERENCES

Allen, T. E. (1986). Patterns of academic achievement among hearing-impaired students: 1974–1983. In A. Schildroth & M. Karchmer (Eds.), *Deaf children in America* (pp. 161–206). San Diego: College Hill Press.

Applebee, A. (1989). *The teaching of literature in programs with reputations for excellence in English.* Albany, NY: Center for the Learning and Teaching of Literature.

Armstrong, K. (2005, October 4). *The battle for God.* Distinguished Speaker Keynote Address, Boise State University, Boise, ID.

Atwell, N. (1987). *In the middle: Writing, reading and learning with adolescents.* Montclair, NJ: Boynton/Cook.

Barnes, D. (1986). *Language, the learner, and the school.* London: Routledge.

Barthes, R. (1986). *Image-music-text* (S. Heath, Trans.). New York: Hill and Wang.

Beck, I. L., & McKeown, M. G. (2006). *QtA: A fresh and expanded view of a powerful approach.* New York, NY: Scholastic.

Belcher, T. (1981). *Mental imagery in basal manuals.* Unpublished manuscript, University of Maryland.

Benton, M. (1983). Secondary worlds. *Journal of Research and Development in Education, 16*(3), 68–75.

Benton, M., & Fox, G. (1985). *Teaching literature, 9–14.* Oxford, UK: Oxford University Press.

Bereiter, C. (2004). Reflections on depth. In K. Leithwood, P. Mcadie, N. Bascia, & A. Rodriguez (Eds.), *Teaching for deep understanding* (pp. 8–12).Toronto, Ontario, Canada: OISE/UT and EFTO.

Bissex, G. (1987). What is a teacher researcher? In G. Bissex & R. Bullock (Eds.), *Seeing for ourselves: Case-study research by teachers of writing* (pp. 3–5). Portsmouth, NH: Heinemann.

Bleich, D. (1975). *Readings and feelings: An introduction to subjective criticism.* Urbana, IL: National Council of Teachers of English.

Bleich, D. (1987). Gender interests in reading and language. In E. Flynn & P. Schweickart (Eds.), *Gender and reading: Essays on readers, texts and contexts* (pp. 234–266). Baltimore: Johns Hopkins University Press.

Bloom, B. (1976). *Human characteristics and school learning.* New York, NY: McGraw-Hill.

Blunt, J. (1977). Response to reading: How some young readers describe the process. *English in Education, 11*(3), 34–47.

Bolt, R. (1996). *A man for all seasons*. Oxford, UK: Heinemann.

Bolter, J. D. (1991). *Writing space: The computer, hypertext and the history of writing*. Hillsdale, NJ: Erlbaum.

Boomer, G. (1987). Addressing the problems of elsewhereness: A case for action research in schools. In D. Goswami & P. Stillman (Eds.), *Reclaiming the classroom: Teacher research as an agency for change* (pp. 4–13). Upper Montclair, NJ: Boynton/Cook.

Booth, W. (1983). A new strategy for establishing a truly democratic criticism. *Daedalus, 112,* 193–214.

Booth, W. (1988). *The company we keep: An ethics of reading*. Berkeley, CA: University of California Press.

Bransford, J. (1979). *Human cognition: Learning, understanding, and remembering*. Belmont, CA: Wadsworth.

Britton, J. (1984). Message and text in poetic utterance. In M. Meek & J. Miller (Eds.), *Changing English: Essays for Harold Rosen* (pp. 220–235). London: Heinemann.

Brown, J., Collins, A., & Duguid, P. (1989). Situated cognition and the culture of learning. *Educational Researcher, 18,* 32–42.

Brown, R. (1991). *Schools of thought: How the politics of literacy shape thinking in the classroom*. San Francisco: Jossey-Bass.

Bruner, J. (1986). *Actual minds, possible worlds*. Cambridge, MA: Harvard University Press.

Burke, K. (1957). *The philosophy of literary form*. New York: Vintage Press.

Carlsen, G. (1980). *Books and the teenage reader*. New York: Harper & Row.

Chambers, A. (1985). *Booktalk*. London: The Bodley Head.

Clark, C., & Rumbold, K. (2006). Reading for pleasure: A research review. London, England: National Literacy Trust. Retrieved from www.literacytrust.org.uk/research/Reading%20for%20pleasure.pdf

Cromer, W. (1970). The difference model: A new explanation for some reading difficulties. *Journal of Educational Psychology, 61*(6, part 1), 471–483.

Csikszentmihalyi, M. (1990). *Flow: The psychology of optimal experience*. New York, NY: Harper & Row.

Culler, J. (1975). *Structuralist poetics: Structuralism, linguistics and the study of literature*. Ithaca, NY: Cornell University Press.

Daneman, M., & Carpenter, P. (1980). Individual differences in working memory and reading. *Journal of Verbal Learning and Verbal Behavior, 19,* 450–456.

Dewey, J. (1916). *Democracy in education*. New York, NY: The Free Press.

Dewey, J., & Bentley, A. (1949). *Knowing and the known*. Boston, MA: Beacon Press.

Dillard, A. (1998). *Pilgrim at Tinker Creek*. New York: Harper Collins.

Dissanayake, E. (1992). *Homo aestheticus: Where art comes from and why*. Seattle, WA: University of Washington Press.

Dixon-Krauss, L. (1996). *Vygotsky in the classroom: Mediated literacy instruction and assessment*. White Plains, NY: Longham.

Dole, J., Duffy, G., Roehler, L., & Pearson, P. (1991). Moving from the old to new: Research on reading comprehension instruction. *Review of Educational Research, 62*(2), 239–264.

Duckworth, E. (1996). *"The having of wonderful ideas" and other essays on teaching and learning*. New York: Teachers College Press.

Durkin, D. (1979). What classroom observations reveal about reading comprehension instruction. *Reading Research Quarterly, 14*(4), 481–533.

Dweck, C. (2006). *Mindset: The new psychology of success*. New York, NY: Ballantine.

Dyson, A. (1984). Reading, writing, and language: Young children solving the written language puzzle. In J. Jensen (Ed.), *Composing and comprehending*. Urbana, IL: National Council of Teachers of English.

Earl, L. (2013). *Assessment as learning: Using classroom assessment to maximize student learning* (2nd ed.). Thousand Oaks, CA: Corwin

Eco, U. (1978). *The role of the reader*. Bloomington: Indiana University Press.

Edmiston, B. (1991). *What have you travelled? A teacher researcher study of structuring drama for reflection*. Unpublished doctoral dissertation, Ohio State University, Columbus.

Eisner, E. (1992). The misunderstood role of the arts in human development. *Phi Delta Kappan, 8*, 591–595.

Eisner, E. (1993). The education of vision. *Educational Horizons, 71*(2), 80–85.

Enciso, P. (1992, December). *Accounting for engagement: Emerging principles for rethinking reading processes*. Paper presented at the annual meeting of the National Reading Conference, San Antonio, TX.

Enciso, P. [nee Edmiston]. (1990). *The nature of engagement in reading: Profiles of three fifth graders' engagement strategies and stances*. Unpublished doctoral dissertation, Ohio State University, Columbus.

Engelmann, S., & Osborn, J. (1976). *DISTAR language: An instructional system*. Chicago: Science Research Associates.

Ericsson, A. (2016). Malcolm Gladwell got us wrong: Our research was key to the 10000 hour rule but here's what got oversimplified. Salon. Retrieved from www.salon.com/2016/04/10/malcolm_gladwell_got_us_wrong_our_research_was_key_to_the_10000_hour_rule_but_heres_what_got_oversimplified/

Fish, S. (1980). *Is there a text in this class? The authority of interpretive communities*. Cambridge, MA: Harvard University Press.

Flower, L., & Hayes, J. (1981). A cognitive process theory of writing. *College Composition and Communication, 32*(4), 21–32.

Flynn, E. (1987). Gender and reading. In E. Flynn & P. Schweickart (Eds.), *Gender and reading: Essays on readers, texts and contexts* (pp. 267–288). Baltimore: Johns Hopkins University Press.

Friedman, T. (2005). *The world is flat*. New York, NY: Farrar, Straus and Giroux.

Galda, L. (1982). Assuming the spectator stance: An examination of the responses of three young readers. *Research in the Teaching of English, 16*(1), 1–20.

Gambrell, L. (1981). Induced mental imagery and the text prediction performance of first and third graders. In J. A. Niles and L. A. Harris (Eds.), *New inquiries in reading research and instruction. Thirty first yearbook of the National Reading Conference* (pp. 131–135). Rochester, NY: National Reading Conference.

Gambrell, L., & Bales, R. J. (1986). Mental imagery and the comprehension-monitoring performance of fourth and fifth grade readers. *Reading Research Quarterly, 21*(4), 454–464.

Gambrell, L. B., & Heathington, B. S. (1981). Adult disabled readers' metacognitive awareness about reading tasks and strategies. *Journal of Reading Behavior, 13*(3), 215–222.

Gambrell, L., & Jawitz, P. (1993). Mental imagery, text illustrations and children's story comprehension and recall. *Reading Research Quarterly, 28*(3), 265–275.

Gardner, H. (1983). *Frames of mind.* New York: Basic Books.

Gilligan, C. (1982). *In a different voice: Psychological theory and women's development.* Cambridge, MA: Harvard University Press.

Giroux, H. (1987). Critical literacy and student empowerment: Donald Graves' approach to literacy. *Language Arts, 64*(2), 175–181.

Giroux, H. (1991). Modernism, postmodernism, and feminism: Rethinking the boundaries of educational discourse. In H. Giroux (Ed.), *Postmodernism, feminism, and cultural politics: Redrawing educational boundaries* (pp. 1–59). Albany, NY: State University of New York Press.

Golden, J., & Guthrie, J. (1986). Convergence and divergence in reader response to literature. *Reading Research Quarterly, 21*(4), 408–421.

Goodlad, J. (1984). *A place called school: Prospects for the future.* New York, NY: McGraw-Hill.

Goodlad, J. I., Mantle-Bromley, C., & Goodlad, S. J. (1994). *Education for everyone: Agenda for education in a democracy.* San Francisco: Jossey-Bass.

Goodman, K. (1982). *Language and literacy* (Vols. 1 and 2) (F. Gollasch, Ed.). London: Routledge and Kegan Paul.

Goodman, K. (1985). Unity in reading. In H. Singer & R. B. Ruddell (Eds.), *Theoretical processes and models of reading* (3rd ed.) (pp. 813–840). Newark, DE: International Reading Association.

Greene, M. (1978). *Landscapes of learning.* New York: Teachers College Press.

Hansen, J. (1981). The effects of inference training and practice on young children's reading comprehension. *Reading Research Quarterly, 16*(3), 391–417.

Hanssen, E., Harste, J., & Short, K. (1990). In conversation: Theory and instruction. In D. Bogdan & S. Shaw (Eds.), *Beyond communication: Reading comprehension and criticism.* Portsmouth, NH: Boynton/Cook-Heinemann.

Harding, D. W. (1937). The role of the onlooker. *Scrutiny, 6*(3), 247–258.

Harding, D. W. (1962). What happens when we read. *British Journal of Aesthetics, 2*(2), 133–147.

Hardy, B. (1977). Towards a poetics of fiction. In M. Meek et al. (Eds.), *The cool web.* London: The Bodley Head.

Hart, L. (1984). *Human brain and human learning.* White Plains, NY: Longman.

Healy, J. (1990). *Endangered minds: Why children don't think and what we can do about it.* New York: Touchstone.

Heathcote, D. (1984). *Dorothy Heathcote: Collected writings on drama and education* (L. Johnson & C. O'Neill, Eds.). London: Hutchinson.

Heathcote, D. (1990). *The fight for drama—The fight for education.* Newcastle upon Tyne, UK: National Association of Teachers of Drama/Printers Inc.

Heathcote, D., & Bolton, G. (1995). *Drama and learning: Dorothy Heathcote's mantle of the expert approach to education.* Portsmouth, NH: Heinemann.

Hillocks, G. (1986a). *Research on written composition: New directions for teaching.* Urbana, IL: National Conference on Research in English/ERIC Clearinghouse on Reading and Communication Skills.

Hillocks, G. (1986b). The writer's knowledge: Theory, research and implications for practice. In D. Bartholomae & A. Petrosky (Eds.), *The Teaching of Writing* (85th Yearbook of the National Society for the Study of Education; pp. 71–94). Chicago, IL: University of Chicago Press.

Hillocks, G. (1987). Literary texts in classrooms. In P. Jackson (Ed.), *From Socrates to software: The teacher as text and the text as teacher* (pp. 135–158). Chicago: National Society for the Study of Education.

Hillocks, G. (1995). *Teaching writing as reflective practice.* New York, NY: Teachers College Press.

Hillocks, G. (1999). *Ways of thinking/ways of teaching.* New York, NY: Teachers College Press.

Hillocks, G., Kahn, E., & Johannessen, L. (1983, October). Teaching defining strategies as a mode of inquiry: Some effects on student writing. *Research in the Teaching of English, 17*(3), 275–284

Hubbard, R., & Power, B. (1993). *The art of classroom inquiry.* Portsmouth, NH: Heinemann.

Hubbard, R., & Power, B. (2003). *The art of classroom inquiry* (2nd ed.). Portsmouth, NH: Heinemann.

Hynds, S. (1990). Reading as a social event: Comprehension and response in the text, classroom and world. In D. Bogdan & S. Shaw (Eds.), *Beyond communication: Reading comprehension and criticism.* Portsmouth, NH: Boynton/Cook-Heinemann.

Iser, W. (1978). *The act of reading: A theory of aesthetic response.* Baltimore, MD: Johns Hopkins University Press.

Jacob, S. (1976). Contexts and images in reading. *Reading World, 15*(3), 167–175.

Jacobs, H. H. (1989). *Interdisciplinary curriculum: Design and implementation.* Washington, DC: Association for Supervision and Curriculum Development.

Johnson, R. (1986). *Inner work.* New York, NY: Harper & Row.

Johnston, P. (1985). Understanding reading disability: A case study approach. *Harvard Education Review, 55*(2), 153–177.

Johnston, P. (1993). Assessment and literate development. *The Reading Teacher, 46*(5), 428–429.

Johnston, P. H. (2012). *Opening minds: Using language to change lives.* Portland, ME: Stenhouse.

Johnston, P., & Winograd, P. (1983, December). *Passive failure in reading.* Paper presented at the annual meeting of the National Reading Conference, Austin, TX.

Joyce, B., & Weil, M., with Calhoun, E. (2014). *Models of teaching* (9th ed.). Boston, MA: Allyn and Bacon.

Knapp, M., Stearns, M., John, M., & Zucker, A. (1988). Prospects for improving K–12 science education from the federal level. *Phi Delta Kappan, 69*(9), 677–683.

Knoblauch, C., & Brannon, L. (1993). *Critical teaching and the idea of literacy.* Portsmouth, NH: Heinemann.

Krashen, S., Lee, S., & McQuillan, J. (2012). Is the library important? Multivariate studies at the national and international level. *Journal of Language and Literacy Education, 8*(1), 26–38. Retrieved from jolle.coe.uga.edu/wp-content/uploads/2012/06/Is-the-Library-Important.pdf

LaGravenese, R. (Director). (2007). *Freedom writers* [Motion picture]. United States: Paramount Pictures.

Land, R., & Meyer, J. H. F. (2003). *Threshold concepts and troublesome knowledge 1—Linkages to ways of thinking and practising in improving student learning—Ten years on* (C. Rust, Ed.). Oxford, UK: Oxford Center for Staff Learning and Development.

Langer, J. (1984). Examining background information and text comprehension. *Reading Research Quarterly, 19*(4), 468–481.

Langer, J. (1989). *The process of understanding literature.* Albany, NY: Center for the Teaching and Learning of Literature.

Langer, J. (1990). The process of understanding: Reading for literary and informative purposes. *Research in the Teaching of English, 24*(3), 229–260.

Lortie, D. (1977). *Schoolteacher: A sociological study.* Chicago, IL: University of Chicago Press.

Manguel, A. (1996). *A history of reading.* New York, NY: Penguin Putnam.

Meek, M., Armstrong, S., Austerfield, V., Graham, J., & Plackett, E. (1983). *Achieving literacy: Longitudinal studies of adolescents learning to read.* London: Routledge and Kegan Paul.

Meyer, J. H. F., & Land, R. (2006). Threshold concepts and troublesome knowledge: Issues of liminality. In J. H. F. Meyer & R. Land (Eds.), *Overcoming barriers to student understanding: Threshold concepts and troublesome knowledge* (pp. 19–32). New York, NY: Routledge.

Miller, J. B. (1976). *Towards a new psychology of women.* Boston: Beacon.

Moore, C. (in preparation). *Creating scientists: Teaching and assessing science thinking and practice.* New York, NY: Routledge.

National Endowment for the Arts. (2004). *Reading at risk: A survey of literary reading in America* (Research Division Report #46). Washington, DC: Author.

Nell, V. (1990). *Lost in a book: The psychology of reading for pleasure.* New Haven: Yale University Press.

Newell, G. (1984). Learning from writing in two content areas: A case study/protocol analysis. *Research in the Teaching of English, 18*(3), 265–287.

Newell, G. (1990). Exploring the relationships between writing and literary understanding: A language and learning perspective. In G. E. Mawisher and A. D. Soter (Eds.), *On literacy and its teaching: Issues in English education* (pp. 111–127). Albany: State University of New York.

Newell, G., MacAdams, P., & Spears-Burton, L. (1987, November). *Process approaches to writing about literary texts: Case studies of three classrooms.* Paper presented at the annual conference of the National Council of Teachers of English, Los Angeles.

Newkirk, T. (2009). *Holding on to good ideas in a time of bad ones: Six literacy principles worth fighting for.* Portsmouth, NH: Heinemann.

Newman, F., & Associates. (1996). *Authentic achievement: Restructuring of schools for intellectual quality.* San Francisco, CA: Jossey-Bass.

Newman, F., & Wehlage, G. (1995). *Successful school restructuring: A report to the public and educators by the Center on Organization and Restructuring of Schools.* Madison, WI: Board of Regents of the University of Wisconsin System and Document service, Wisconsin Center for Education Research.

Nickerson, R. S. (1985). Understanding understanding. *American Journal of Education, 93,* 201–239.

Nystrand, M. (1997). *Opening dialogue: Understanding the dynamics of language and learning in the English classroom.* New York, NY: Teachers College Press.

Ornstein, A. (1990). The arts and the learning of high-risk individuals. *Design for Arts in Education, 92*(1), 15–28.

Perfetti, C. A., & Lesgold, A. M. (1979). Coding and comprehension in skilled reading and implications for instruction. In L. B. Resnick & P. A. Weaver (Eds.), *Cognitive processes in comprehension* (pp. 141–183). Hillsdale, NJ: Erlbaum.

Perkins, D. N. (1986). *Knowledge as design.* Mahwah, NJ: Erlbaum.

Pianta, R. C., Belsky, J., Houts, R., Morrison, F., & The National Institute of Child Health and Human Development (NICHD) Early Child Care Research Network. (2007, March 30). TEACHING: Opportunities to learn in America's elementary classrooms. *Science,* pp. 1795–1796.

Pierce, C. S. (1931/1958). *Collected papers of Charles Sanders Pierce.* (Vols. 1–6: C. Hartshorne & P, Weiss, Eds.; Vols. 7, 8: A. W. Burks, Ed.). Cambridge, MA: Harvard University Press.

Poulet, G. (1969). Phenomenology of reading. *New Literary History, 1,* 53–68.

Pressley, M. (1977). Imagery and children's learning: Putting the picture in developmental perspective. *Review of Educational Research, 47,* 585–622.

Probst, R. (1988). *Response and analysis: Teaching literature in junior and senior high school.* Portsmouth, NH: Boynton/Cook.

Purcell-Gates, V. (1991). On the outside looking in: A study of remedial-readers' meaning-making while reading literature. *Journal of Reading Behavior, 23*(2), 235–254.

Purves, A. (1973). *Literature education in ten countries: An empirical study.* New York: Wiley.

Rabinowitz, P. (1987). *Before reading: Narrative conventions and the politics of interpretation.* Ithaca, NY: Cornell University Press.

Rabinowitz, P. J., & Smith, M. W. (1998). *Authorizing readers: Resistance and respect in the teaching of literature.* New York: Teachers College Press.

Radway, J. (1984). *Reading the romance.* Chapel Hill: University of North Carolina Press.

Raphael, T. (1982). Question answering strategies for children. *Reading Teacher, 36*(2), 186–190.

Ravitch, D. (2000). *Left back: A century of battles over school reform.* New York, NY: Touchstone.

Ravitz, J., Becker, H., & Wong, Y. (2000, July). Constructivist-compatible beliefs and practices among U.S. teachers. *Teaching, Learning, and Computing: 1998 National Survey Report #4.* Center for Research on Information Technology and Organizations, University of California, Irvine & University of Minnesota.

Reid, D. K. (1988). *Teaching the learning disabled: A cognitive, developmental approach.* Boston: Allyn & Bacon.

Ricoeur, P. (1984, 1985, 1988). *Time and narrative* (Vols. 1–3). Chicago, IL: The University of Chicago Press.

Rogers, T. (1988). *Students as literary critics: The interpretive theories, processes and experiences of ninth grade students.* Unpublished doctoral dissertation, University of Illinois at Urbana-Champaign.

Rogoff, B., Matusov, E., & White, C. (1996). Models of teaching and learning: Participation in a community of learners. In D. R. Olson & N. Torrance (Eds.), *Handbook of education and human development* (pp. 388–414). Oxford, UK: Blackwell. Retrieved from citeseerx.ist.psu.edu/viewdoc/download?doi=10.1.1.467.1369&rep=rep1&type=pdf.

Rosenblatt, L. (1978). *The reader, the text, the poem: The transactional theory of the literary work.* Carbondale: Southern Illinois University Press.

Rosenblatt, L. (1982). The literary transaction: Evocation and response. *Theory into Practice, 21*(4).

Rosenblatt, L. (1983). *Literature as exploration.* New York: The Modern Language Association of America. (Original work published 1938)

Rumelhart, D. E. (1985). Toward an interactive model of reading. In H. Singer & R. B. Ruddell (Eds.), *Theoretical processes and models of reading* (3rd ed.) (pp. 722–750). Newark, DE: International Reading Association.

Sadoski, M. (1985). The natural use of imagery in story comprehension and recall: Replication and extension. *Reading Research Quarterly, 20*(5), 658–667.

Schank, R. (1990). *Tell me a story.* New York: Scribners.

Schuster, E. (2003). *Breaking the rules: Liberating writers through innovative grammar instruction.* Portsmouth, NH: Heinemann.

Selman, R., & Byrne, D. (1974). A structural-developmental analysis of levels of role-taking in middle childhood. In *Child Development, 45*(81), 803–806.

Shulman, L. (1986). Those who understand: Knowledge growth in teaching. *Educational Researcher, 15*(2), 4–14.

Shulman, L. (1987). Knowledge and teaching: Foundations of a new reform. *Harvard Educational Review, 57,* 1–22.

Smagorinsky, P. (2011). *Vygotsky and literacy research: A methodological framework.* Rotterdam, The Netherlands: Sense Publishers.

Smagorinsky, P., & Coppock, J. (1994). Cultural tools and the classroom context: An exploration of an artistic response to literature. *Written Communication, 11,* 283–310.

Smith, F. (1978). *Understanding reading: A psycholinguistic analysis of reading and learning to read* (2nd ed.). New York: Holt, Rinehart and Winston.

Smith, F. (1988). *Joining the literacy club: Further essays into education.* Portsmouth, NH: Heinemann.

Smith, M. (1989). Teaching the interpretation of irony in poetry. *Research in the Teaching of English, 23*(3), 254–272.

Smith, M. (1991). *Understanding unreliable narrators.* Urbana, IL: National Council of Teachers of English.

Smith, M. (1992). Submission versus control in literary transactions. In J. Many & C. Cox (Eds.), *Reader stance and literary understanding: Exploring the theories, research and practice.* Norwood, NJ: Ablex.

Smith, M. W., & Wilhelm, J. (2002). *"Reading don't fix no Chevys": Literacy in the lives of young men.* Portsmouth, NH: Heinemann.

Smith, M. W., & Wilhelm, J. (2006). *Going with the flow: How to engage boys (and girls) in their literacy learning.* Portsmouth, NH: Heinemann.

Smith, M. W., & Wilhelm, J. (2007). *Getting it right: Fresh approaches to teaching grammar and language use.* New York: Scholastic.

Smith, M. W., & Wilhelm, J. (2010). *Fresh takes on teaching literary elements.* New York, NY: Scholastic.

Smith, M. W., Appleman, D., & Wilhelm, J. (2014). *Uncommon core: Where the authors of the standards get it wrong and how you can get it right.* Thousand Oaks, CA: Corwin.

Squires, J., & Applebee, R. (1966). *A national study of English programs with a reputation for excellence in the teaching of literature.* Cooperative Research Project No. 1994, University of Illinois.

Steinberg, J. (1996). *Beyond the classroom: Why school reform has failed and what parents need to do.* New York, NY: Simon and Shuster.

Sullivan, A., & Brown, M. (2013). *Social inequalities in cognitive scores at age 16: The role of reading.* London, England: Centre for Longitudinal Studies.

Thomson, J. (1987). *Understanding teenagers' reading: Reading processes and the teaching of literature.* Maryborough: Australian Association of Teachers of English.

Tierney, R., & Pearson, P. (1983). Toward a composing model of reading. *Language Arts, 60*(5), 568–586.

Tolkien, J. R. R. (1964). *Tree and leaf.* London: Allen and Unwin.

Vipond, D., & Hunt, R. (1984). Point-driven understanding: Pragmatic and cognitive dimensions of literary reading. *Poetics, 13,* 261–277.

Vygotsky, L. (1978). *Mind in society* (M. Cole, V. John-Steiner, S. Scribner, & E. Souberman, Eds.). Cambridge, MA: Harvard University Press.

Wade, S. (1983). A synthesis of the research for improving research in social sciences. *Review of Educational Research, 53*(4), 461–479.

Wiggins, G., & McTighe, J. (2006). *Understanding by design.* Washington, DC: Association for Supervision and Curriculum Development.

Wilhelm, J. D. (1992). Literary theorists, hear my cry? *English Journal, 81*(7), 50–56.

Wilhelm, J. D. (1996). *Standards in practice, 6–8.* Champaign, IL: National Council of Teachers of English.

Wilhelm, J. D. (2003). *Action strategies for deepening comprehension.* New York: Scholastic.

Wilhelm, J. D. (2004). *Reading IS seeing.* New York: Scholastic.

Wilhelm, J. D. (2007). *Engaging readers and writers with inquiry.* New York, NY: Scholastic.

Wilhelm, J. D. (2012a). *Action strategies for deepening comprehension.* New York, NY: Scholastic.

Wilhelm, J. D. (2012b). *Reading IS seeing.* New York, NY: Scholastic.

Wilhelm, J. D. (in preparation). *Reading manipulatives: To make reading visible.* New York, NY: Scholastic.

Wilhelm, J. D., Baker, T. N., & Dube-Hackett, J. (2001). *Strategic reading: Guiding students to lifelong literacy.* Portsmouth, NH: Heinemann.

Wilhelm, J. D., & Edmiston, B. (1998). *Imagining to learn: Inquiry, ethics, and integration through drama.* Portsmouth, NH: Heinemann.

Wilhelm, J. D., Fry, S., & Douglas, W. (2014). *The activist learner: Inquiry, literacy and service to make learning matter.* New York, NY: Teachers College Press.

Wilhelm, J. D., & Novak, B. (2011). *Teaching literacy for love and wisdom: Being the book and being the change.* New York, NY: Teachers College Press.

Wilhelm, J. D., & Smith, M. W. (2014). *Reading unbound: Why kids need to read what they want, and why we should let them.* New York, NY: Scholastic.

Wilhelm, J. D., & Smith, M. W. (2016). *Diving deep into nonfiction: Transferable tools for any nonfiction text/reader's rules of notice.* Thousand Oaks, CA: Corwin.

Wilhelm, J. D., Smith, M. W., & Fredricksen, J. (2013). *Get it done: Writing and analyzing informational texts to make things happen.* Portsmouth, NH: Heinemann.

Woods, M. L., & Moe, A. J. (1989). *Analytical Reading Inventory* (4th ed.). Columbus, OH: Merrill.

Zeichner, K., & Tabachik, B. (1981). Are the effects of university teacher education "washed out" by school experience? *Journal of Teacher Education, 32*(3), 7–11

Zickuhr, K., & Rainie, L. (2014). A snapshot of reading in 2013. *Pew Research Center.* Retrieved from www.pewinternet.org/2014/01/16/a-snapshot-of-reading-in-america-in-2013/

STORIES AND POEMS CITED IN THE TEXT

CB

Adams, R. (1974). *Watership down.* New York: Macmillan.
Aiken, J. (1992). Lob's girl. In *A fit of shivers* (pp. 63–75). New York: Delacorte.
Alcott, L. M. (1982). *Little women.* Franklin Center, PA: Franklin Library.
Alexander, L. (1968). *The high king.* New York: Holt, Rinehart & Winston.
Arthur, R. (1960). Larceny and old lace. In O. Niles et al. (Eds.), *Skills for reading* (pp. 91–97).Glenview, IL: Scott, Foresman.
Bemelmans, L. (1939). *Madeline.* New York: Viking.
Bemelmans, L. (1953). *Madeline's rescue.* New York: Viking.
Bemelmans, L. (1957). *Madeline and the bad hat.* New York: Viking.
Blos, J. (1990). *A gathering of days.* New York: Macmillan.
Blume, J. (1987). *Just as long as we're together.* New York: Orchard.
Bolt, R. (1996). *A man for all seasons.* Oxford, UK: Heinemann.
Burnett, F. (1987). *The secret garden.* Mahwah, NJ: Watermill.
Burnsford, S. (1960). *The incredible journey.* New York: Bantam Starfire.
Carroll, L. (1965). *Alice's adventures in Wonderland.* New York: Random House.
Ciardi, J. (1975). The shark. In *Fast and slow* (p. 10). New York: Houghton Mifflin.
Clancy, T. (1987). *Patriot games.* New York: Putnam.
Clancy, T. (1989). *A clear and present danger.* New York: Putnam.
Clancy, T. (1991). *The sum of all fears.* New York: Putnam.
Cole, B. (1989). *Celine.* New York: Farrar, Strauss & Giroux.
Corbett, J. (1985). *Man eaters of Kumaon.* Oxford, UK: India Books.
De Marino, L. (1989). *The Odyssey project.* New York: Pageant Books.
Flanagan, T. (1979). *The year of the French.* New York: Holt, Rinehart, & Winston.
Frank, A. (1978). *Anne Frank: The diary of a young girl.* New York: Pocket Books.
Gage, N. (1983). *Eleni.* New York: Random House.

Gitlin, T. (1987). *The sixties: Years of hope, days of rage.* New York: Bantam.

Gourley, C. (1992). Pandora's box. *Read, 42*(5), 18–29.

Grahame, K. (1908). *The wind in the willows.* New York: Scribners.

Grisham, J. (1991). *The firm.* New York: Doubleday.

Grisham, J. (1992). *The pelican brief.* New York: Doubleday.

Hawthorne, N. (2004). *The scarlet letter* (2nd ed.) (J. S. Martin, Ed.). Peterborough, ON: Broadview Press.

Hawthorne, N. (2007). Young Goodman Brown. Retrieved September 5, 2007, from www.classicshorts.com

Hinton, S. E. (1971). *That was then, this is now.* New York: Viking.

Ishiguro, K. (1989). *The remains of the day.* New York: Knopf.

Lee, H. (1988). *To kill a mockingbird.* New York: Warner.

London, J. (1980). *White fang.* Mahwah, NJ: Watermill.

Longfellow, H. W. (1952). The wreck of Hesperus. In D. L. George (Ed.), *The family book of best-loved poems.* Garden City, NY: Hanover House.

Matute, A. (1968). The little boy whose friend died on him. In *Los ninos tontos* (p. 16). Madrid: Ediciones Destino.

Montgomery, L. M. (1976). *Anne of Green Gables.* New York: Bantam.

O'Flaherty, L. (1923). The sniper. In E. J. O'Brien & J. Corimos (Eds.), *The best British short stories of 1923* (pp. 242–246). Boston: Small, Maynard & Co.

Paterson, K. (1978). *The great Gilly Hopkins.* New York: Harper & Row.

Paterson, K. (1988). *Park's quest.* New York: Puffin.

Paterson, K. (1991). *Lyddie.* New York: Dutton.

Paton, A. (1953). *Too late the phalarope.* New York: Scribners.

Quammen, D. (1985). The Republic of Cockroaches. In *Natural acts* (pp. 53–60). New York: Dell.

Robinson, G. (1991). Swish. *Read, 40*(10), 16–19.

Schwartz, A. (1992). High beams. In *Scary stories* (pp. 66–69). New York: HarperCollins.

Spiegelman, A. (1986). *Maus: My father bleeds history.* New York: Pantheon.

Spiegelman, A. (1991). *Maus II: A survivor's tale, and here my troubles began.* New York: Pantheon.

Taylor, M. (1976). *Roll of thunder, hear my cry.* New York: Dial.

Voigt, C. (1986). *Come a stranger.* New York: MacMillan.

Walker, A. (1982). *The color purple.* New York: Harcourt, Brace, Jovanovich.

Westlake, D. (1970). The winner. In H. Harrison (Ed.), *Nova, 1* (pp. 44–48). London: Knox, Burger Associates, Ltd.

White, R. (1973). *Deathwatch.* New York: Dell.

Wilder, L. I. (1981). *Little house in the big woods.* New York: Harper & Row.

Wilhelm, H. (1988). *Waldo goes to the zoo.* Reinbek: Carlsen Verlag.

INDEX

CB

Accelerated Reader, 242
Action Strategies for Deepening Comprehension (Wilhelm), 173–174
Action strategies, for drama, 156–159, 173–182
Activist Learner, The (Wilhelm et al.), 245–246
Actual Minds, Possible Worlds (Bruner), 26–27
Adams, R., 57
Aesthetic stance (Rosenblatt), 31–33, 34–35, 147, 148, 156, 191
Agency, as readers, 55, 234
Aiken, J., 120–121
Alcott, L. M., 57
Alexander, L., 57
Alice's Adventures in Wonderland (Carroll), 57
Allen, T. E., 190
American Girls series, 151, 186
Analogy dramas, 158, 166, 167
Analytical Reading Inventory (ARI), 150, 151, 185–187
Anne Frank: The Diary of a Young Girl (Frank), 57
Anne of Green Gables (Montgomery), 57, 94, 112
Anthologies, literature, 22, 32, 155
Applebee, A., 26, 61
Applebee, Roger, 26
Appleman, D., xvii, 17
Apprenticeship of observation (Lortie), 66
Armstrong, Karen, 139–140
Armstrong, S., 1–2, 35, 125
Art. *See* Visual arts
Arthur, Robert, 189–190
Arts education, aims of, 192
Assessment. *See* Evaluation and assessment

Association-driven readings (M. Smith), 89–90
Asterix comics, 193, 194
Attention Deficit Hyperactivity Disorder (ADHD), students with, 48, 150
Atwell, N., 82
Austerfield, V., 1–2, 35, 125
Authorial reading, 50–51, 137–142
Authority of practice (Wilhelm), xxiv–xxv, 65, 72–74

Baby-sitters Club series, 151
Baker, T. N., 43–47
Bakhtin, Mikhail, 139
Bales, R. J., 147, 188
Barnes, D., 148
Barthes, R., 118, 146, 155
Basal readers, 3, 24, 188
Becker, H., 37
Beck, I. L., 139
Belcher, T., 188
Belsky, J., 38
Bemelmans, Ludwig, 6–7
Bentley, Arthur, 246
Benton, M., 101–102, 145, 160, 192
Bereiter, C., xxiv, 136
Bernini, Gian Lorenzo, 219
Biographies, 14, 56–57
Bissex, G., 52
Bleich, David, 31, 96–97
Bloom, Benjamin, 74
Blos, J., 57, 100–101
Blume, Judy, 102, 115, 121–122
Blunt, J., 159
Boise State Writing Project (BSWP), 68–70
Bolter, Jay David, 245
Bolton, G., 176
Bolt, Robert, 74

Boomer, G., 234
Booth, Wayne, 139, 247
Bosch, Hieronymus, 212
Bottom-up approach to reading, 23–27, 28.
    See also Phonics
Bradbury, Ray, 60
Brannon, L., 231, 233
Bransford, J., 148
Bricolage, xx, 71
Britton, J., 145
Brown, J., 176
Brown, M., xxiii, 245
Brown, R., 62
Brueghel, 212
Bruner, Jerome, 26–27, 63, 95, 96, 113, 146,
    155, 204
Bryson, Bill, 218
Burke, Kenneth, 73
Burnett, F., 57, 94
Burnsford, Sheila, 94, 123, 153–154,
    157–168, 185, 200, 205, 263–268
Byrne, D., 102

Calhoun, E., 12
Calvin and Hobbes, 187, 190
Canon, literary, expansion of, 57, 243–245
Carlsen, G., 60
Carpenter, P., 147
Carroll, L., 57
Celine (Cole), 57, 106
Chambers, Aidan, 27, 52, 58, 61, 63, 89,
    249n
Character books, 29
Characters
    imagining lives of, 177
    learning from events and, 114–116
    relating to, 87, 99–105, 163–165,
        198–201, 251–253
Children's literature, 58, 243
Ciardi, John, 207–209
Clancy, Tom, 57, 101, 124, 126–127, 189
Clark, C., 245
Classics Illustrated series, 186, 190, 193
Classics Junior series, 190
Classroom projects, 19
Close readings, 26
The club of clubs (F. Smith), 5
Coaching, athletic, 5
Cole, Brock, 57, 106
Collages, 195, 207–208

Collins, A., 176
Come a Stranger (Voigt), 57, 106
Comic books, 3, 57, 58, 186, 187, 190,
    193–194, 226
Common Core State Standards (CCSS), xiv,
    xv–xviii, 238, 239
    authority of teachers and, 72–74
    impact on teachers, 17–18
    in shift toward inquiry as cognitive
        apprenticeship, 37–38
Company We Keep, The (Booth), 139
Conferences, 49, 52
Connecting literature to life, 88, 113–117
    analogy dramas, 158, 166–167
    learning from characters and events,
        114–116
    role-playing, 116–117
    telling others, 117
Connective dimensions of response to
    reading, 88, 108–117
Conscious competence, 21, 66
Constrained knowledge, xvi
Context, drama in providing, 171–172,
    176–177
Cooperative learning, 34, 126–128, 212
Coppock, J., 149
Corbett, Jim, 116–117
Correspondence concept, 134, 136
Correspondence dramas, 158, 159, 160,
    162–163, 179, 200
Critical inquiry, 177
Critical literacy, 231, 233–237, 240
Critical teaching, 231
Critical Teaching and the Idea of Literacy
    (Knoblauch & Brannon), 231, 233
Cromer, W., 147
Crutcher, Chris, 56
Csikszentmihalyi, M., 172
Cued protocols, 9, 189–190
Cued-response protocols, 83
Culler, J., 34
Cultural factors, 16–20, 40
Curriculum-centered teaching. *See*
    Information-transmission teaching

Daneman, M., 147
Deaf children, 190
Deathwatch (White), 3–4, 57
Decoding, 24, 147–148, 155, 170. *See also*
    Word identification

De Marino, Lawrence, 101, 107, 111–112
Democratic classroom, 238–248
Developmental model of response, 88, 156, 159
Dewey, John, 240–241, 246
Dialogic space (Armstrong), 139–140
Diary entries, 161
Diary of a Young Girl (Frank), 57
Dillard, Annie, xxv
Dimensions of response to reading, 87–128, 134–135
  category overview, 87–88
  classroom research methods, 81–87
  connecting literature to life, 88, 113–117, 166–167, 256
  considering significance, 88, 118–121, 201–205, 209, 257–258
  in drama, 159–167, 227–228
  elaboration, 88, 90, 109–113, 165–166, 254–255
  entering the story world, 87, 92–98, 159–161, 196–198, 249–250
  evaluating an author, and the self as reader, 88, 126–128, 135, 260–261
  questions and activities for, 249–261
  recognizing literary conventions, 88, 121–123, 135, 258–259
  recognizing reading as a transaction, 88, 123–126, 135, 259–260
  relating to characters, 87, 99–105, 163–165, 198–201, 251–253
  seeing the story world, 87, 105–108, 161–163, 253–254
  showing interest in the story action, 87, 98–99, 250–251
  in visual arts, 195–206, 227–228
"Dinner Party, The" (Gardner), 189
Discovery learning, 38, 43–47
Discussion dramas, 178–179
Dissanayake, Ellen, 247
DISTAR (Direct Instructional System for Teaching Reading), 24, 155
Dixon-Krauss, L., 176
Dole, J., 35
Douglas, W., 74, 133, 140, 176–177, 245–246
Drama, 29–30, 130, 143–182, 234. *See also* Story drama
  action strategies for, 156–159, 173–182
  context in, 171–172, 176–177

  defined, 157
  dimensions of response to reading, 159–167, 227–228
  discussion dramas, 178–179
  effects on reading, 167–169
  effects on writing, 161
  engaged reading as, 145–146
  in framing curriculum, 174, 176–177
  in making meaning for children, 117
  mantle of the expert, 176–177, 179
  misconceptions of, 174–175
  preparing for, 152–156
  reader response theory and, 143, 156, 219–220
  in reading process, 145–149
  with reluctant/struggling readers, 146–147, 150–170
  revolving role, 157–168, 185, 263–268
  role-playing, 116–117, 158–160, 163–165, 175–176, 178
  simulation activity, 3–4
  and SRI, 85, 192–193
  as way of gaining entry to text, 169–170
Drama-in-education activities, 175
Dramatic play, 158
Drama world (Edmiston), 147
Drawing, 29, 186, 191–192, 202–205, 207–208, 235. *See also* Protocols, visual; Visual arts
  as a memory aid, 205–206
  student illustration of stories, 194–195
Dube-Hackett, J., 43–47
Duckworth, Eleanor, 67
Duffy, G., 35
Dugget, Willard, 62
Duguid, P., 176
Durkin, D., 10–11, 25
Dweck, Carol, xix, 19–20, 67, 74
Dyson, Anne, 235–236

Earl, L., 20
Eco, Umberto, 144, 155
Edmiston, Brian, 147, 157, 173
Effective teaching, 12, 19–20
Efferent stance (Rosenblatt), 31–33, 35
Eisner, E., 190, 192, 237
Elaboration, 88, 90, 109–113, 254–255
  extratextual imagined events, 112–113
  filling textual gaps, 110–112, 165–166
  intertextual, 109–110

Eleni (Gage), 56–57
Emotional disturbance (ED), students with, 48, 150–170
Empathy, 164, 225
Enciso, Patricia, 84, 99–100, 101, 113, 145–146, 155, 156
Engaged reading, 53–62, 236–237
    characteristics of, 53–55
    dimension responses of. *See* Dimensions of response to reading
    as drama, 145–146
    engaged readers versus less engaged readers, 49–50, 108, 122, 130–131, 144–149, 225–226, 231, 232
    intensity of engagement, 56
    joy of reading in, xiv–xv
    as missing piece of Common Core State Standards (CCSS), xvii–xviii
    nature of, xiv, 145–146
    pleasure reading in, xxii–xxiv, 13, 15, 167–168
    questions about, 10–11, 36
    reading aloud to children, 4, 6–7, 8
    teaching for, 133–136
Engelmann, S., 155
English as a Second Language (ESL) students, 48, 49–50, 184–190, 206, 241–242
Entry into a textual world, 169–170
Ericsson, Anders, xxiv
Erikson, Erik, 15
Essential questions, 41, 68, 177
Evaluation and assessment
    Analytical Reading Inventory (ARI), 150, 151, 185–187
    attitude inventories, 10–11, 148
    grading, 49, 54, 95, 102
    of reading, 54–55, 121, 150, 151, 185–187
    Smarted Balanced Assessment Consortium (SBAC), 19
    standardized testing, xxii, 18–20, 228–230, 235
    teacher role in assessment process, 19–20
Evocative dimensions of response to reading, 87, 92–108
Exceptional education needs (EEN), students with, 150–170
Experience, reading as, 55, 156

Fantasy, 58, 60
Far Side, The, 187
Field and Stream, 151
Filling textual gaps, 110–112, 165–166
Firm, The (Grisham), 110, 124
Fish, S., 31, 126
Flanagan, T., 4
Flower, L., 82
Flynn, E., 96–97
Formulaic fiction, 59–61, 124–126
Fox, G., 101–102
Framing, 174, 176–177
Frank, Anne, 57
Frankenstein (Shelley), 244
Fredricksen, J., 137, 138, 217
Free-choice reading, xiii–xiv, 3, 22, 34, 152, 167, 186, 187, 190, 194, 242–243
Free-response protocols, 82
Friedman, T., 245
Frost, Robert, 240
Fry, S., 74, 133, 140, 176–177, 245–246
Functional literacy, 52, 62, 234

Gage, N., 56–57
Galda, L., 118
Gallese, Vittorio, 219
Gambrell, L. B., 147–148, 188
Garden of Earthly Delights (Bosch), 212
Gardner, Howard, 213
Gardner, Mona, 189
Gathering of Days, A (Blos), 57, 100–101
Gender differences
    in reading, 4, 95–97
    teacher support in learning process, xix–xx, 13–14
Genre, literary, 56–62
Gilligan, Carol, 57
Giroux, H., 74, 234
Gitlin, T., 56–57
Gladwell, Malcolm, xxiv
Goals of teaching, expanding, 245–246
Golden, J., 102
Goodlad, J. I., xxii, 140
Goodlad, S. J., 140
Goodman, Ken, 28, 156
Gourley, C., 197, 198, 200, 206
Grahame, K., 57
Graham, J., 1–2, 35, 125
Great Gilly Hopkins, The (Paterson), 124, 125, 127–128

Greene, Maxine, 234
Grisham, John, 57, 110, 124
Grounded theory, 133–135
Guided imagery, 158
Guthrie, J., 102

Hansen, J., 148
Hanssen, E., 235
Harding, D. W., 56, 145
Hardy, B., 62
Hardy Boys series, 60
Harste, J., 235
Hart, L., 213
Hayes, J., 82
Healy, J., 61–62
Heathcote, D., 157, 176
Heathington, B. S., 147–148
Hermeneutic challenges (Iser), 118, 125
"High Beams" (Schwartz), 107, 120
High Interest-Easy Reading books, 58
High King, The (Alexander), 57
Hillocks, George, 10–11, 12, 25, 37, 38
Hinton, S. E., 32–33
Historical fiction, 58
History of Reading, A (Manguel), xiv, xviii
Hmong culture, 184–185, 186, 200–202, 206
Horror fiction, 58
Hotseating, 175–176, 178, 180–182
House of the Scorpion (Farmer), 244
Houts, R., 38
Hubbard, R., 64
Human factor in teaching, 12–16
"Human Frailty," 204–205
Hunt, R., 209
Hynds, Susan, 235
Hypermedia, 30, 34, 131

Iconic response, 149
Illustrated books, 193–194, 226
Illustration of stories by students, 194–195
Imagination
    in learning process, xxii–xxiv, 190
    social, 59, 233, 237
Imagining to Learn (Wilhelm & Edmiston), 173
Immersive play pleasure, xxiii
Implied author, 126–128, 260–261
Implied reader, 126–128, 260–261

Incredible Journey, The (Burnsford), 94, 123, 153–154, 200, 205
    revolving role drama, 157–168, 185
    revolving role drama lesson plans, 263–268
Individualized education programs (IEPs), 15
Information-driven reading, 209
Information-transmission teaching, 37, 42, 43–47, 73, 136, 155, 239
Inner work pleasure, xxiii
Inquiry as cognitive apprenticeship, xxii, xxiv, 12, 36–39, 43–46, 134, 172, 176
Inquiry themes, 177
Integrated curriculum, 48, 200
Intellectual pleasure, xxiii
Interactive model of reading, xiii, 28–30
Interpretations, revising, 120–121
Interpretive communities, 30, 126–128
Interrogating the text, 119–120
Intersubjectivity, 139, 140
Intertextual elaborations, 109–110
Irony, 122
Iser, Wolfgang, 89, 113, 118, 125, 132, 144, 155, 249n
Ishiguro, K., 5

Jacob, S., 188
Jacobs, H. H., 41
Jawitz, P., 188
Jaws (movie), 208
Johannessen, L., 38
John, M., 148
Johnson, Eric, 39
Johnson, R., 247
Johnston, P., 19–20, 147, 148, 233–234, 237
Journals, student, 3, 19, 34, 127, 161. *See also* Teacher journals
Joyce, B., 12
Jung, Carl, 247
Just as Long as We're Together (Blume), 102, 115, 121–122

Kafka, Franz, 61
Kahn, E., 38
Kettering, Charles, 64
King Lear (Shakespeare), xiv
King, Stephen, 60, 97
Knapp, M., 148
Knoblauch, C., 231, 233
Krashen, S., xxiii

Land, R., xvi, 38
Landscape of action (Bruner), 95, 146, 160, 204
Landscape of consciousness (Bruner), 96, 146, 155, 160, 204
Langer, J., 88, 148, 159
"Larceny and Old Lace" (Arthur), 189–190
Learning
    cultural factors in, 16–20
    discovery, 38, 43–47
    imagination in learning process, xxii–xxiv, 190
    relational, 12, 13, 40, 42, 246
    social, 28–30, 40–42
    as struggle, xviii–xx, 1–4, 18–19
    theories of teaching and learning, 43–47
    through teacher research, xxiv–xxv, 66–72
Learning disabilities (LD), students with, 22–24, 48, 49–50, 108, 150–170, 184–190, 206–209, 213, 225, 227
Lee, Harper, 27, 70
Lee, S., xxiii
Lee, Spike, 109–110
Legend, Eskimo, 154
Le Guin, Ursula, 60
Lesgold, A. M., 147
Liminality, 175
Literacy, 59
    as civil rights and social justice issue, xv
    critical, 231, 233–237, 240
    expanding notions of, 245
    functional, 52, 62, 234
    importance of, xiv–xv
    robust vision of, xv
Literacy of thoughtfulness (Brown), 62
Literal reading, 152–154
Literary conventions, recognizing, 88, 121–123, 135
    questions and activities, 258–259
Literary letters, 3, 34, 52, 82, 86, 90, 104, 158, 159, 160, 162–163, 186
Literary theory, 131–142
Literature
    connecting to life, 88, 113–117
    expanding the definition of, 3, 56–62, 226–227, 243–245
    literary theory in teaching, 132–133
    marginalization of, in schools, 49
    multicultural, 59
    purpose of, 62–64

Literature as Exploration (Rosenblatt), 31, 191
Literature circles, 34
"Little Boy Whose Friend Died on Him, The" (Matute), 202, 204
Little House in the Big Woods (Wilder), 186
Little Women (Alcott), 57
"Lob's Girl" (Aiken), 120–121
Logs, reading, 186
Longfellow, Henry Wadsworth, 100
Lortie, Dan, 66
Ludic reading, 93
Lyddie (Paterson), 124

MacAdams, P., 26
Madeline (Bemelmans), 6–7
Madeline and the Bad Hat (Bemelmans), 6–7
Madeline's Rescue (Bemelmans), 6–7
Magazines, 3, 30, 34, 56
Man Eaters of Kamaon (Corbett), 116–117
Man for All Seasons, A (Bolt), 74
Manguel, Alberto, xiv, xviii
Manson, Marilyn, 14
Mantle-Bromley, C., 140
Mantle of the expert dramas, 176–177, 179
Martin, Steve, 26
Matusov, E., 12
Matute, Ana Maria, 202, 204
Maus (Spiegelman), 57, 193, 194
Mauss II (Spiegelman), 57, 193, 194
McKeown, M. G., 139
McQuillan, J., xxiii
McTighe, J., xvi, 215
Meaning-making, reading as, xvii–xviii, xxii, 10–11, 28–30, 35, 62–64, 129, 156, 170, 210–212
Medvedev, P. N., 139
Meek, Margaret, 1–2, 35, 125
Memory, drawing as memory aid, 205–206
Merging with text, 169
Metacognition, 87, 206, 214
Meyer, J. H. F., xvi, 38
Miller, Jean Baker, 57
Milton, John, 239
Missing scene scripts, 158
Modeling, by teachers, 20–21
Moe, A. J., 150, 186–187
Montgomery, L. M., 57, 94, 112
Moore, C., 12
Moore, Chris, 72

Morgan, Emily, 68–70
Morrison, F., 38
Motivation, xxii, 12, 171–172
Multicultural literature, 59
Multimedia texts, 20
Multiple intelligences, 212–213
Murals, 212, 235
Mutual perspective-taking (Selman &
    Byrne), 102, 256
Mysteries, 58, 59–60

Nancy Drew series, 56, 60, 101, 126,
    151
National Endowment for the Arts, 243
National Institute of Child Health and
    Human Development (NICHD) Early
    Child Care Research Network, 38
National Writing Project (NWP), xiv, xx,
    1, 16–17, 18, 40, 65, 67, 68–70, 238,
    239, 245
Nell, V., 93
Never Cry Wolf (movie), 154
New Criticism, 24–27, 30
Newell, G., 26, 82
Newkirk, Tom, 18
Newman, Fred, 38
Newscast dramas, 159, 160
Newspapers, 3, 34
Newsweek, 30
Next-generation standards, xv–xviii, 238
    authority of teachers and, 72–74
    impact on teachers, 17–18
    in shift toward inquiry as cognitive
        apprenticeship, 37–38
Nickerson, R. S., 136
Nonfiction texts, xv, 57, 58, 132, 134–135,
    137–138, 176, 205, 215–218, 226
Nonvisual information, 29
Note-making, visual, 83–84, 195, 220–221,
    222
Novak, Bruce, 133, 140, 176, 245–246,
    247
Nystrand, M., 139

Odyssey Project, The (De Marino), 101,
    107, 111–112
O'Flaherty, Liam, 98, 103, 110, 112,
    115–116, 119, 124, 202–203, 206
Ornstein, A., 213
Osborn, J., 155

"Pandora's Box" (Gourley), 197, 198, 200,
    206
Parallel focus (Enciso), 99
Park's Quest (Paterson), 124
Participant stance, 145
Passive reading, 154–156, 169, 210
Past made present (Ricouer), 247
Paterson, Katherine, 56, 123, 124, 125,
    127–128
Paton, A., 5
Pearson, P., 35, 102
Pedagogical content knowledge
    defined, xv
    need for, xv, 73–74
Pelican Brief, The (Grisham), 124
Perfetti, C. A., 147
Perkins, David N., 247
Perseus, myth of, 206
Perspective-taking, 87, 98, 99–105, 114–
    116, 158, 161, 189–190, 233–234
Pew Foundation, 243
Phenomenology, 209
Philosophy, Anglo-American, 26–27
Phonics, 23–24, 28. *See also* Bottom-up
    approach to reading
Pianta, R. C., 38
Picture books, 20, 58, 155, 191, 193–195,
    215, 226
Picture mapping, 195, 205–206, 220–221,
    222
Pierce, C. S., 149
Pilcher, Rosamunde, 60
Pilgrim at Tinker Creek, A (Dillard), xxv
Place holding function, of representation
    (Eisner), 192
Plackett, E., 1–2, 35, 125
Plato, 23, 26
Pleasure reading, xxii–xxiv, 13, 15, 167–168
Poetry, 14, 25, 27, 31, 100, 207, 208–209
Portfolios, 19, 87
Poulet, Georges, 209
Power, B., 64
PowerPoint slide shows, 222
Predictions, during reading, 87, 92, 98
Present made future (Ricouer), 247
Present made past (Ricouer), 247
Pressley, M., 188
Prior knowledge, 29, 152–153
Problem-solving, xx, 122–123
Probst, Robert, 33

Procedural feedback, 67–68, 75–76
Professionalism, 66, 72–74, 239–240
Professional Learning Communities (PLCs), 41
Projects, classroom, 19
Protocols, 52, 85, 90, 224
  audiotaped, 9
  authorial reading, 137–142
  cued, 9, 189–190
  cued-response, 83
  free-response, 82
  steps for modeling, 140–141
  visual, 83–84, 193, 202–205
  as way to share strategies, 86–87
  written, 83
Psycholinguistics, 28, 30–33, 156
Purcell-Gates, V., 147, 188
Purves, Alan, 32

Quammen, David, 137, 205–206
Questioning the Author (QtA), 139, 141–142

Rabinowitz, Peter J., 34, 98, 118, 136, 137, 209
Radway, J., 60–61
Rainie, L., 243
Raphael, T., 209
Ravitch, D., 12
Ravitz, J., 37
Reader response theory, 27, 30–33, 35–36, 225–226. *See also* Dimensions of response to reading; Rosenblatt, Louise; Transactional approach to reading
  drama and, 143, 156, 219–220
  visual arts and, 210–212, 215–216, 219–220
Reader, the Text, the Poem, The (Rosenblatt), 31, 191
Reading. *See also* Dimensions of response to reading
  active participation in, 147–149
  at-home versus in-school, 7–8, 29–30, 49
  authorial, 50–51, 137–142
  balancing shared and individualized, 116
  bottom-up approach to, 23–27, 28. *See also* Phonics
  comparison of interpretations, 126–128
  creation of secondary worlds, 56, 93, 99, 105, 108, 109, 113, 138, 145, 147, 154, 156, 160, 192, 203, 209, 225

  definition of, 11
  developmental model of response, 88, 156, 159
  as engagement. *See* Engaged reading
  evaluation and assessment of, 54–55, 121, 150, 151, 185–187
  as experience, 55, 156
  free-choice, xxiii–xiv, 3, 22, 34, 152, 167, 186, 187, 190, 194, 242–243
  gender differences, 4, 95–97
  interactive model, xiii, 28–30
  interpretations, 86–87
  literal, 152–154
  and maturity, 59
  as meaning-making, xvii–xviii, xxii, 10–11, 28–30, 35, 62–64, 129, 156, 170, 210–212
  metaphors for, 55
  passive, 154–156, 169, 210
  personal reading by teacher, 4–5
  pleasure, xxii–xxiv, 13, 15, 167–168
  predictions during, 87, 92, 98
  professional reading by teacher, 236–237
  purposes for, 62–64, 89
  reading process becomes curriculum, 224–225
  remedial, 2–4, 8, 146–147
  spectator role, 145
  strategies for, xv–xvi, 10–11, 28–29, 30, 34–35, 36, 147–149, 167, 169–170, 224–225. *See also* Drama; Visual arts
  students' attitudes toward, 2–4, 10–11, 22–24, 49–50, 54–55, 150–152, 169–170
  sustained silent reading (SSR), 84
  theories of, 24–33
  time spent on, 61–62
  top-down approach to, 28, 30–33
  transactional approach to, xiv, 30–33, 35–36, 55, 57, 59–61, 62–64, 88, 123–126, 132–133, 135, 144, 227, 246–248, 259–260
  transformative, xiv, 61
  value of rereading, 6–7, 107–108
Reading aloud
  to children, 4, 6–7, 8
  students' response to, 4
Reading at Risk (National Endowment for the Arts), 243

"Reading Don't Fix No Chevys" (Smith & Wilhelm), 13
Reading IS Seeing (Wilhelm), 215–216
Reading partners/friends, 83, 91, 117, 126–127, 131, 186, 208
Reading the Romance (Radway), 60–61
Reading Unbound (Wilhelm & Smith), xxiii–xxiv, 15, 172, 244
Reading workshop, 22, 34
Real reader test (Schuster), 136
Real writer test (Schuster), 136
Reciprocal learning, 12, 40, 139, 176–177
Reciprocity (Bakhtin), 139
Reenactments, 178
Reflective dimensions of response to reading, 88, 117–128
Reflective teaching, xx–xxii, 66, 71, 72–73, 133
Reid, D. K., 148
Relational learning, 12, 13, 40, 42, 246
Remains of the Day, The (Ishiguro), 5
Remedial reading, 2–4, 8, 146–147
"Republic of Cockroaches, The" (Quammen), 205–206
Rereading, value of, 6–7, 107–108
Research, teacher. *See* Teacher research
Resilience, xviii–xx, 1–4, 18–19
Response journals, 3, 19, 34, 127, 161. *See also* Teacher journals
Response to reading. *See* Dimensions of response to reading; Reading
Restructuring Schools Study (Newman et al.), 38
Revising interpretations, 120–121
Revolving role drama
    The Incredible Journey (Burnsford), 157–168, 185, 263–268
    lesson plans, 263–268
    nature of, 157–158
Ricoeur, Paul, 246, 247
Robinson, G., 199
Roehler, L., 35
Rogers, T., 102
Rogoff, B., 12
Role-playing, 116–117, 158–160, 163–165, 175–176, 178
Roll of Thunder, Hear My Cry! (Taylor), 104–105, 110–111, 112–113, 114–115, 128, 207, 211
Romances, 59–60, 186

Romeo and Juliet (Shakespeare), 69, 241–242
Rorty, Richard, 26–27
Rosenblatt, Louise, 30–35, 50–51, 55, 132–133, 143–145, 147, 148, 156, 191, 246
Rules of notice (Rabinowitz), 98, 209
Rules of signification (Rabinowitz), 118, 209
Rumbold, K., 245
Rumelhart, David E., 28
Ryan, Jack (Tom Clancy character), 101, 102–103, 114, 127

Sadoski, M., 188
Salience of the traditional (Zeichner), 39, 66, 173, 239, 248
Scary Stories series, 56, 194
Schank, R., 62
Schema, 29, 97, 152–153, 156. *See also* Prior knowledge
Scholastic, 173–174, 175
Schools, purpose of, 62, 228
Schuster, Edgar, 136
Schwartz, A., 107, 120
Schwarzenegger, Arnold, 110
Science, 38, 41
Science fiction, 60, 204–205
Scientific literacy, 217, 218
Secondary worlds, reading in creating, 56, 93, 99, 105, 108, 109, 113, 138, 145, 147, 154, 156, 160, 192, 203, 209, 225
Secret Garden, The (Burnett), 57, 94
Self-efficacy, 171–172
Selman, R., 102
Semiotic theory, 149
"Seven Daughters, The," 200–202, 206
"Shadow" self, 175
Shakespeare, William, xiv, xvi, 26, 69, 226–227, 241–242
"Shark, The" (Ciardi), 207–209
Shell Seekers, The (Pilcher), 60
Short, K., 235
Short stories, 3, 85
Shulman, L., xv, 73–74
Significance, 88, 118–121
    interrogating the text, 119–120
    questions and activities, 257–258
    revising interpretations, 120–121
    rules of signification (Rabinowitz), 118, 209
    visual arts and, 201–205

Sixties, The (Gitlin), 56–57
Smagorinsky, P., 149
Smarter Balanced Assessment Consortium
    (SBAC), 19
Smith, Dallas, 41
Smith, Frank, 5, 28, 29
Smith, Michael W., xi, xiii, xv, xvii, xix–
    xx, xxii–xxiv, 13, 15–17, 41, 68, 89,
    122–123, 131, 132, 134, 136–138,
    169, 171, 172, 176, 177, 209, 215,
    217, 218, 244, 247
Snapshot dramas, 158, 162
"Sniper, The" (O'Flaherty), 98, 103,
    110, 112, 115–116, 119, 124–125,
    202–203, 206
Social contract, 13–16
Social imagination, 59, 233, 237
Social learning, 28–30, 40–42
Social pleasure, xxiv
Sociocultural learning-centered teaching. *See*
    Inquiry as cognitive apprenticeship
Spears-Burton, L., 26
Spectator role in reading, 145
Speech class, 2
Spiderman comics, 190
Spiegelman, Art, 57, 193, 194
Spin, 56
Squires, J., 26
SRI (symbolic story representation). *See*
    Symbolic story representation (SRI)
Standardized testing, xxii, 18–20, 228–230,
    235
Stearns, M., 148
Steinberg, J., xxii
Stine, R. L., 56, 60
Story drama, 145, 156–159. *See also* Drama
    analogy dramas, 158, 166–167
    correspondence, 158, 159, 160, 162–163,
        179, 200
    defined, 157
    dramatic play, 158
    guided imagery, 158
    hotseating, 175–176, 178, 180–182
    missing scene scripts, 158
    newscast dramas, 159, 160
    revolving role drama, 157–158, 185,
        263–268
    snapshot dramas, 158, 162
    tableaux dramas, 158, 162, 179, 195,
        221–223

"To Tell the Truth" game, 158, 163–164,
    166
Story theater. *See* Drama; Story drama
Strategies for reading, xv–xvi, 10–11,
    28–29, 30, 34–35, 36, 147–149, 167,
    169–170, 224–225
Student-centered teaching/discovery learning,
    38, 43–47
Students
    attitudes toward reading and writing, 2–4,
        10–11, 22–24, 49–50, 54–55, 68,
        150–152, 169–170
    attitudes toward school, 22
    collaboration in teacher research, 9–10,
        67–68, 231, 232
    engaged readers versus less engaged
        readers, 49–50, 108, 122, 130–131,
        144–149, 225–226, 231, 232
    English as a Second Language (ESL), 48,
        49–50, 184–190, 206, 241–242
    expectations for teachers, xix–xx, 13–14
    importance of teacher support, xix–xx,
        13–16
    learning as struggle, xviii–xx, 1–4, 18–19
    with learning disabilities, 22–24, 48,
        49–50, 108, 150–170, 184–190,
        206–209, 213, 225, 227
    listening to, xxiv–xxv
    preferences of engaged readers, 58–61
    procedural feedback for, 67–68, 75–76
    quality of experiences at school, xxii
    response to reading aloud, 4
    selection of case study students in teacher
        research, 48, 53–54, 150–152
Submission to text, 169, 209
Sullivan, A., xxiii, 245
Superman comics, 190
Sustained silent reading (SSR), 84
"Swish" (Robinson), 199
Symbolic representation interviews (SRI), 84
Symbolic story representation (SRI), 52,
    91–92, 93, 95, 96, 107, 111, 224–225
    described, 84–87
    drama in, 85, 192–193
    visual arts in, 192–193, 196–201,
        205–206, 215, 217–219, 222–223

Tabachik, B., 39, 66
Tableaux, 158, 162, 179, 195, 221–223
Taking inferential walks (Eco), 144

Taylor, Mildred D., 104–105, 110–111, 112–113, 114–115, 128, 207, 211
Teacher education, 22, 25, 26, 32–33, 58
Teacher journals, 1, 3–4, 27, 32–33, 36, 51, 82, 86–87, 91–92, 94, 148–149, 184, 188–189, 190, 196, 197, 198, 199, 214, 228, 236
Teacher research, 51–53, 64–79. *See also* Dimensions of response to reading
  benefits of, 129–131, 232
  collaboration with students, 9–10, 67–68, 231, 232
  conversations about, 64–66, 73–74
  criteria for methods, 68–69
  emerging themes of, 50–51
  importance of, 9–10
  inquiry as cognitive apprenticeship, xxii, xxiv, 12, 36–39, 43–46, 134, 172, 176
  methods, 10–11, 52, 67–73, 81–87
  personal importance of, xx–xxii, 66–72
  planning worksheet, 78–79
  possibilities of, 230–231
  procedural feedback, 67–68, 75–76
  professional culture for, 16–18, 232
  protocols. *See* Protocols
  research questions, 7–8, 11, 36, 37, 149, 170
  research techniques as instructional tools, 224–225
  selection of case study students, 48, 53–54, 150–152
  teacher learning in, xxiv–xxv, 129–131
  traditional research and, 236
Teachers. *See also* Teacher research; Teaching
  authority of practice (Wilhelm), xxiv–xxv, 65, 72–74
  conscious competence of, 21, 66
  empowerment of, 9–10, 231
  importance of support for students, xix–xx, 13–16
  leadership role of, 240
  modeling by, 20–21
  personal reading by, 4–5
  professional autonomy of, 19–20, 230–231
  Professional Learning Communities (PLCs), 41
  professional reading by, 236–237

  qualifications versus abilities of, 38
  role of, 57–58, 62, 214–215, 228–231
  student expectations for, xix–xx, 13–14
  teaching as struggle, xviii–xx, 1–4, 18–19
Teaching
  comparison with baseball, 240
  cultural factors in, 16–20, 40
  effective, 12, 19–20
  for engaged reading, 133–136
  expanding goals of, 245–246
  human factor in, 12–16
  information-transmission, 37, 42, 43–47, 73, 136, 155, 239
  inquiry as cognitive apprenticeship, xxii, xxiv, 12, 36–39, 43–47, 134, 172, 176
  as profession, 66, 72–74
  reflective, xx–xxii, 66, 71, 72–73, 133
  social contract in, 13–16
  as struggle, xviii–xx, 1–4, 18–19
  team, 48
  theories of teaching and learning, 43–47
  with urgency, xxi–xxii
Teaching Literacy for Love and Wisdom (Wilhelm & Novak), 245–247
Team teaching, 48
"Tell me" framework (Chambers), 75–76, 89, 154–156, 249–261
Terminator movies, 110
Testing, standardized, xxii, 18–20, 228–230, 235
Textbooks, 243–244
Text, expanding notions of, 243–244
Textual constraints, 138
Textual indices (Barthes), 118
That Was Then, This Is Now (Hinton), 32–33
Theories of reading. *See also* Reader response theory
  classical, 25
  New Criticism, 24–27, 30
Theories of teaching and learning, 43–47
Think-aloud protocols. *See* Protocols
Thinking partners, xix, 69, 70
Thomson, Jack, 88, 123–124, 146, 159. *See also* Developmental model of response
"Three Little Pigs, The," 29–30
Threshold knowledge, xvi, 36–37, 38
Tierney, R., 102
Tintin comics, 193, 194

To Kill a Mockingbird (Lee), 27, 70
Tolkien, J. R. R., 145, 192
Too Late the Phalarope (Paton), 5
Top-down approach to reading, 28, 30–33
Topical research (Wilhelm), 177
"To Tell the Truth" game, 158, 163–164, 166
Transactional approach to reading, xiv, 30–33, 35–36, 55, 57, 59–61, 62–64, 88, 123–126, 132–133, 135, 144, 227, 246–248, 259–260
Transactional consciousness (Dewey), 246
Transformative reading, xiv, 61
Troilus and Cressida (Shakespeare), 26

Uncommon Core (Smith et al.), xviin

Valid reading (Rosenblatt), 50–51
Video, 30, 34, 57, 85, 131, 159
Video games, 244
Vipond, D., 209
Visual arts, 29, 130, 131, 146–147, 183–223. *See also* Drawing
   aims of art education in, 192
   dimensions of response to reading, 195–206, 227–228
   multiple intelligences and, 212–213
   reader response theory and, 210–212, 215–216, 219–220
   with reluctant/struggling readers, 187–223
   and SRI, 192–193, 196–201, 205–206, 215, 217–219, 222–223
Visual-data displays, 216–217
Visualization, 83–84, 95, 98, 99, 105–108, 114, 153, 161–162, 187–209, 214–223, 225–226
Visual protocols, 83–84, 193, 202–205
Vocabulary lists, 24
Voigt, Cynthia, 57, 106
Vygotsky, Lev, 20, 40, 41, 74, 140, 148

Wade, S., 148
Waldo Goes to the Zoo (Wilhelm), 6
Walker, Scott, 18
Watership Down (Adams), 57
Wehlage, G., 38

Weil, M., 12
Westlake, Donald, 202–203, 204
West, Rebecca, xiv
"What If?" questions, 109, 163–164
White, C., 12
White Fang (movie), 154
White, Robb, 3–4, 57
Whole language, 28
Whole text, 24–27
Wide-awakeness (Greene), 234, 237
Wiggins, G., xvi, 215
Wilder, L. I., 186
Wilhelm, Fiona, 6–7, 29–30, 40–41, 71–72
Wilhelm, Hans, 6
Wilhelm, Jasmine, 7, 29
Wilhelm, Jeffrey D., xiii, xv, xvii, xix–xx, xxii–xxiv, 13, 15, 17, 41, 43–47, 68, 74, 86, 111, 132–134, 136–138, 140–142, 146, 171–174, 176–177, 180–182, 215–219, 241, 244–247
Wilhelm, Peggy Jo, xviii–xix, 5, 60, 232
Wind in the Willows, The (Grahame), 57
"Winner, The" (Westlake), 202–203, 204
Winograd, P., 148
Wong, Y., 37
Woods, M. L., 150, 186–187
Word identification, 147–148, 187. *See also* Decoding
Work pleasure, xxiii
Worksheets, 24
"Wreck of the Hesperus, The" (Longfellow), 100
Writing workshop, 34
Written protocols, 83

X-Men comics, 57

Year of the French, The (Flanagan), 4
YM, 56
Young adult literature, 20, 56, 57, 58, 226, 243

Zeichner, Ken, 39, 66
Zickuhr, K., 243
Zucker, A., 148

ABOUT THE AUTHOR

છૈ

JEFFREY WILHELM is an internationally known teacher, author, and presenter. A full-time classroom teacher for 13 years, he is currently a distinguished professor of English Education at Boise State University. He works as a thinking partner, co-teacher, and fishbowl teacher in local schools as part of a Professional Development Site Network sponsored by the Boise State Writing Project. He teaches middle or high school students each spring.

Jeff has devoted his professional career to helping teachers help their students. He is particularly devoted to assisting students who are considered to be reluctant, struggling, or at-risk.

He is the founding director of both the Maine Writing Project and the Boise State Writing Project. BSWP currently supports over 3,000 teachers each year with over 110,000 contact hours annually of professional development.

He is a highly-regarded author or co-author of over 36 books about literacy and literacy education, and has edited several nonfiction series for late elementary, middle school and high school students. He has won the two top research awards in English Education: the NCTE Promising Research Award for *"You Gotta BE the Book"* and the Russell Award for Distinguished Research for *"Reading Don't Fix No Chevys."* He is also the recipient of the initial International Literacy Association's Thought Leader in Adolescent Literacy Award. He enjoys speaking, presenting, and working with students and schools.

On the personal side, Jeff is an avid whitewater rafter and kayaker, backpacker, marathon Nordic skier, photographer, traveler, reader, and writer.